Impact on Issues 2022 – 2024

Introduction...1

Taking Action...2

    Working Together to Influence Public Policy 2

Principles...10

Summary of Public Policy Positions..11

    Representative Government 11

    International Relations 12

    Natural Resources..13

    Social Policy 14

REPRESENTATIVE GOVERNMENT..16

Voting Rights...23

    Citizen's Right to Vote..23

    DC Self-Government and Full Voting Representation 32

The Election Process...35

    Apportionment...35

    Redistricting..38

    Money in Politics..42

    Selection of the President...49

    Voter Representation/Electoral Systems..51

Citizen Rights..52

    Citizen's Right to Know/Citizen Participation......................................52

    Individual Liberties...55

    Public Policy on Reproductive Choices...57

Evaluating Constitutional Amendment Proposals and Constitutional Conventions.....61

    Constitutional Amendment Proposals 61

    Constitutional Conventions...62

Congress and the Presidency...63

    Congress..63

    The Presidency..66

Privatization..67

Digital Equity..69

INTERNATIONAL RELATIONS...70

    United Nations..71

    Trade...77

    US Relations with Developing Countries..80

    Arms Control...84

    Military Policy and Defense Spending...87

(Continued on next page)

NATURAL RESOURCES.. 90

Resource Management.. 93

Environmental Protection and Pollution Control........................ 96

Air Quality... 96
Energy.. 97
Land Use.. 97
Water Resources.. 98
Waste Management.. 99
Nuclear.. 100

Transfer of Federal Public Lands... 109

Climate Change 110

Public Participation 112

Federal Agriculture Policies 114

SOCIAL POLICY.. 118

Criminal Justice.. 120

Equality of Opportunity.. 122

Employment 125
Fair Housing 126

Federal Role in Public Education.. 132

Fiscal Policy.. 134

Health Care... 137

Immigration... 143

Meeting Basic Human Needs.. 145

Child Care.. 151

Early Intervention for Children at Risk... 152

Violence Prevention.. 153

Gun Policy.. 153

Urban Policy... 155

Death Penalty 157

Sentencing Policy.. 157

Human Trafficking.. 158

Introduction

Impact on Issues is designed to help League members use LWVUS public policy positions effectively at the national, state, local, and regional levels. The intention is to inspire Leagues to use national positions to act in their own communities.

Impact on Issues has been organized so that "Taking Action" is front and center, followed by the League Principles. Then, for quick reference, the LWVUS public policy Positions in Brief summarize the more detailed positions presented in the sections that follow. For each of the major issue areas, the listing gives the full official statement of position in bold type. The history sections provide background for each position and trace significant actions and achievements.

Since 1920, the League of Women Voters has been an activist, grassroots organization whose leaders believed that people should play a critical role in democracy. The League of Women Voters was founded by Carrie Chapman Catt in 1920, just six months before the 19th Amendment to the US Constitution was ratified, giving women the right to vote.

Throughout the years, the League has continued its dual purposes of education and advocacy, engaging in studies on representative government, international relations, natural resources, and social policy. Although our history of advocacy goes back to our beginnings, this version of Impact on Issues covers our advocacy efforts beginning in the 1960s.

Impact on Issues is an indispensable resource for League members. A clear understanding of LWVUS positions, how they interrelate, and how they can complement and reinforce state, local, and regional Inter-League Organization (ILO) positions, strengthens the League's impact on issues at all levels of government.

In applying LWVUS positions to national, state, local, and regional issues, each appropriate League board — depending on the level of action — is responsible for determining whether member understanding and agreement exists and whether the action makes sense in terms of timing, need, and effectiveness.

Taking Action

WORKING TOGETHER TO INFLUENCE PUBLIC POLICY

In the League, we tend to focus our efforts on influencing legislative measures in the US Congress and state and local legislative bodies by preparing testimony, lobbying legislators, and initiating advocacy campaigns on issues of interest to our members. We also file lawsuits, file "friend of the court" (amicus) briefs in court cases, and monitor and comment when regulations are being written for executive branch agencies. The following guidelines apply to all these activities.

General Guidelines

This section is organized with general guidelines for action, followed by the role of the national office and staff in advocacy, then how to use Impact on Issues to take action at the state and local levels, and finally how state and local Leagues can request permission to take national action on non-priority federal issues.

The goal is to work collaboratively among the levels of League with consistent messages and strategies. Effective advocacy efforts on national issues depend on a partnership at all League levels — lobbying in Washington and constituent lobbying at home. This one-two punch reinforces the League's impact in influencing national and state legislation.

Working Together to Influence Public Policy

The process used in formulating positions and acting at the grassroots level makes the League unique and sets the League apart from other organizations. The fact that we are members of not only a local League, but a state League and the League of Women Voters of the United States, makes us a powerful force.

Speaking with One Voice

"Speaking with one voice" is one of the most important tenets of the League. The national League is responsible for determining strategies and action policies that ensure that the League's message on national issues is consistent throughout the country. Similarly, state Leagues are responsible for a consistent state message, and local Leagues must cooperate with one another to ensure that regional issues are addressed in a manner consistent with neighboring Leagues. Typically, the president of the national, state, or local League is the only person who speaks for the League in an official capacity, unless another person has been designated as the official spokesperson on a specific issue. This may be a League expert, a senior staff person, or a former board member. The key is that this designation is explicitly made by the appropriate Board. This helps to ensure that the League speaks with one voice, which is essential for our effectiveness as an advocacy and lobbying organization.

Voter Service

The League's nonpartisan voter services activities and lobbying activities must be kept separate and voters' guides and other voter service materials and publications must not contain statements of League positions.

League Lobbying

League lobbying is based on member study and agreement on selected issues and involves concerted efforts to achieve public policies consistent with League positions. League Boards at every level set their own priorities. League lobbying promotes or opposes specific pieces of legislation. The LWVUS public policy positions are the official statements of positions for each issue area and reflect the program adopted by the most recent national convention.

Advocacy vs. Lobbying

Advocacy is a broader concept than lobbying. Advocacy activities are often considered "educational." This is the case even when only one side of an issue is presented if no action on a piece of legislation is requested. Such activities can include: (1) developing public policy briefs that analyze issues and provide detailed information and recommendations for addressing them through specific reforms and (2) providing forums for discussing issues and educating policymakers and the public. Speaking in support of the organization is also advocating (i.e., for the overall cause of the organization).

Lobbying is defined as an attempt to influence specific legislation, both legislation that has been introduced and specific legislation that has been proposed. Lobbying includes actions that transmit a point of view on a specific piece of legislation to elected officials or their staffs, as well as actions urging the public to contact their legislators about a specific piece of legislation. It also includes communications to the general public expressing a view on specific referenda or other ballot measures.

Applying Diversity, Equity, and Inclusion (DEI) Lens to Our Work

Applying a DEI lens is a way of examining a program, process, product, or otherwise with an eye toward how it will be perceived by a variety of communities, voices, and perspectives, and what barriers may exist that prevent it from being equitable or inclusive to everyone. We recommend Leagues apply a DEI lens to any position that they utilize. When examining your work through a DEI lens you should ask these key questions:

1. Who is involved in the process? Leagues should consider whether this work impacts a group or community, if the voice of the impacted community is represented, and how diverse the group of decision-makers who represent a variety of relevant viewpoints is.

2. Who will be impacted? Leagues should consider who benefits or could be harmed, whether it helps meet the needs of underserved voters, how we considered various, specific marginalized groups, and how they'll be impacted.

3. What are the likely intended and unintended outcomes? Leagues should consider the issue we are trying to address, what we hope will happen, the potential negative impacts, who could be hurt by this, the supporting data or evidence, and how it might be perceived by others.

4. Does this align with our vision for an equitable and inclusive organization? Leagues should consider how equity is addressed, what barriers it might place in the way of achieving equity, and how it impacts the organization's culture.

5. What changes could we make to improve equity? Leagues should consider the short- and long-term goals, policies or bylaws that need to be added or amended, the benefits to members, and the benefits for partners and/or members of the community.

Leagues should be aware that this process will take more time in the beginning, but as the DEI lens is regularly applied it will become easier to move through the questions, identify opportunities, and react in a way that bolsters DEI. In instances where Leagues go through the questions and find that the DEI is not present fully or partially, Leagues should work to include as many factors as possible, consider obstacles that led to gaps in one area versus others, and determine how to continue to build on this work any time the League takes action. When applying the DEI lens to events, Leagues should consult the DEI checklist on the League Management Site.

Following the 2020 Convention, the DEI board committee met with other board members to review nine positions to provide additional insight into how Leagues could apply the DEI lens to the work. The positions reviewed were Selection of the President, Climate Change, Death Penalty, Equality of Opportunity/Equal Rights, Gun Policy, Health Care, Immigration, Sentencing Policy, and Violence Prevention.

These positions are indicated with a 🔍 symbol throughout this document.

The following takeaways emerged:
- Editorial changes were needed for the Gun Policy position, which included outdated language describing the types of guns.
- Editorial changes were needed for the Immigration position, which included the term "undocumented workers" and did not reflect current criminal law.
- Editorial changes were not needed for the Sentencing Policy and Violence Prevention positions, since both will be augmented by the new Criminal Justice position adopted at Convention 2022.
- The updated Health Care position, also adopted at Convention 2022, will replace and clarify language regarding the impact of health care access for communities of color.
- The Death Penalty position, Selection of the President, and Climate Change met DEI review.
- The Equality of Opportunity/Equal Rights position needed more in-depth, substantive changes.

Advocacy at the National Level

Establishing National Priorities

To guide its work in Congress, the LWVUS Board adopts lobbying priorities every year. The goal is to maintain focus on issues of primary importance identified by LWVUS.

The goals are to:
- Project a focused and consistent message.
- Enhance the League's effectiveness and impact.
- Build the League's credibility and visibility.
- Ensure that the League has sufficient issue and political expertise.
- Reflect program decisions made at convention and/or council.
- Build on strong member interest and support.
- Enable the League to manage resources effectively.

LWVUS Advocacy and Litigation Team

The Advocacy and Litigation team works together to ensure the League's advocacy and litigation reflect our public policy positions.

The advocacy team, working in collaboration with the LWVUS Board, is responsible for developing and implementing strategies for lobbying and advocating on national issues. LWVUS staff lobbyists carry out the day-to-day monitoring and action plans for the League and oversee the LWVUS Lobby Corps. Advocacy staff work with LWV leaders and activists in targeted states and congressional districts to help develop and implement grassroots lobbying strategies.

The litigation team engages with state and national legal cases, researches national litigation and litigation trends, creates legal resources to educate Leagues, and consults with Leagues and legal partners in support of LWVUS priorities. Litigation staff work with LWV leaders and activists to help align litigation across the country, offering legal resources to state and local Leagues.

Action Alerts

The LWVUS advocacy team sends out regular Action Alerts based on League priorities detailing the subject under consideration, the proposed action steps, and the individuals to be contacted. Action Alerts are sent to the League's online grassroots supporter list and state and local League presidents, who are expected to respond with the appropriate action.

LWVUS Lobby Corps

The Lobby Corps (LC) is made up of Washington, DC-area League member volunteers who lobby each month on a targeted assignment at the direction of LWVUS advocacy staff when Congress is in session.

Grassroots Lobbying

Advocacy staff work with LWV leaders and activists in targeted states and congressional districts to help develop and implement grassroots lobbying strategies. In addition to working directly with staff on targeted requests, members can join the LWVUS online grassroots support list. League members with email addresses on file are automatically subscribed to this list. The list also includes activists and other interested members of the public who believe in the League's mission.

State and Local Advocacy and Lobbying on LWVUS Priority Issues

Once LWVUS has identified its legislative priorities, state and local Leagues are requested to act on those issues under guidance from LWVUS. Optimally, state and local Leagues should encourage members to contact their national legislators on key League national issues following LWVUS guidance. Lobbying in Washington is vitally important, but direct lobbying of members of Congress by constituents is often the key to persuading them to support the League's position. The conversations that League leaders and members have with their representative or senators can make the difference in how they vote.

On key issues, LWVUS may call on League presidents to take state-specific actions before critical votes in Congress. LWV presidents also will receive sample messages for use on issues on which the organization is actively lobbying.

Each state and local League president is expected to take whatever official action is requested in response to the requests.

Local Leagues and Members

While the LWVUS Board takes the lead in national action and keeps League action synchronized with the US Congress, there is a role for every League in national legislation in many circumstances. For example, when responding to an LWVUS action alert, a local League president sends a message on behalf of the organization (i.e., on League letterhead). Members are also encouraged to respond to Action Alerts. Please note that using the Action Alert tool to send a letter to your representatives does not require the submission of a Federal Action Request form.

State and Local Action on Federal Issues

A state or local League wishing to act on an issue at the national level must consult with the LWVUS. **The state League must support a local League's action request.** Leagues and League members must lobby only their own legislators. Individual members are welcome to act on their own behalf without any mention of or attribution to the League. For regional issues, which touch multiple Leagues, all the Leagues in the affected region must be part of the decision-making process. LWVUS often helps to facilitate such regional efforts, particularly when the situation involves federal law.

Federal Action Request Form

For League convenience and to ensure a prompt reply, LWVUS has developed an online form that goes directly to the Advocacy and Litigation team at LWVUS. The federal action request process exists to solicit LWVUS approval to take an action related to any federal office. All action at the federal level, relating to federal law or in federal court, must be authorized by the LWVUS office. This includes any effort aimed at influencing a decision on a federal issue, such as communicating with an elected or appointed official, joining a coalition, taking part in a press conference or rally, writing a letter to the editor, or signing with a legal partner using the LWV brand. Effective action on national legislative and litigation issues depends on a partnership at all League levels.

The Federal Action Request Form should be used any time a League would like to act at the federal level or is contemplating litigation in the federal courts. The form can be found on the LWVUS League Management Site at the following URL: https://www.lwv.org/federal-action-request-form

A state or local League wishing to take a federal advocacy action or participate in federal litigation should consult with LWVUS about the intended action. Depending on the action, the state/local League is asked to provide the following information, which is outlined in the Federal Action Request Form:

Advocacy
- The proposed action and the message to be conveyed.
  - If you are requesting to send or co-sign a letter, please attach that letter in the appropriate section of this form.
- The LWVUS position on which the action is based.
- The timeline for the action (e.g., sending the message, the deadline for signing the letter).

- Details about other groups that are involved in this effort.
- Evidence that the issue is a priority for that state or local League.
  - Evidence of an existing policy position is required. If a local League is requesting permission to contact its US Senator(s) on an issue that has not been the subject of an LWVUS Action Alert, it should provide evidence that the action has been authorized by its state League. If a local League is joining a coalition letter at the state level, it must also have sign-off from its state League.
- Any relevant additional supporting documents.

Litigation

Leagues are encouraged to consult the League Guidance for Assessing Litigation Opportunities.

- The proposed litigation and basis for action (e.g., voting rights, improving elections, redistricting, money in politics, health care).
- Details about other groups that are involved in this effort.
- Name of legal partner(s).
- US court where lawsuit would be filed.
- Deadline for confirming participation.

LWVUS staff will review the advocacy and litigation requests to determine whether they are consistent with League positions, confirm that the proposed activities will not interfere with LWV actions in other federal spaces, and determine whether the matter involves a priority issue that does not compromise the overall national advocacy and litigation portfolio.

LWVUS's approval process for a federal action request outside of the Campaign for Making Democracy Work® includes assessing whether the action:

1. is an unforeseen or unexpected crisis, and
2. requires an immediate response, or
3. addresses a significant risk of harm to many.

When the League decides to work on issues outside of the Campaign for Making Democracy Work, we seek to ally with similar nonpartisan organizations that lead on those issues. Often our allyship takes the form of cosigning a letter written by an allied organization that has the expertise and credibility to lead on the issue. One common type of federal action request is League wanting to send a letter to a federal official or suggesting that LWVUS sign a letter. League members should use the Federal Action Request Form to request LWVUS approval for local or state Leagues to co-sign another organization's letter or send a letter of their own that is addressed to any office at the federal level. The state League must support a local League's action request.

Offices Leagues Can Contact

Leagues may send a letter or communicate only with the office of an official who represents their jurisdiction. For example, a local League may communicate with its representative in the House of Representatives, but it must receive approval from the state chapter. The level of the League should be aligned with the level of government, so a local League wishing to contact one of its state's senators in Congress should do so through its state League. Local Leagues should coordinate with the state League office before submitting a federal action request to LWVUS.

Level of League	Federal Offices That May Be Contacted	Chapter(s) That Must Approve
Local	District representative in US House of Representatives Executive branch offices/federal agencies	State and National
State	State representatives and senators in US House and Senate Executive branch offices/federal agencies	National
National	US Congress, executive branch offices/federal agencies	LWVUS Board and through membership agreement from Impact on Issues Policy positions

Regional Advocacy

In the event that the issue in question impacts multiple local Leagues or multiple state Leagues, it is imperative that all the Leagues in the affected region be part of the decision-making. Prior to submitting a Federal Action Request for a regional issue, please coordinate with all Leagues in the affected region to ensure that all parties agree to take that action. After confirming the participation of all affected Leagues, a Federal Action Request Form may be submitted with the name of the point of contact at each League that agreed to participate and their contact information. Rather than first acquiring LWVUS approval and then coordinating affected League participation, this process prioritizes local decision-making on local issues. Leagues considering engaging in regional advocacy should thoughtfully review the criteria in the next section for acting in the community to determine whether to accept an opportunity to partner on the issue or to request that other Leagues in the region partner on the advocacy.

State and Local Action Using Impact on Issues

Using National Positions at the Regional, State, and Local Levels

Both the Principles (broad statements of beliefs) and Positions (specific statements and guidelines) can be used at the state and local levels to develop support for actions taken at those levels. Impact on Issues, while often citing the federal level of government, is also designed as a guide to encourage state and local Leagues to develop plans for acting at the community level.

League positions at the national level are by their very nature broad and general in scope; they are guides for acting. Local Leagues are responsible for determining action at the local level, and state Leagues are responsible for determining action at the state level and ensuring that the action is consistent throughout the state. Therefore, state and local Leagues must determine that members understand and generally agree with actions taken based on League positions; they should ensure that the action reflects the unique circumstances of the affected community. As with other action, when there are ramifications beyond a League's own governmental jurisdiction, that League must consult other Leagues that may be affected.

Typical actions include any effort aimed at influencing a decision on a federal issue, such as communicating with an elected or appointed official, joining a coalition, taking part in a press conference or rally, or writing a letter to the editor.

Acting in the Community

Interpretation of a League position is the responsibility of the board wishing to take action based on a position. Local League boards are responsible for interpreting local, state, and/or national positions before acting. State boards interpret state, regional, and/or national positions; the national board interprets national positions. Interpretation may be influenced by local conditions. LWVUS staff is available for consultation related to national positions. A League contemplating action on a community issue should consider the following questions:

- Does the League have a position that supports the proposed action?
- Is there broad member understanding and agreement?
- Is it a priority for the League?
- Does the League have a unique role to play or a chance to take the lead?
- Are other organizations or a coalition already working on the issue?
- Is this the best use of the League's resources (time and money) or would they be better spent on other activities?
- Is the timing right? Is action likely in the near future?
- What kind of community involvement would best support the League's efforts?

Principles

The League of Women Voters believes in representative government and in the individual liberties established in the Constitution of the United States. The League of Women Voters of the United States believes that all powers of the US government should be exercised within the constitutional framework of a balance among the three branches of government: legislative, executive, and judicial.

The League of Women Voters believes that democratic government depends upon informed and active participation in government and requires that governmental bodies protect the citizen's right to know by giving adequate notice of proposed actions, holding open meetings, and making public records accessible.

The League of Women Voters believes every citizen should be protected in the right to vote; every person should have access to free public education that provides equal opportunity for all; and no person or group should suffer legal, economic, or administrative discrimination.

The League of Women Voters believes efficient and economical government requires competent personnel, the clear assignment of responsibility, adequate financing, and coordination among the different agencies and levels of government.

The League of Women Voters believes responsible government should be responsive to the will of the people; government should maintain an equitable and flexible system of taxation, promote the conservation and development of natural resources in the public interest, share in the solution of economic and social problems that affect the general welfare, promote a sound economy, and adopt domestic policies that facilitate the solution of international problems.

The League of Women Voters believes cooperation with other nations is essential in the search for solutions to world problems and that development of international organization and international law is imperative in the promotion of world peace.

Summary of Public Policy Positions

League of Women Voters® of the United States

REPRESENTATIVE GOVERNMENT

Promote an open governmental system that is representative, accountable, and responsive.

Voting Rights

Citizen's Right to Vote. Protect the right of all citizens to vote; encourage all citizens to vote.

DC Self-Government and Full Voting Representation. Secure for the citizens of the District of Columbia the rights of self-government and full voting representation in both houses of Congress.

Election Process

Apportionment. Support apportionment of congressional districts and elected legislative bodies at all levels of government based substantially on population.

Redistricting. Support redistricting processes and enforceable standards that promote fair and effective representation at all levels of government with maximum opportunity for public participation.

Money in Politics. (formerly Campaign Finance) Support campaign finance/MIP regulations that enhance political equality for all citizens, ensure transparency, protect representative democracy from distortion by undisclosed contributions and big money, and combat corruption and undue influence in government. Support campaign spending that is restricted but not banned. Support public financing, full disclosure, abolishing super PACs, and creating an effective enforcement agency.

🔍 **Selection of the President.** Promote the election of the President and Vice-President by direct popular vote. Support uniform national voting qualifications and procedures for presidential elections. Support efforts to provide voters with sufficient information about candidates.

Voter Representation/Electoral Systems. Support electoral systems at each level of government that encourage participation, are verifiable and auditable, and enhance representation for all voters.

Citizen Rights

Citizen's Right to Know/Public Participation. Protect the citizen's right to know and facilitate informed understanding and public participation in government decision-making.

Individual Liberties. Oppose major threats to basic constitutional rights.

Public Policy on Reproductive Choices. Protect the constitutional right of privacy of the individual to make reproductive choices.

Evaluating Constitutional Amendment Proposals and Constitutional Conventions

Amendment Proposals. Consider whether a proposal addresses matters of abiding importance, makes our political system more democratic, protects individual rights, could be achieved by a constitutional amendment or legislative proposal, and is consistent with other League positions.

Constitutional Conventions. Hold constitutional conventions only when certain conditions are in place, including limited to a specific topic, full transparency, delegates selected by population, and voting by delegates not by states.

Congress and the Presidency

Congress. Support responsive legislative processes characterized by accountability, representativeness, decision-making capability, effective performance, and transparency.

The Presidency. Promote a dynamic balance of power between the executive and legislative branches within the framework set by the Constitution.

Privatization

Ensure transparency, accountability, positive community impact, and preservation of the common good when considering the transfer of governmental services, assets, and/or functions to the private sector.

Digital Equity

High-speed affordable internet access is an essential service that should be readily available to all US residents and businesses.

INTERNATIONAL RELATIONS

Promote peace in an interdependent world by working cooperatively with other nations and strengthening international organizations.

United Nations

Support a strong, effective United Nations to promote international peace and security and to address the social, economic, and humanitarian needs of all people.

Trade

Support US trade policies that reduce trade barriers; expand international trade; and advance the achievement of humanitarian, environmental, and social goals.

Developing Countries

Promote US policies that meet long-term social and economic needs of developing countries.

Arms Control

Reduce the risk of war through support of arms control measures.

Military Policy and Defense Spending

Work to limit reliance on military force. Examine defense spending in the context of total national needs.

NATURAL RESOURCES

Promote an environment beneficial to life through the protection and wise management of natural resources in the public interest.

Resource Management

Promote the management of natural resources as interrelated parts of life-supporting ecosystems. Promote resource conservation, stewardship, and long-range planning, with the responsibility for managing natural resources shared by all levels of government. Preserve the physical, chemical, and biological integrity of the ecosystem with maximum protection of public health and the environment.

Environmental Protection and Pollution Control

The League supports the preservation of the physical, chemical, and biological integrity of the ecosystem and maximum protection of public health and the environment.

Air Quality. Promote measures to reduce pollution from mobile and stationary sources.

Energy. Support environmentally sound policies that reduce energy growth rates, emphasize energy conservation, and encourage the use of renewable resources.

Land Use. Promote policies that manage land as a finite resource and that incorporate principles of stewardship.

Water. Support measures to reduce pollution in order to protect surface water, groundwater, and drinking water, and set up a process to evaluate inter-basin water transfers.

Waste Management. Promote policies to reduce the generation of solid and hazardous wastes and promote their reuse and recycling.

Nuclear. Promote the maximum protection of public health and safety and the environment.

Transfer of Federal Public Lands

Promote policies that keep federal public lands under the jurisdiction of the federal government.

⚲ Climate Change

Support climate goals and policies that are consistent with the best available climate science and that will ensure a stable climate system for future generations.

Public Participation

Promote public understanding and participation in decision making as essential elements of responsible and responsive management of our natural resources.

Federal Agriculture Policies

Support environmentally sound farm practices, and increased reliance on the free market while promoting adequate supplies of food at reasonable prices and regulations to all animal and aquaculture production. Enforce federal antitrust laws to ensure competitive agricultural markets, provide financial support to subsidize agriculture in specific instances. Support the federal government's funding of basic agricultural research to ensure adequate safety of our food supply.

SOCIAL POLICY

Secure equal rights and equal opportunity for all. Promote social and economic justice and the health and safety of all Americans.

Criminal Justice

Support a criminal justice system that is just, effective, equitable, transparent, and that fosters public trust at all stages, including policing practices, pre-trial procedures, sentencing, incarceration, and re-entry.

⌕ Equality of Opportunity

Equal Rights. Support ratification of the Equal Rights Amendment and efforts to bring laws into compliance with the goals of the ERA. Support equal rights for all under state and federal law regardless of race, color, gender, religion, national origin, age, sexual orientation, or disability.

Education, Employment, and Housing. Support equal access to education, employment, and housing.

Federal Role in Public Education. Support federal policies that provide an equitable, quality public education for all children from pre-K through grade 12.

Fiscal Policy

Federal Deficit. Promote responsible deficit policies.

Funding of Entitlements. Support a federal role in providing mandatory, universal, old-age, survivors, disability, and health insurance.

Tax Policy. Support adequate and flexible funding of federal government programs through an equitable tax system that is progressive overall and that relies primarily on a broad-based income tax.

⌕ Health Care

Promote a health care system for the United States that provides affordable access to a basic level of quality care for all US residents, including behavioral health that is integrated with and achieves parity with the physical health care system.

⌕ Immigration

Promote reunification of immediate families; meet the economic, business, and employment needs of the United States; be responsive to those facing political persecution or humanitarian crises; and provide for student visas. Ensure fair treatment under the law for all persons. In transition to a reformed system, support provisions for individuals already living in the country without legal permission to earn legal status.

Meeting Basic Human Needs

Support programs and policies to prevent or reduce poverty and to promote self-sufficiency for individuals and families.

Income Assistance. Support income assistance programs, based on need, that provide decent, adequate standards for food, clothing, and shelter.

Support Services. Provide essential support services.

Housing. Support policies to provide a decent home and a suitable living environment for every American family.

Child Care

Support programs and policies to expand the supply of affordable, quality child care for all who need it.

Early Intervention for Children at Risk

Support policies and programs that promote the well-being, development, and safety of all children.

🔍 Violence Prevention

Support violence prevention programs in communities.

🔍 Gun Policy

Protect the health and safety of citizens through limiting the accessibility and regulating the ownership of handguns and semi-automatic weapons. Support regulation of firearms for consumer safety.

Urban Policy

Promote the economic health of cities and improve the quality of urban life.

🔍 Death Penalty

Support abolition of the death penalty.

🔍 Sentencing Policy

Support the exploration and utilization of alternatives to imprisonment, taking into consideration the circumstances and nature of the crime. Oppose mandatory minimum sentences for drug offenses.

Human Trafficking

Oppose all forms of domestic and international human trafficking of adults and children, including sex trafficking and labor trafficking.

Whatever the issue, the League believes that efficient and economical government requires competent personnel, the clear assignment of responsibilities, adequate financing, coordination among levels of government, effective enforcement, and well-defined channels for citizen input and review.

IMPACT ON ISSUES

Representative Government

Promote an open governmental system that is representative, accountable, and responsive.

Founded by the activists who secured voting rights for women, the League has always worked to promote the values and processes of representative government. Protecting and enhancing voting rights for all Americans; assuring opportunities for citizen participation; and working for open, accountable, representative, and responsive government at every level—all reflect the deeply held convictions of the League of Women Voters.

In the 1950s, the League worked courageously to protect fundamental rights and individual liberties against the threats of the McCarthy era. In the 1960s, attention turned to securing "one person, one vote" through apportionment of legislative districts based substantially on population. In the 1970s, members worked to reform the legislative process and open it to scrutiny, and to balance congressional and presidential powers. The League also sought to reform the campaign finance system to reduce the dominance of special interests, affirmed support for the direct election of the President, and fought for full voting rights in Congress for the residents of the District of Columbia.

In the 1980s and 1990s, the League worked to break down the barriers to voting, first through multiple reauthorizations of the *Voting Rights Act* (VRA), and then through a campaign for passage and implementation of the landmark *National Voter Registration Act* (NVRA). Campaign finance reform, with a focus on public financing and closing loopholes, again was a major activity at the federal and state levels, with the goal of enhancing the role of Americans in the election and legislative processes. In the late 1990s, the fight for DC voting rights was reinvigorated. During that same period, the League worked to ensure the constitutional right of privacy of the individual to make reproductive choices and opposed term limits for legislative offices.

In the mid- to late 1990s, the League launched its Campaign for Making Democracy Work®, focusing on five key indicators of a healthy democracy: voter participation, campaign finance reform, diversity of representation, civic education and knowledge, and civic participation. The 1998 Convention added "full congressional voting representation for the District of Columbia" to the campaign. State and local Leagues measured the health of democracy in their communities, reported the results, and worked with other groups to seek change. The LWVUS report, Charting the Health of American Democracy, took a nationwide measure and made recommendations for change.

In the 2000s, this campaign continued. Convention 2002 decided to update the position on the Selection of the President, focusing not only on the electoral process, but on the other factors that affect the presidential race (e.g., money, parties, the media). The position was expanded and formally approved at Convention 2004.

In the second half of the 2000s, the League supported legislation to reform the lobbying process and rebuild public confidence in Congress. In 2008, the House passed new ethics guidelines, including new ethics rules, disclosure requirements for campaign contributions "bundled" by lobbyists, and a new ethics enforcement process. The League also continued its work seeking full enforcement of the *National Voter Registration Act*.

In late 2010 and again in 2012, the League and coalition partners urged the Speaker to preserve and strengthen House ethics rules and standards of conduct.

Campaign Finance in the 2000s

The five-year fight for campaign finance reform paid off in March 2002 when President George W. Bush signed the *Bipartisan Campaign Reform Act* (BCRA) into law. The League was instrumental in developing this legislation and pushing it to enactment, and we remain vigilant in ensuring the law is enforced and properly interpreted in the courts.

In the late 2000s, LWVUS filed amicus briefs in two pivotal US Supreme Court cases: *Caperton v. Massey* and *Citizens United v. FEC*. In the latter case, the League argued that corporate spending in elections should not be equated with the First Amendment rights of individual citizens.

In 2010, the League reacted swiftly and strongly to the Supreme Court's adverse decision in the *Citizens United* case, which allowed unlimited "independent" corporate spending in candidate elections. The League president testified before the relevant House committee on the key steps that can be taken to respond, focusing on the importance of including tighter disclosure requirements. The League continues to urge passage of the *DISCLOSE Act* to ensure that corporate and union spending in elections is fully disclosed.

With the explosion of supposedly "independent" spending by outside groups in the years since *Citizens United*, the League is pushing for tougher rules on coordination, because much of the outside spending is not independent, and instead is coordinated with candidate campaigns. In addition, the League continues to push for legislation to protect and refresh the presidential public financing system and to institute congressional public financing. The League is also working to reform the dysfunctional Federal Election Commission (FEC), which has refused to enforce the law.

Election Administration in the 2000s

When the disputed 2000 elections exposed the many problems facing our election administration system, the League leaped into action. Bringing our coalition allies together, the League worked to ensure that key reforms were part of the congressional debate. In October 2002, the *Help America Vote Act* (HAVA) was signed into law, creating the Election Assistance Commission and authorizing funds for each state to improve the operation of elections according to federal requirements.

The League continues to fight to ensure that the requirements of HAVA are implemented in ways to assure voter access. The League created the 5 Things You Need to Know on Election Day public awareness campaign in 2004 to educate voters about the new requirements and the steps each voter could take to protect access. The campaign was highly successful and has continued in subsequent election seasons with a particular emphasis on providing high-quality voting information to first-time voters and other impacted communities.

Convention 2006 clarified the League's stance on voting systems to assure that they would be secure, accurate, recountable, accessible, and transparent.

Voter Protection in the 21st Century

In 2006, the League launched its highly successful Public Advocacy for Voter Protection (PAVP) project and by the early 2010s, the PAVP project had expanded to more than 20 states as the League engaged in targeted state-based advocacy. LWVUS collaborates with state Leagues to enhance their public education and advocacy campaigns to fight barriers to voter participation and ensure election laws and processes are applied in a uniform and non-discriminatory manner.

Since its inception, the PAVP project has helped to remove or mitigate barriers to voting by underserved populations and to advance the capacity of state Leagues to become even more effective advocates in five focus areas identified by the League as essential to protecting the votes of all citizens and improving election administration overall: (1) oppose photo ID and documentary proof of citizenship; (2) improve administration of statewide database systems; (3) guard against undue restrictions on voter registration; (4) improve polling place management; and (5) improve poll worker training.

League work includes advocating for compliance with existing laws and regulations, such as the *National Voter Registration* Act, advocating for key reforms through education and advocacy, and pursuing litigation when necessary. League action has been directed toward legislators, state/local elections officials, other policy makers, the media, and concerned citizens, as appropriate.

One of the most significant threats tackled by Leagues through the PAVP project is onerous and restrictive voter photo ID requirements. As late as 2008, as many as 21 million Americans did not have government-issued photo identification, with communities of color and individuals with limited income disproportionately less likely to have photo ID showing a current address. The League's efforts to combat voter suppression require issue monitoring and action by League advocates, often over multiple state legislative sessions, countless articles and opinion pieces placed in national and regional media, and multiple steps in the state and federal courts. League leaders and their partners have worked every step of the way to ensure all eligible voters have the opportunity to participate and have the tools necessary to overcome the confusion that results from these drawn-out battles.

During the 2011 – 2012 cycle, the League's efforts resulted in the defeat of five strict voter photo ID bills during state legislative sessions (CO, IA, ME, MO, and NC); successful court action to block restrictive ID laws from implementation in four more states (SC, TX, PA, and WI); and success of the "People's Veto" in ME in protecting same-day voter registration.

On Election Day in 2012, Minnesota voters were the first in the country to soundly reject a proposed constitutional amendment that would have required government-issue voter photo ID and eliminated Election Day registration in future elections. The League and its partners were instrumental in securing this success for voters.

In the late summer and fall of 2012, the League was also a leader in pushing back against illegal purging of voters from voter registration lists in Colorado and Florida. Through additional court action, the League succeeded in overturning onerous restrictions on voter registration and quickly moved to fill the gap created by limits to independent voter registration in Florida.

The 2013 – 2014 period brought renewed national and state legislature attempts to restrict voting. LWV staff assisted 31 state League affiliates as they encountered voter suppression issues, and Leagues were instrumental in advocating against approximately 25 strict voter photo ID bills during the 2013 – 2014 state legislative sessions.

LWVUS and state Leagues across the country undertook court action to block restrictive laws in Kansas, North Carolina, Ohio, South Carolina, Wisconsin, and other states, with several major victories prior to Election Day

2016. We distributed an updated "ID Toolkit" to ensure that Leagues across the country disseminated a unified, comprehensive, and sustained message. The toolkit includes national overview of photo ID laws, overview of major court cases across the country, and a host of useful advocacy suggestions and templates.

The Ohio League received support in a challenge to reinstate the "golden week" of early voting that overlapped with open voter registration following the legislature's action to cut it. In Georgia, a League-led coalition successfully stopped legislation that would have significantly reduced the early voting period.

In early 2013, the US Supreme Court heard two important cases challenging the *Voting Rights Act* and the *National Voter Registration Act*, and their ruling eliminated key voting rights safeguards that have been in place for decades. LWVUS submitted an amicus brief in each case, and the Arizona state League was a plaintiff in the NVRA challenge. The League strongly supported the enforcement mechanism in the VRA and, in support of the NVRA, continued its opposition to a documentary proof-of-citizenship requirement for voter registration.

During the 2014 – 2016 biennium, LWVUS with state Leagues successfully challenged purging rules in Florida and sought to reverse a decision by the new executive director of the US Election Assistance Commission to allow documentary proof-of-citizenship requirements in Arizona, Georgia, and Kansas.

State Leagues in Kansas, North Carolina, Ohio, and Wisconsin were active participants and leaders in a variety of lawsuits seeking to block voting restrictions in those states.

During the 2016 – 2018 biennium, LWVUS partnered with state Leagues in challenging illegal purging practices and strict voter ID laws in Arizona, Florida, Georgia, Ohio, Texas, and Wisconsin.

Preventing Election Day Barriers

In the lead-up to Election Day 2016, League volunteers worked around the clock to protect the rights of voters. They staffed English and Spanish language hotlines answering voters' questions and troubleshooting for them. They set up poll observation programs, served as poll workers, and reported challenges to the national Election Protection Coalition, all with the goal of ensuring votes were successfully cast and counted. In states where restrictive photo ID laws had passed and were implemented, the League actively sought out and provided assistance to individuals who could have difficulty getting the required ID. Assistance included education about the requirements, transportation to Department of Motor Vehicles offices, and help in obtaining—and in some instances paying for—underlying documentation (e.g., birth certificates). As part of this effort, LWV printed tens of thousands of state-specific voter education materials. In 2016 alone, the League's work to protect and mobilize voters was featured in more than 35,000 news stories.

Leagues also regularly met with election officials to encourage Election Day preparedness, poll worker training (especially in states where changes have been made), and fair distribution of resources so that all polling places were staffed and prepared for voters. In all, Leagues had more than 1,000 meetings with election officials. Across the country, hundreds of League volunteers staffed hotlines and worked as election observers to ensure voters' rights were protected on Election Day itself.

In 2018, LWVUS along with a legal partner worked with state Leagues in Alabama, Indiana, and Maine to successfully combat purging practices in violation of the NVRA. Letters were sent to each secretary of state specifically asking for a commitment in writing that these purging practices would not be implemented during the midterm election cycle.

LWVUS staff also renewed its activity in the Election Protection coalition, serving as lead for states with a history of voter suppression. The work done on Election Day influenced lawsuits that were successful in keeping polls open for disenfranchised voters in the South.

In all, the League protected more than 4.2 million voters through its advocacy, litigation, and education efforts throughout 2018.

When possible, Leagues also worked to improve voter registration database matching criteria; ensure students' right to vote using their campus address; increase the effectiveness of public assistance office voter registration; and ensure fair and equitable implementation of early voting and vote centers. LWVUS has promoted key proactive election reform priorities since 2013, including secure online voter registration, permanent and portable statewide voter registration, expansion of early voting, improvement of polling place management, and electronic streamlining of election processes.

COVID-19 Pandemic

As the world dealt with the COVID-19 pandemic and prepared for the 2020 election, a host of states quickly adjusted their election and registration rules. The pandemic created ample opportunity for anti-voter rules, such as reduced mail-in voting options and last-minute election changes, to thrive. Leagues across the US fought these rules by initiating or joining dozens of cases focused on expanding voting options through added protections for in-person voting; the elimination or relaxation of discriminatory ID requirements; support for the US Postal Service; increased opportunities for early and mail-in voting; and much more. League litigation pushed for expanded options for mail-in voting and no-excuse absentee voting, as well as increased accessible drop boxes, to balance health and safety with the right to vote. Ultimately, the League protected 25,831,538 voters through legal actions in 2020, which was among the League's largest voter protection results in recent history. Nonetheless, an explosion of anti-voter laws emerged following the 2020 election, and the League jumped into action to counter ongoing discrimination, voter intimidation, and suppression.

Key Structures of Democracy

At the 2014 Convention, delegates voted on an ambitious program to examine three key structures of democracy: redistricting reform, amending the Constitution, and money in politics. Through League studies, new positions were developed on Money in Politics, Considerations for Evaluating Constitutional Amendment Proposals, and Constitutional Conventions under Article V of the US Constitution. A League task force recommended a new position on Redistricting to Convention 2016, and it was adopted by concurrence.

Based on these new positions and the positions on Voting Rights, LWV launched a Campaign for Making Democracy Work® for the 2016 – 2018 biennium. Voter registration, education, mobilization, and protection are key parts of this campaign, which extends to legislative reform at the state and local levels as well as the national level.

Campaign for Making Democracy Work

The 2018 convention reaffirmed the League's commitment to the Campaign for Making Democracy Work (CMDW) and updated the program to include advocacy of the National Popular Voter Interstate Compact as resources allowed. LWVUS initiated an NPV task force in early 2019 to assess viability of this reform. In November 2019, the League signed on to a report by the Leadership Conference on Civil and Human Rights (LCCHR), Vision for Democracy, which details the massive systemic reforms needed to protect and improve our democracy. These reforms include preventing barriers to the ballot box, ending felony disenfranchisement, expanding voter registration, increasing voter participation and access, strengthening election security, and creating structural reform (addressing gerrymandering, DC statehood, and money in politics).

The CMDW was reaffirmed as part of the program by Convention in 2020 and 2022. As part of the campaign, LWVUS launched People Powered Fair Maps™, a project to build fair and transparent redistricting processes in all fifty states and DC, following the disappointing decisions in *Rucho v. League of Women Voters of North Carolina*. The League also started work at the federal level to support legislation like the *For the People Act*, *the Freedom to Vote Act*, and the *John R. Lewis Voting Rights Advancement Act*.

When the COVID-19 pandemic stalled the nation in the spring of 2020, the League was forced to pivot to seeing elections through a lens of pandemic preparedness. The 2020 elections created unique challenges that required new thinking and forced elections officials to expand voting options to protect public health. Many states expanded no-excuse absentee voting or extended mail-in ballots to all voters. The League was at the forefront, fighting for funding to aid election workers facing unique challenges and informing voters about their options to participate in a way that made them feel comfortable. With the US Postal Service beginning wide-scale changes just before an election, the national League joined partners to file a lawsuit against the postmaster general and US Postal Service asserting that recent changes to the postal service and procedures and equipment presented an undue burden on the fundamental right to vote, infringed on free speech rights, and violated the Administrative Procedures Act (APA). Within a week after filing our lawsuit, the postmaster general issued an announcement that the agency would suspend certain "operational initiatives" until after the election.

While the pandemic expanded opportunities for voters, it also created stress for the 2020 Census. The League was a partner with the US Census Bureau, helping to share information on the ground and through social media about the importance of the 2020 Census. When the US Census Bureau was forced to shut down enumeration and then restart on a shortened timeline, LWVUS and three state Leagues joined partners to file a lawsuit to protect the Census count. We argued that the Trump administration's decision to stop collecting data on September 30, 2020, rather than October 31, 2020, was an attempt to exclude undocumented immigrants and would result in an undercount of minority communities. We requested that the timeline be restored so that a full count could be completed. The lawsuit resulted in eleven additional days of counting before finally being shut down on October 15, 2020.

Following the 2020 election, and in the face of lack of protections from the *Voting Rights Act*, states began enacting changes to roll back the expansion of voting that occurred during the COVID-19 pandemic. State Leagues in Georgia, Texas, Florida, and other states were forced to fight back against omnibus voting laws.

Voting Rights

CITIZEN'S RIGHT TO VOTE

The League's Position

Statement of Position on Citizen's Right to Vote, as announced by the national board, March 1982:

The League of Women Voters of the United States believes that voting is a fundamental citizen right that must be guaranteed.

League History

The Voting Rights Act of 1965

The right to vote for every eligible American has been a basic League principle since its origin. Early on, many state Leagues adopted positions on election laws. But at the national level, despite a long history of protecting voting rights, the League found itself during the civil rights struggle of the 1960s without authority to take national legislative action on behalf of the *Voting Rights Act of 1965* (VRA). Stung by the League's powerlessness to act on such a significant issue, the 1970 Convention adopted a bylaws amendment enabling the League to act "to protect the right to vote of every citizen" without the formality of adopting voting rights in the national program. This unusual decision reflected member conviction that protecting the right to vote is indivisibly part of the League's basic purpose.

When the 1974 Convention amended the Bylaws to provide that all League Principles could serve as authority for action, the separate amendment on voting rights was no longer needed and in the 94th Congress (1975 – 1977) the League was part of a successful coalition effort to extend the VRA and expand its coverage to language minorities. The 1976 Convention's adoption of voting rights as an integral part of the national Program and the 1978 confirmation of that decision underlined the already existing authority under the Principles for the League to act on this basic right.

In May 1982, the LWVUS Board made explicit the League's position on voting rights, and the 1982 Convention added voting rights to the national program. In the 97th Congress (1981 – 1983), the League was a leader in the fight to strengthen the VRA and extend its major provisions for 25 years. The 1986 Convention affirmed that a key element of protecting the right to vote is encouraging participation in the political process. The 1990 Convention affirmed that LWVUS should continue emphasis on protecting the right to vote by working to increase voter participation.

In the 102nd Congress (1991 – 1993), the League successfully sought reauthorization of the language assistance provision for an additional 15 years. In 2006, the League sponsored a major public initiative to support the *Fannie Lou Hamer, Rosa Parks, and Coretta Scott King Voting Rights Act Reauthorization and Amendments Act of 2006*. After months of action by Leagues across the country, the bill was passed and signed into law.

The League has played a role in every major reauthorization of the Voting Rights Act. After the 2013 decision in *Shelby County v. Holder*, in which the League participated with an amicus brief, the League again joined with coalition partners to restore the VRA. The League participated in the 50th Anniversary of the March on Washington with President Obama and all other living presidents, as well as leaders from the civil rights movement, Congressman John Lewis, and other elected leaders. The League continued to push for action on the Voting Rights Advancement Act during the 115th and 116th Congresses.

In response to threats to voting rights, the League has actively pursued litigation and administrative advocacy. In 1985, the League filed comments objecting to proposed regulations that would weaken the administrative enforcement provisions of Section 5 of the Act. And with other amici curiae, the League successfully urged the US Supreme Court to adopt a strong interpretation of Section 2 for challenges to minority vote dilution.

From 1984 to 1989, building on a 1982 pilot project to monitor compliance with the *Voting Rights Act* in states covered by Section 5 of the Act, LWVEF conducted projects to apply monitoring techniques in jurisdictions considering bailout from Section 5, to establish the League as a major source of information on bailout and compliance issues. Since 1988, LWVEF has worked with state and local Leagues to encourage full participation in each census and to ensure that subsequent reapportionment and redistricting complies with one-person, one-vote requirements and the *Voting Rights Act*.

In 1996 and 1998, LWVUS worked against congressional "English-only" legislation that would have effectively repealed the minority language provisions of the *Voting Rights Act*.

National Voter Registration Act (NVRA)

In 1990, LWVEF convened a symposium of scholars, journalists, campaign consultants, and activists to examine the role of negative campaigning in the decline in voter participation and possible grassroots remedies. The symposium led to a comprehensive effort to return the voter to the center of the election process. The Take Back the System campaign coordinated League activities to make voter registration more accessible, provide voters with information about candidates and issues, and restore voters' confidence and involvement in the electoral system. The program included LWVUS efforts on voter registration and campaign finance reform; an LWVEF presidential primary debate; a national voter registration drive; voter registration efforts aimed at young people; a Campaign Watch pilot project to help voters deter unfair campaign practices; and grassroots efforts to register, inform, and involve voters. The League's grassroots campaign to secure national legislation to reform voter registration resulted in the 1990 House passage of the *National Voter Registration Act* (NVRA) — also known as the "motor-voter" bill — but the bill did not reach the Senate that year.

In 1991, the effort to pass national motor-voter legislation intensified, and the *National Voter Registration Act of 1991* was introduced in the Senate. Leading a national coalition, the League executed a high-visibility, multifaceted, grassroots drive, resulting in passage by both houses in 1992, but President George H. W. Bush vetoed the bill and the Senate failed to override.

In May 1993, the years of concerted effort by the League and other organizations paid off when both houses passed, and President Clinton signed, the *National Voter Registration Act*. The President gave one of the signing pens to LWVUS and saluted the League and other supporters as "fighters for freedom" in the continuing effort to expand American democracy. The motor-voter bill enabled voter registration at motor vehicle agencies automatically, as well as by mail and at public and private agencies that service the public.

In 1994, LWVEF launched the Wired for Democracy project, anticipating the potential of the internet for providing voter education and opening government to citizens. In 1996, the League focused its energies on getting voters to the polls.

League members also quickly turned to ensuring effective implementation of the NVRA by states and key federal agencies. In early 1994, LWVEF sponsored the Motor Voter Alert conference of representatives from more than 30 state Leagues, other grassroots activists, and representatives of civil rights and disability groups. Throughout 1994, while LWVUS successfully lobbied the President and the Justice Department for strong federal leadership, state Leagues kept the pressure on their legislatures to pass effective enabling legislation by the January 1995 deadline. On September 12, 1994, the President issued an executive order requiring affected federal agencies to cooperate to the greatest extent possible with the states in implementing the law by providing funds, guidance, and technical assistance to affected state public assistance agencies and agencies serving the disabled.

A report on the first-year impact of the NVRA indicated that 11 million eligible Americans registered to vote under required NVRA motor-voter, agency-based, and mail-in programs in 1995. State Leagues and other organizations joined the Justice Department in filing lawsuits against states that refused to implement the NVRA. By the summer of 1996, Illinois, Pennsylvania, California, South Carolina, Virginia, Michigan, and Kansas had lost Tenth Amendment states-rights arguments against the NVRA in federal court.

In 1995 and 1996, state and local Leagues worked to ensure effective state enforcement of the NVRA, as LWVUS lobbied against congressional amendments that would have weakened or undermined the new federal law.

A noncompliance suit filed by the state League against New Hampshire was dropped early in 1996 when Congress passed a legislative rider exempting New Hampshire and Idaho from the NVRA by extending the law's deadline for state exemptions based on having Election Day registration programs. LWVUS opposed the New Hampshire exemption.

LWVUS urged state election officials and Congress to give the NVRA a chance to work before proposing changes. The League opposed a Senate NVRA "unfunded mandate" amendment that would have blocked state compliance by requiring the federal government to pay for implementation. The League also opposed amendments that required proof of citizenship to register to vote. All but the New Hampshire exemption were defeated or withdrawn.

While the NVRA helped more Americans register to vote for the 1996 election than at any other time since records have been kept, LWVUS continued to fight congressional attempts to cripple the law. For example, the League lobbied and testified against the *Voter Eligibility Verification Act*, which sought to create a federal program to verify the citizenship of voter registrants and applicants, arguing that the program was not necessary, would not work, and would depress voter participation.

On related issues, the League has supported efforts to increase the accessibility of registration and voting for people with disabilities in federal elections and undertaken major efforts to encourage participation in the electoral process. Since 1988, LWVEF has been coordinating broad-based voter registration drives, combining national publicity and outreach with grassroots activities by state and local Leagues, other groups, and public officials.

The League also has worked to change aspects of the coverage and conduct of campaigns that might frustrate voter participation. From 1980 to 1985, LWVUS sought to pressure broadcasters not to air projections of election results before all the polls in a race closed.

Since 2012, the League has served on the national working committee that oversees National Voter Registration Day, a major national initiative that has brought together thousands of partners to register hundreds of thousands of voters each September. In 2016, more than 350 Leagues from 45 states participated and registered more than 19,000 individuals to vote on National Voter Registration Day. In 2018, Leagues from 40 states hosted more than 400 events and registering more than 32,000 individuals to vote—making the League the single largest on-the-ground participant for the seventh year in a row.

Voter Engagement and Turnout

Original research sponsored by LWVEF found that voters and nonvoters differ in several key respects: nonvoters are less likely to grasp the impact of elections on issues that matter to them, nonvoters are more likely to believe they lack information on which to base their voting decisions; nonvoters are more likely to perceive the voting process as difficult and cumbersome; and nonvoters are less likely to be contacted by organizations encouraging them to vote.

In 1996, armed with the message, "It's about your children's education, your taxes, your Social Security, your Medicare, and your safe streets. It's about you and your family. Vote," Leagues nationwide conducted targeted, grassroots get-out-the-vote (GOTV) campaigns. Focusing on racial and ethnic minorities and other underrepresented populations, Leagues worked in coalition with other organizations to expand their reach and let voters know they have a stake in the system. Despite an overall downturn in voter participation in 1996, precincts targeted by the League's effort posted increased voting rates.

In the 2000 elections, LWVEF worked with state and local Leagues on intensive GOTV campaigns in 30 communities, targeting impacted voters. Training highlighted new ways to engage citizens to work in coalitions with diverse communities. The League also participated in forming the Youth Vote 2000, a nonpartisan coalition of organizations committed to encouraging greater participation in the political process and promoting a better understanding of public policy issues among youth.

Also in 2000, the League launched its Take a Friend to Vote (TAFTV) campaign, based on research showing that nonvoters are most likely to vote if asked by a friend, family member, neighbor, or someone else they respect. The TAFTV campaign featured toolkits with reminder postcards and bumper stickers, a website, PSAs on Lifetime Television, and "advertorials" in major magazines featuring celebrities and their friends talking about the importance of voting.

Help America Vote Act

When the 2000 election exposed the many problems facing the election system, the League began to work relentlessly on election reform and bringing its importance to national attention. LWVUS helped draft and pass the *Help America Vote Act of 2002* (HAVA), working closely with a civil rights coalition in developing amendments and lobbying for key provisions.

LWVUS took a leadership role in forming an election reform coalition to develop recommendations on HAVA implementation and testified before the House and Senate, stressing the importance of substantial new federal funding for election reform efforts. The League used its special expertise to argue for improved voting systems and machines, provisional balloting and other safeguards, and improvements in voter registration systems and poll worker training and administration.

LWVEF worked to heighten public awareness about election administration problems and provide informational and action materials to state and local Leagues. In 2001, LWVEF hosted three Focus on the Voter symposia and worked with Leagues to design and conduct a survey of election administration practices in local jurisdictions. Four hundred and sixty Leagues from 47 states and the District of Columbia responded to the survey. A report of the findings was released at a post-election symposium in November 2001 and concluded that "good enough is not good enough."

In 2001 and 2002, we made Election Administration Reform: A Leader's Guide for Action, the Election 2001 Toolkit, and Navigating Election Day: What Every Voter Needs to Know available to state and local Leagues for voter education activities. In late 2002, LWVEF convened a conference, sponsored by the McCormick Tribune Foundation, to explore emerging issues in election reform.

In the 108th Congress (2003 – 2005), the key issue was funding for HAVA, as President George W. Bush initially proposed that HAVA not be fully funded. A joint lobbying effort of state and local government organizations, civil rights groups, and the League prevailed in achieving full funding for the first two years of implementation.

The League issued several publications following the passage of HAVA to support effective implementation of the bill. In mid-2003, LWVEF published Helping America Vote: Implementing the New Federal Provisional Ballot Requirement, which examined and made key policy recommendations for states and localities in implementing HAVA's provisional balloting requirement. The second report, Helping America Vote: Safeguarding the Vote, followed in 2004, outlining a set of recommended operational and management practices for state and local election officials to enhance voting system security, protect eligible voters, manage statewide voter registration databases, and ensure that valid votes are counted. A third report, published in in June 2005 by LWVEF, was Helping America Vote: Statewide Voter Registration Databases. And a fourth and final report was Helping America Vote: Thinking Outside the Ballot Box, published in 2006 by LWVEF.

In the early 2000s, the League made available its attractive VOTE brochure, a succinct, step-by-step guide to voting and Election Day, designed to reach out to new, young, and first-time voters. Our 5 Things You Need to Know on Election Day card provided hundreds of thousands of voters with simple steps to ensure their vote is counted.

At the 2004 Convention, the League determined that to ensure integrity and voter confidence in elections, LWVUS supports the implementation of voting systems and procedures that are secure, accurate, recountable, and accessible. State and local Leagues may support a particular voting system appropriate to their area, but should evaluate them based on the "secure, accurate, recountable, and accessible" criteria. While LWVUS has not commented on specific voting systems, Leagues should continue to consult with LWVUS before taking a stand on a specific type of voting system to ensure that the League speaks with a consistent voice. Leagues should also consult standards developed by the Election Assistance Commission (EAC) pertaining to voting systems when studying or improving their own voting systems.

At Convention 2006, delegates further clarified this position with a resolution stating that the Citizens' Right to Vote be interpreted to affirm that LWVUS supports only voting systems that are designed so that:

- They employ a voter-verifiable paper ballot or other paper record, said paper being the official record of the voter's intent.
- The voter can verify, either by eye or with the aid of suitable devices for those who have impaired vision, that the paper ballot/record accurately reflects his or her intent.
- Such verification takes place while the voter is still in the process of voting.
- The paper ballot/record is used for audits and recounts.
- The vote totals can be verified by an independent hand count of the paper ballot/record.
- Routine audits of the paper ballot/record in randomly selected precincts can be conducted in every election, and the results published by the jurisdiction.

At Convention 2010, delegates added the principle of transparency, so that the League supports voting systems that are secure, accurate, recountable, accessible, and transparent.

Also, in 2004, the League of Women Voters conducted a survey of local and state election officials in a number of target states to identify potential problems with HAVA implementation that could put the votes of eligible voters at risk. The League identified the top five risks to eligible voters in 2004, including voter registration problems, erroneous purging, problems with the new ID requirement, difficulties with voting systems and a failure to count provisional ballots, and asked election officials for resolution before the election. League leaders in various states were at the forefront of high-profile battles over HAVA's implementation.

In 2006, the League released Thinking Outside the Ballot Box: Innovations at the Polling Place, a comprehensive report aimed at sharing successful election administration stories with local officials throughout the country.

As a complement, not a substitute, to the NVRA, the League continues to support shortening the period between registration and voting or same-day voter registration. LWVUS has worked with state Leagues interested in promoting such reforms.

Choosing the President

The League's respected voter education tool, Choosing the President: A Citizen's Guide to the Electoral Process, was revised in 2004 and 2008. The 2008 edition was also translated into Russian and Arabic and was the basis for Electing the President, a 16-page education supplement created and distributed to schools in collaboration with the Newspapers in Education Institute. We updated Electing the President in 2012 and in 2016 and again distributed it to schools in collaboration with the Newspapers in Education Institute.

Additionally, we appointed an Election Audit Task Force to report to the LWVUS Board on the auditing of election procedures and processes. The 2009 report is available at www.lwv.org. Leagues should find this report useful in talking with their legislatures and elections officials about election auditing.

League Investment in Online Voter Information

In 1998, the League was a visionary, recognizing that the way of the future for voter education would be online. It tested two systems to transform its trusted, nonpartisan voters' guides and make them readily available online. LWVEF chose the DemocracyNet (DNet) as its nationwide online voter information platform and worked with state and local Leagues to expand the system to all 50 states for the 2000 elections. By the 2004 election, DNet was the most comprehensive source of voter information and one of the top online sites for unbiased election information, offering full coverage of all federal races as well as thousands of state and local contests.

In 2006, the League launched the next generation of online voter education with VOTE411.org, a "one-stop shop" for election-related information, providing nonpartisan information to the public with both general and state-specific information including a nationwide polling place and ballot drop box locator, absentee ballot information, ballot measure information, comprehensive candidate information, and other important resources. In 2008, 2012, and 2019, LWVEF accomplished consecutive overhauls and improvements to this award-winning voter education website, and in 2020 VOTE411 launched in Spanish, continuing the tradition of making it the most comprehensive, easy-to-use online tool for voters. The site is at the heart of the League's campaign to prepare voters.

Since we launched VOTE411 in 2006, more than 53.6 million people have benefited from the information available on the site. VOTE411 has expanded access to information about candidates at the state and local levels with every election year. In partnership with hundreds of state and local Leagues, VOTE411 provides voters with information on where tens of thousands of candidates stand on the issues and up-to-date election rules for all 50 states in every election year. And in 2016 for the first time, the statements from the presidential candidates were available in English and Spanish.

In 2022, VOTE411.org served nearly 5 million individuals and proved to be one of the most stable, reliable, comprehensive, and accessible platforms throughout the primary season as well as on Election Day.

Opposing Voting Barriers

In 2006, the League launched the Public Advocacy for Voter Protection (PAVP) project, and since then, the League has undertaken concerted nationwide efforts to promote voter protection and education to prevent the development of processes and laws that threaten to disenfranchise voters, educate the public on new election procedures, and provide voters with the information they need to cast a vote and be sure that vote is counted.

As part of the PAVP effort, in 2007, the League opposed state legislation that would require documentary proof of citizenship or picture ID to register to vote and to vote. The League also filed an amicus brief in a Supreme Court case regarding ID requirements in Indiana. In 2009, the League filed an amicus brief in the Arizona voter ID case, *Gonzalez v. Arizona*, asking the 9th Circuit Court of Appeals to recognize that the *National Voter Registration Act of 1993* prohibits a proof-of-citizenship requirement when using the national mail voter registration application form. The League again filed an amicus brief when the case was argued before the Supreme Court in 2013. The League and its allies finally prevailed. In the renamed *ITCA v. Arizona*, the Court agreed that the NVRA preempts state law.

2014 and 2016 brought unprecedented challenges and successes to the PAVP program, with participating Leagues ultimately defeating dozens of onerous barriers that threatened the right to vote. For the first time in 2016, LWVEF supported state Leagues' efforts to call more than 100,000 people to encourage their participation in the 2016 election and make sure they had accurate information about early voting and identification rules.

Since its inception, the PAVP project has helped to remove or mitigate barriers to voting by underserved populations and advance the capacity of state Leagues to become even more effective advocates. The League identified five focus areas as essential to protecting the votes of all citizens and improving election administration overall: (1) oppose photo ID and documentary proof of citizenship, (2) improve administration of statewide database systems, (3) guard against undue restrictions on voter registration, (4) improve polling place management, and (5) improve poll worker training.

Expanding the National Voter Registration Act and Increasing Participation

In 2008, the League worked to support voting rights by publicly requesting that secretaries of state across the country designate veterans' health facilities as voter registration agencies as provided for in the *National Voter Registration Act*. In 2012 – 2014 this work continued as LWVUS and many state Leagues worked to ensure the state health care exchanges created under the *Affordable Care Act* were designated as voter registration agencies.

This same year, LWVEF produced Engaging New Citizens as New Voters: A Guide to Naturalization Ceremonies, which detailed how Leagues could get involved in such ceremonies. Starting in 2012, LWVEF built on this effort and supported targeted local Leagues with grant funding and strategic support to register new citizens at naturalization ceremonies and underrepresented community colleges. In 2014, LWVEF released a brand-new toolkit designed to support Leagues in their work to engage new citizens as first-time voters. Leveraging this toolkit in 2016, LWVEF launched its largest nationwide grant-funded effort to support state and local Leagues in registering newly naturalized citizens, ultimately resulting in in tens of thousands of new registrants at hundreds of citizenship ceremonies nationwide. In 2022, this work resulted in Leagues registering more than 34,000 new citizens at more than 650 naturalization ceremonies, and ceremony participants took home more than 21,700 voter registration applications for their friends and family.

Since 2010, the League has aimed through its national Youth Voter Registration Project to bring more young people, especially in communities of color, into the democratic process. Local Leagues in dozens of target communities have received LWVEF grant funding and strategic support to assist approximately 150,000 students to register to vote. The League used data and feedback provided by participating Leagues to determine effective strategies and produced a groundbreaking and widely used 2011 training manual, Empowering the Voters of Tomorrow, for Leagues and other groups interested in registering high school students. The guide was updated and republished in early 2013, 2015, and again in 2018.

All aspects of the League's 2012 – 2022 work were part of three major national initiatives, Power the Vote, Women Power the Vote, and Women Power Democracy. Through these initiatives, Leagues worked at all levels to protect, register, educate, and mobilize voters to participate. The League summarized its 2012 – 2014 efforts in the whitepaper, Power the Vote: How a new initiative launched results for millions of voters. It and many corresponding training and planning resources are available at www.lwv.org.

Opposing Voter Suppression

In 2013, the Supreme Court reversed key voting rights protections that had been in place for decades in the case of *Shelby County v. Holder*. The Court ruled that the *Voting Rights Act* formula for determining which jurisdictions had to clear their election law changes with the federal government was based on old data and was therefore unconstitutional.

The League immediately acted, urging Congress to repair and restore the effectiveness of the VRA. This work continued into 2015 and 2016, with active participation from state and local Leagues in target districts backing up the LWVUS lobbying efforts to enact a new *Voting Rights Advancement Act*, restoring key elements of the VRA while extending new protections nationwide.

Also, in the 2010s, Leagues worked in their state legislatures with other concerned organizations for bills to re-enfranchise formerly incarcerated individuals, believing that excessive disenfranchisement undermines voting rights as well as reintegration into the community. In 2018, Leagues were successful in working with a broad coalition of individuals and organizations to re-enfranchise 1.4 million formerly incarcerated individuals. This success is paving the way for similar efforts in Leagues across the country.

In 2017 – 2018 the League actively opposed the creation of the Pence-Kobach Election "Integrity" Commission. President Trump created the commission to address the so-called voter fraud in the 2016 election. The League opposed moves by the commission to collect voter registration data from all 50 states and create a national database of registration names because of voter data privacy issues. State Leagues across the country spoke with their chief election officials about the concerns over data privacy and some filed letters of intent or lawsuits with their officials over the state's intent to share data. LWVUS worked with civil rights groups at the federal level to participate in civil disobedience events and collect and deliver comments to the commission from League members and activists around the country. The commission met twice but was unable to justify the unfounded claims of voter fraud in the 2016 election and disbanded in spring of 2018.

The For the People Act and the Freedom to Vote Act

In December 2018, the League began working with members of Congress and a new coalition, the Declaration for American Democracy (DFAD), on comprehensive legislation to address voting rights, money in politics, and ethics reform in Congress. The legislation, known as the *For the People Act (FTPA)*, was introduced in the 116th Congress (2019 – 2021) and passed the House in March 2019, but never received a committee hearing or made it to the floor of the Senate. Despite lack of movement in the Senate, the League continued to meet with lawmakers and build grassroots support for the legislation around the country.

LWVUS launched grants to key target states to run full-page ads on Easter weekend urging senators in eight states to move the legislation forward for a hearing. The ads reached hundreds of thousands of people and were complemented by an action alert, events, letters to the editor, and postcards parties around the country. The Leagues worked to pressure lawmakers into taking action and continued to build support for the legislation at the local level.

The *For the People Act* was introduced again in the 117th Congress (2021 – 2023). The League lobbied legislators in Washington, DC, engaged grassroots supporters through action alerts, and helped facilitate meetings with state and local League members and their elected officials. In the summer of 2021, the League launched another grant to 12 states and passed through more than $100K to Leagues to continue to build support for the legislation.

As part of the Campaign for Making Democracy Work, the League continued focusing on the protection and enforcement of voting rights in the 117th Congress, including FTPA, the *Freedom to Vote Act (FTVA)*, and the *John R. Lewis Voting Rights Advancement Act (JLVRAA)*.

If passed, this national voting rights legislation would set minimum uniform standards for conducting federal redistricting, voting, and elections across the county. The bills would hold states and bad actors accountable for attempts to restrict voting and would prevent voter suppression efforts. Collectively, these two pieces of legislation would bring us closer to a democracy that is representative of all Americans.

LWVUS staff, grassroots membership, and LWVUS Lobby Corps contacted their representatives and senators in support of this legislation. LWVUS convened a congressional panel in June 2021 to discuss the future of democracy with a focus on federal legislation.

Later in the summer and fall, LWVUS President Dr. Deborah Turner and CEO Virginia Kase Solomón, joined by Leagues from across the country, participated in actions at the White House and on Capitol Hill to demand passage of the legislation through the No More Excuses: Voting Rights Now arc of escalation rallies.

Alongside national voting and civil rights partners, LWVUS supported hundreds of Leagues in leading and joining distributed actions around the country in support of federal voting rights legislation, resulting in hundreds of actions and thousands of voters engaged.

The FTPA passed the House of Representatives but did not achieve the 60-vote threshold to move forward on all three votes in the Senate. In the fall of 2021, Senators put together new legislation, the *Freedom to Vote Act*, which combined parts of the *For the People Act* as they pertained to voting rights and money in politics with the *John R. Lewis Voting Rights Advancement Act*. The legislation was brought up for a vote in the Senate three times, but it was unable to overcome the filibuster.

In January 2022, the Senate finally got the bill to the floor, when Senator Chuck Schumer (D-NY) used a procedural motion to bypass the filibuster and bring the bill to the floor for the first time since it had been introduced. Ultimately, the legislation failed to move from debate to final passage, when two senators voted against a rule change that would have lowered the filibuster threshold.

DC SELF-GOVERNMENT AND FULL VOTING REPRESENTATION

The League's Position

Statement of Position on DC Self-Government and Full Voting Representation, as revised by the national board, March 1982 and June 2000:

The League of Women Voters of the United States believes that citizens of the District of Columbia should be afforded the same rights of self-government and full voting representation in Congress as are all other citizens of the United States. LWVUS supports restoration of an annual, predictable federal payment to the District to compensate for revenues denied and expenses incurred because of the federal presence.

League History

The League of Women Voters began early to seek redress for another disenfranchised group: the citizens of the District of Columbia (DC). The League has supported DC self-government since 1938. Realization of these goals has been slow, but since 1961 DC residents have made some gains in the drive for full citizenship rights. The remaining goals—voting representation in both the House and Senate and full home-rule powers—were made explicit in the LWVUS program in March 1982.

The League has applied a wide variety of techniques, including a massive petition campaign in 1970, to persuade Congress to change the status of the "Last Colony." League support has been behind each hard-won step: the right of District citizens to vote for President and Vice President, through ratification of the 23rd Amendment to the Constitution in 1961; the right to elect a non-voting delegate to Congress in 1970; a 1974 limited home-rule charter providing for an elected mayor and city council, based on the 1973 *DC Self Government and Governmental Reorganization Act*. The League supported the last two reforms as interim steps until voting representation in Congress and full home-rule powers are achieved.

On August 22, 1978, the Senate confirmed the House-approved constitutional amendment providing full voting representation in Congress for citizens of the District of Columbia. State and local Leagues took the lead in ratification efforts. However, when the ratification period expired in 1985, only 16 states of the necessary 38 had ratified the amendment.

In 1993, at the request of the LWV of the District of Columbia, the LWVUS Board agreed that statehood for the District would "afford the same rights of self-government and full voting representation" for citizens of the District as for other US citizens. Accordingly, the League endorsed statehood as one way of implementing the national League position.

The 1998 Convention agreed to incorporate "full congressional voting rights for the District of Columbia" in the Campaign for Making Democracy Work®. In September 1998, DC League members were among the plaintiffs in a federal suit, *Alexander et al. v. Daley et al.*, challenging the denial of full voting representation for citizens of the District in Congress. This and a related suit were rejected 2-1 by a three-judge panel of the court in March 2000. The case was appealed to the Supreme Court, and LWVUS filed an amicus brief in September 2000. Later in 2000, the Supreme Court rejected voting rights in Congress for District of Columbia citizens.

LWVUS was instrumental in the formation of the Coalition for DC Representation in Congress (now DC Vote), which seeks to build a national political movement supporting full representation in Congress and full home-rule powers for the citizens of DC.

In April 2000, the LWUVS Board agreed that the existing LWVUS position on DC voting rights also includes support for autonomy for the District in budgeting locally raised revenue and for eliminating the annual congressional DC appropriations budget-approval process. Convention 2000 adopted a concurrence to add to the LWVUS position support for the "restoration of an annual, predictable federal payment to the District to compensate for revenues denied and expenses incurred because of the federal presence."

While such congressional review remains in force, the League continues to urge members of Congress to oppose appropriations bills that undermine the right of self-government of DC citizens, including restrictions on abortion funding.

In the 108th Congress (2003 – 2005), the League worked with DC Vote to develop legislation providing voting rights in Congress to DC residents. The House Committee on Government Reform held hearings in spring 2004 to discuss four different legislative approaches to gaining representation in Congress. In 2005, members of Congress took on the DC voting rights issue with more enthusiasm than had been seen in years. Under a new legislative plan, Utah would receive an additional fourth seat in Congress, while congressional voting rights in the House of Representatives would be provided for Americans living in Washington, DC. This balanced approach, developed by Rep. Tom Davis (R-VA) and supported by the DC City Council and mayor, would provide voting rights for District residents without upsetting the partisan balance of the House. As momentum for this plan increased, the League worked tirelessly to encourage members of Congress and the public to act on DC voting rights.

In 2006, with support from the DC government, LWVEF launched a DC Voting Rights Education project, aimed at building public awareness of the unique relationship between Congress and District of Columbia citizens, specifically their lack of full voting rights. As part of the project, selected Leagues throughout the country began work to educate voters and local leaders on the DC voting rights issue through summer 2007.

Despite the League's hard work and progress in the 109th (2005 – 2007) and 110th (2007 – 2009) congressional sessions toward passing DC congressional voting rights legislation, supporters were not successful.

In 2016, LWVEF relaunched efforts to build awareness about the need for DC representation in Congress through a grant from the DC government. With ongoing support from the DC government, this effort continued through 2022, with LWVEF staff and LWVDC volunteers working to raise awareness and educate the public about the need for DC voting rights throughout the entire country, working with grass tops leaders, hosting public events, building a social media campaign, and providing leadership development. From 2016 through 2022, LWVEF received grant funds from the DC government to raise awareness about the struggle for DC voting rights and statehood and build support for the necessary reforms.

In the 116th session (2019 – 2021) of Congress, LWVUS worked closely with national partners and the DC League to continue to push for statehood as well as preventing the rights of DC residents from being undermined through federal government action. In 2019, the League submitted a letter to the House and Senate appropriations committees supporting Fiscal Year 2020 appropriations and asking Congress to ensure that no riders that would infringe on the rights of DC residents would be added to the package. In 2019, as a result of LWVUS advocacy and work around statehood, DC Vote recognized LWVUS as a Champion of Democracy. Additionally, LWVUS and LWVDC joined as amici to support a lawsuit that would expand voting rights for DC residents. The lawsuit, *Castanon v. United States* was filed in federal court against federal officials for violation of the equal protection and due process guarantees of the Constitution.

2020 – 2022 were exceptional years for the DC statehood fight. For the first time ever, the House of Representatives voted to pass HR51, *Washington DC Admission Act*. In advance of this vote, LWVUS urged Congress to support the passage and mobilized our base through an action alert to contact their representatives. LWVUS and

LWVDC also co-hosted a highly successful watch party to view the initial committee hearing outside the Rayburn House office building as well as an event to watch the final vote; both events had hundreds of attendees.

2020 was also the beginning of the COVID-19 pandemic. In its efforts to mobilize aid, Congress passed the CARE ACT. The package treated the District of Columbia as a territory. This misclassification meant the District was overlooked for nearly $725 million in needed aid. LWVUS joined coalition partners to demand that in the subsequent relief packages, DC be made whole and awarded funds on the same basis as states.

In the 117th Congress (2021 – 2022), HR51 was reintroduced in January and passed the House chamber that April. The League elevated attention to this vote by helping to organize, with the DC League, "Honk for Statehood" events in every ward of DC and a virtual watch party for the Oversight & Reform Committee hearing. LWVUS also launched a successful action alert activating our membership to contact their representatives.

LWVUS was also a valued partner and member of the DC Kitchen Sink Coalition conversations in support of statehood that brought together organizations including LWVUS, LWVDC, DC Vote, Indivisible, Leadership Conference on Civil Rights, ACLU DC, Neighbors United for DC Statehood, American Progress, The Hub Project, Stand up America, and Civic Nation.

LWVUS also acted when statehood was taken up in the Senate in 2021. LWVUS's volunteer lobby corps mobilized in June to encourage support for the bill among senators. LWUVS sent a letter to Senator Gary Peters, the then Chairman of the Homeland Security and Governmental Affairs Committee, urging him to have the committee take up the issue. In a victory, for only the second time in history (the first in 2014), the Senate held a hearing to discuss DC statehood in June 2021. LWVUS submitted testimony in favor of the legislation.

Between the fall of 2019 and the spring of 2021, LWVUS and LWVDC worked on a petition to demonstrate support across the country for DC statehood. In collaboration with ACLU-DC and DC Vote, LWVUS and LWVDC organized a petition delivery day in October 2021 to deliver signatures. The League contributed 13,000 signatures from all 50 states, among a petition amounting to 37,000 signatures to members of Congress.

The Election Process

APPORTIONMENT

The League's Position

Statement of Position on Apportionment, as announced by the national board, January 1966, and revised March 1982:

The League of Women Voters of the United States believes that congressional districts and government legislative bodies should be apportioned substantially on population. The League is convinced that this standard, established by the Supreme Court, should be maintained, and that the US Constitution should not be amended to allow for consideration of factors other than population in apportionment.

League History

The apportionment of election districts was a state issue until 1962 and 1964 Supreme Court rulings, requiring that both houses of state legislatures must be apportioned substantially on population, transferred the issue to the national arena. These rulings, spelling out the basic constitutional right to equal representation, prompted introduction in Congress of constitutional amendments and laws to subvert the Court's one-person, one-vote doctrine. Leagues in 33 states already had positions on the issue when, in 1965, the League's national council adopted a study on apportionment. By January 1966, the League had reached national member agreement on a position that both houses of state legislatures must be apportioned substantially on population. The 1972 Convention extended the position to cover all voting districts.

League action at both the national and state levels during the late 1960s had a significant role in the defeat of efforts to circumvent the Court's ruling. The League first lobbied in Congress against the Dirksen Amendment, which would have allowed apportionment of one legislative house based on factors other than population, and later worked to defeat resolutions to amend the Constitution by petition of state legislatures for a constitutional Convention. Successful efforts to fend off inadvisable constitutional amendments have left the responsibility for work on this position at the state and local levels. Successive League Conventions have reaffirmed the commitment to an LWVUS apportionment position to be available for action should the need arise. After the 1980 Census, state and local Leagues used this position to work for equitable apportionment of state and local representative bodies.

Since 1988, LWVEF has worked with state and local Leagues to encourage full participation in the census and to ensure that subsequent reapportionment and redistricting complied with one-person, one-vote requirements under the *Voting Rights Act*. Leagues conducted projects to encourage the widest possible participation in the 1990 Census as a way to ensure the most accurate population base for apportionment and redistricting. Leagues also work for equitable apportionment and redistricting of all elected government bodies, using techniques from public education and testimony to monitoring and litigation.

Behind the League position on apportionment is the conviction that a population standard is the most equitable way of assuring that each vote is of equal value in a democratic and representative system of government. The term "substantially" used in Supreme Court decisions allows adequate leeway for districting to provide for any necessary local diversities and to protect minority representation under the League's voting rights position.

In 1998 and 1999, the League urged Congress to fully fund the 2000 Census and support scientific sampling as the means to ensure the most accurate count. State Leagues also have worked to ensure that scientific sampling is used for redistricting within the states.

In 2009, LWVEF was an official partner of the US Census, with the goal of getting everyone counted. LWVEF staff worked closely with national partners (e.g., civil rights and Latino groups) and provided information and support to state and local Leagues in their efforts to minimize an undercount.

The League also submitted an amicus brief in the US Supreme Court case *Evenwel v. Abbott*. The case addressed the question of whether states are required to use a metric other than total population, such as registered voters or citizen voting age population (CVAP) when apportioning districts for state legislative districts. The League's brief in this case supported the current practice of drawing district lines based on population counts, and the Court upheld this practice.

Ahead of the 2020 Census, LWVUS worked to encourage participation and provide guidance for state and local Leagues wishing to participate in Complete Count committees. This included producing a Census Action Kit with printable materials for engaging communities in census activities. LWVUS also acted as a partner in the Census Counts campaign and an official partner of the 2020 Census.

The League also engaged in efforts to remove a citizenship question from the 2020 Census. LWV of New York joined one of six lawsuits across the country challenging the inclusion of the question. LWVUS joined an amicus as the suit headed to the US Supreme Court, challenging the question's inclusion without proper vetting. LWVUS also lobbied Congress, engaged the LWVUS Lobby Corps, and activated its grassroot network, yielding the most successful engagement campaign of 2018, to raise awareness of the damaging effects this question would have on communities around the country. In June 2019, the US Supreme Court ruled that there was no rational basis by the government to include a citizenship question and it had to be removed for the 2020 Census questionnaire.

In 2020, the League joined two census-related cases. The first dealt with extending the timeline for completing the census in light of COVID. In a flurry of lawsuits, the court first ruled that the count had to continue through October 31, but on appeal the Circuit Court ruled that the count could end immediately and thus counting wrapped on October 15, 2020. The League did an all-out social media campaign to educate the public on the new deadline and to ensure as many people participated as possible. In the second, the League drafted an amicus that was filed in New York, California, and District of Columbia dealing with an executive order excluding undocumented immigrants from the census. All three cases in federal court ruled that the census required a count of every person in the country regardless of citizenship, and the case has been appealed to the US Supreme Court.

With respect to apportionment data, the League responded to the structural issue of prison gerrymandering. In 2021, the LWVUS, along with the Campaign Legal Center and Washington Lawyers' Committee, co-authored and signed onto a letter addressed to Attorney General Merrick Garland and the US Department of Justice urging the adoption of a new routine use exception under the *Privacy Act*. Such a measure would allow the Federal Bureau of Prisons to share data necessary for states and localities to implement pro-democracy reforms like universal enfranchisement and abolishing prison-based gerrymandering, in which inmates are counted as residents of the district where the prison is located instead of at their home addresses.

Due to the pandemic's delay of census operations in 2020, the Census Bureau completed its operation in April of 2021 and delivered apportionment data to the Bureau's secretary later that month. The Bureau scheduled a release of high-quality redistricting data by August 16, 2021, then transmitted a more user-friendly representation of that data by September 30, 2021. Considering the delays and constant shifting of the census timeline and despite the pandemic's effects, the League advocated for the codification of a more predictable process and timeline for the release of such data in the future. To that end, in 2021, the League joined with 104 other state and national organizations in signing onto a letter authored by the Leadership Conference in support of *The Bipartisan 2020 Census Deadline Extensions Act (S. 1267)* which was sent to US senators, urging them to pass and codify new deadlines for the census data release.

See also the position on Voting Rights that applies to apportionment issues. Leagues applying the Apportionment position should be aware that the Voting Rights position (and League actions supporting the Voting Rights Act) recognizes that both the Constitution and the Voting Rights Act require that reapportionment not dilute the effective representation of minority citizens.

REDISTRICTING

The League's Position

Statement of Position on Redistricting, as adopted by concurrence, June 2016:

1. **Responsibility for redistricting preferably should be vested in an independent special commission, with membership that reflects the diversity of the unit of government, including citizens at large, representatives of public interest groups, and members of minority groups.**

2. **Every redistricting process should include:**
   a. **Specific timelines for the steps leading to a redistricting plan.**
   b. **Full disclosure throughout the process and public hearings on the plan proposed for adoption.**
      i. **Redistricting at all levels of government must be accomplished in an open, unbiased manner with citizen participation and access at all levels and steps of the process.**
      ii. **Should be subject to open meeting laws.**
   c. **A provision that any redistricting plan should be adopted by the redistricting authority with more than a simple majority vote.**
   d. **Remedial provisions established in the event that the redistricting authority fails to enact a plan. Specific provisions should be made for court review of redistricting measures and for courts to require the redistricting authority to act on a specific schedule.**
      i. **Time limits should be set for initiating court action for review.**
      ii. **The courts should promptly review and rule on any challenge to a redistricting plan and require adjustments if the standards have not been met.**

3. **The standards on which a redistricting plan is based, and on which any plan should be judged, must:**
   a. **Be enforceable in court.**
   b. **Require:**
      i. **Substantially equal population.**
      ii. **Geographic contiguity.**
      iii. **Effective representation of racial and linguistic minorities.**
   c. **Provide for (to the extent possible):**
      i. **Promotion of partisan fairness.**
      ii. **Preservation and protection of "communities of interest."**
      iii. **Respect for boundaries of municipalities and counties.**
   d. **Compactness and competitiveness may also be considered as criteria so long as they do not conflict with the above criteria.**

    e.   **Explicitly reject:**
        i.   **Protection of incumbents, through such devices as considering an incumbent's address.**
       ii.   **Preferential treatment for a political party, through such devices as considering party affiliation, voting history and candidate residence.**

This position does not supersede any existing state League redistricting position.

League History

Partisan and racial gerrymandering distorts and undermines representative democracy by allowing officials to select their voters rather than voters to select their officials. When done for purposes of racial discrimination or to ensure the dominance of one political party, or even to ensure the election of a specific legislator, gerrymandering runs counter to the principle of equal voting rights for all.

For much of the League's history, redistricting has been considered a state and local issue, but as state Leagues have become more active—and the political gerrymandering of the US Congress and state legislative districts have become more apparent—LWVUS has provided assistance and, in the 2014 – 2016 biennium, developed a nationwide position statement.

Before the adoption of a specific position on redistricting, the national board affirmed that Leagues at all levels may act under LWVUS positions relating to redistricting. Using the positions on Apportionment, Citizen's Right to Vote, and Congress, Leagues should work to achieve three goals consistent with those positions: (1) congressional districts and government legislative bodies should be apportioned substantially on population ("one person, one vote"); (2) redistricting should not dilute the effective representation of minority citizens; and (3) efforts that attempt or result in partisan gerrymandering should be opposed.

In 2006, the League joined other groups in holding a nonpartisan redistricting conference in Salt Lake City. As a result of that meeting, the League and partners released a report, Building a National Redistricting Reform Movement, which looks at lessons learned from unsuccessful redistricting reform attempts in 2005 and suggests strategies to pursue and pitfalls to avoid in future reform efforts.

Leagues across the country continue to press for redistricting reform at the state level, and LWVUS has gone to the Supreme Court with amicus briefs in landmark cases against partisan and racial gerrymandering. In 2009, LWVEF hosted a unique redistricting conference that convened experts and stakeholders from across the nation to discuss how to work together to influence the results of the state redistricting processes following the 2010 Census. The participants agreed on several core principles and wrote a report emphasizing the importance of transparency in the redistricting process.

In the 2010s the League expressed concern about prison-based gerrymandering. Working with other organizations, the League sought better information from the Census Bureau to support the push to end this practice.

In 2011 and 2012, state Leagues played pivotal roles in advocating for improved redistricting processes through the nationwide funded Shining a Light project. Leagues hosted public events, delivered much-quoted testimony before decision-making bodies, presented alternative maps, launched major public education and media campaigns, and engaged key allies to promote transparent and fair redistricting processes. Key League priorities included advocating for adequate public comment periods before and after the introduction of redistricting proposals; disclosure of committee timelines and other important details; and opportunities for community groups, especially those representing diverse voices, to get involved.

Following the 2011 redistricting process, several state Leagues engaged in litigation or statewide ballot initiative campaigns to challenge unsatisfactory redistricting outcomes. The Texas League and LWVEF jointly submitted comments urging the US Department of Justice to object to the removal of preclearance protections covered under Section 5 of the *Voting Rights Act* for what the League deemed a discriminatory redistricting proposal. Elsewhere, the North Carolina League joined other civil rights groups in challenging a redistricting plan that would negatively impact minorities and other voters, the Arizona League filed an amicus brief that successfully urged the state Supreme Court to protect that state's independent redistricting commission, and the Pennsylvania League participated in a successful citizens' appeal of a state plan.

In California, League leaders worked throughout 2011 and 2012 to defend and ensure success for that state's new Independent Citizens Commission process and provided a detailed analysis of and recommendations for future redistricting commissions. In Florida, the League spearheaded multiple legislative and legal efforts to ensure the integrity of new, groundbreaking redistricting criteria would be upheld. The League prevailed in court when it challenged the 2010 redistricting plan for violating the new criteria. The Florida League garnered an impressive array of statewide and national media coverage for its efforts.

In early 2012, LWVEF published Shining a Light: Redistricting Lessons Learned, which lays out key League priorities related to redistricting reform. The publication has been widely shared with Leagues and partners nationwide. In Ohio, the League led a high-profile effort to pass a November 2012 ballot initiative that would have instituted an independent redistricting commission; unfortunately, that effort was unsuccessful.

Public opinion polling has shown high public support for taking the redistricting process out of the hands of partisan legislatures, and many Leagues continue to consider how best to achieve more representative processes. Leagues remain engaged in pending legal challenges or appeals in several states and continue to pursue a range of opportunities to reform the redistricting process.

Wishing to give redistricting a higher profile for League action, the 2014 national program on Key Structures of Democracy called for a Task Force on Redistricting, which surveyed existing state League positions and recommended a new concurrence statement to the 2016 Convention.

League action on redistricting ramped up during the 2016 – 2018 biennium. Leagues built and participated in coalitions for reform efforts in states all across the country. In 2018, Leagues in Colorado, Michigan, Missouri, Ohio, and Utah were instrumental in passing ballot initiatives that created more independent redistricting processes. Other states also participated in LWVUS and LWVEF redistricting grants, which invited specific Leagues to apply for grant funding related to redistricting efforts. In addition to the five states that passed ballot initiatives, Leagues worked to build support and educate voters about the need for redistricting reform in 12 states.

The League was a plaintiff and filed amicus briefs in key litigation efforts around the country. The League filed an amicus brief in the case of *Gill v. Whitford* before the Supreme Court in 2018. The League's own case in North

Carolina, *League of Women Voters of North Carolina v. Rucho*, was also found to be an unconstitutional partisan gerrymander by the lower courts, and the US Supreme Court agreed in March 2019 to hear it. Following the 2018 election, LWVMI began discussion with the Michigan Secretary of State about settling *League of Women Voters of Michigan v. Benson*, which included redrawing 11 state legislative districts that the League challenged as partisan gerrymanders. All these cases were still pending in June 2019, when the court declined to rein in partisan gerrymandering, ruling that that partisan gerrymandering was a political question and thus, federal courts would no longer hear cases dealing with the issue.

People Powered Fair Maps®

Following the disappointing decision in *Rucho v. League of Women Voters of North Carolina*, a case that was consolidated with two other cases, the League launched People Powered Fair Maps (PPFM), a multi-focus national campaign focused on redistricting reform. The areas included ballot initiatives, state constitutional options, state legislative fix, and federal legislative fix.

Civic education and engagement were foundational components of the program, and it became an integral part of the PPFM story. The League achieved great success by outpacing all its quantitative metrics and had trackable influence across the country over all three years of PPFM. The first year of PPFM consisted of state Leagues working on reform initiatives across all 50 states and DC; the second year was primarily focused on educating and equipping advocates with knowledge of and tools around redistricting as well as building partnerships at both state and national levels; and the third and final year consisted of implementing redistricting advocacy strategies across participating states, including drafting, proposing, and testifying on maps.

Over the course of its three years and in the face of a global pandemic, PPFM engaged 1.4 million people, 2,446 partners, and 24 underrepresented communities. The League held 3,669 educational events and trainings through a combination of in-person and virtual events. It also held 4,699 meetings with key stakeholders to advance redistricting reforms throughout communities in the United States, with a total of five maps submitted and implemented by the League. The League was also a key collaborator in national redistricting advocacy efforts as a founding member of the Coalition Hub for Advancing Redistricting and Grassroots Engagement (CHARGE). Through CHARGE, the League contributed resources to help communities on the ground train volunteers to draw maps, propose maps and reforms, and testify throughout the 2021 – 2022 redistricting cycle.

The League was engaged in 24 redistricting-related lawsuits. The League joined 11 state lawsuits and six federal cases challenging congressional and state gerrymandered maps in California, Florida, Georgia, Maryland, Michigan, New York, Ohio, Pennsylvania, Texas, Utah, and Wisconsin. As of June 2022, the League litigated in federal racial gerrymandering cases in Georgia, Texas, and Wisconsin. On the state level, partisan gerrymandering suits were litigated in Ohio, New York, Wisconsin, and Utah.

Following the end of the 2022 redistricting cycle, the League will continue its work as a CHARGE partner and will continue to advance civic education around redistricting. The League is expected to relaunch PPFM in 2025 ahead of the 2030 Census and the 2031 redistricting cycle.

MONEY IN POLITICS

The League's Position

Statement of Position on Campaign Finance, as announced by the national board, April 2016:

The League of Women Voters of the United States believes that the methods of financing political campaigns should: Enhance political equality for all citizens; ensure maximum participation by citizens in the political process; protect representative democracy from being distorted by big spending in election campaigns; provide voters sufficient information about candidates and campaign issues to make informed choices; ensure transparency and the public's right to know who is using money to influence elections; enable candidates to compete equitably for public office; ensure that candidates have sufficient funds to communicate their messages to the public; and combat corruption and undue influence in government.

The League believes that political corruption includes the following: A candidate or officeholder agrees to vote or work in favor of a donor's interests in exchange for a campaign contribution; an officeholder or staff gives greater access to donors; an officeholder votes or works to support policies that reflect the preferences of individuals or organizations in order to attract contributions from them; a candidate or office holder seeks political contributions implying that there will be retribution unless a donation is given; and the results of the political process consistently favor the interests of significant campaign contributors.

In order to achieve the goals for campaign finance regulation, the League supports: Public financing of elections, either voluntary or mandatory, in which candidates must abide by reasonable spending limits; enhanced enforcement of campaign finance laws that includes changes to ensure that regulatory agencies are properly funded, staffed, and structured to avoid partisan deadlock in the decision-making process; abolishing Super PACs and abolishing spending coordinated or directed by candidates (other than a candidate's own campaign committee); and restrictions on direct donations and bundling by lobbyists, which may include monetary limits as well as other regulations.

Until full public financing of elections is enacted, limits on election spending are needed in order to meet the League's goals for protecting democratic processes. Among the different entities that spend money to influence elections, the League supports the following comparative limits:

- Higher spending limits for political parties, genuinely non-partisan voter registration and get-out-the-vote organizations and activities, and candidates spending money raised from contributors.
- Mid-level spending limits for individual citizens (including wealthy individuals), Political Action Committees (with funds contributed by individuals associated with the sponsoring organization, such as employees, stockholders, members, and volunteers), and candidates spending their own money.
- Lower spending limits for trade associations, labor unions and nonprofit organizations from their general treasury funds.
- Severely restricted spending by for-profit organizations spending from their corporate treasury funds.
- No limits on spending by bona fide newspapers, television, and other media, including the internet, except to address partisan abuse or use of the media to evade campaign finance regulations.

This position is applicable to all federal campaigns for public office — presidential and congressional, primaries, and general elections. It also may be applied to state and local campaigns.

League History

The 1973 Council — spurred by spending abuses in congressional and presidential campaigns — focused on campaign finance. An accelerated study and agreement in 1973 led to the Campaign Finance position, which applied League Principles supporting an open and representative government to political campaigns.

The League initiated a petition drive and lobbied intensively for the campaign reforms embodied in the *Federal Election Campaign Act of 1974 (FECA)*. When the law was challenged in court, the League, together with other organizations, intervened as defendants. In 1976, the US Supreme Court upheld portions of the law providing for disclosure, public financing, and contribution limits, but it overturned limits on candidates' spending if they used private financing and limits on independent expenditures. The court also ruled that the method of selection of the Federal Election Commission (FEC) was unconstitutional because it allowed Congress to encroach on the President's appointment power. After the court's decision, the League successfully lobbied for a new law creating an independent and constitutionally acceptable FEC.

From 1989 to 1992, the League fought for comprehensive campaign finance reform to address the abuses in the existing system, supporting bills that curbed special interest contributions and providing public financing for candidates who accepted voluntary spending limits. The League called for limits to PAC and large contributor donations, for closing the soft-money loophole, and for public benefits for candidates, such as reduced postage and reduced broadcasting costs.

Both houses of Congress enacted reform bills in 1990, but a conference committee was unable to resolve the differences before the adjournment of the 101st Congress (1989 – 1991). Both houses passed strong reform measures in 1992, and the bill that emerged from the conference committee promised the most far-reaching campaign finance reform since Watergate. President George H. W. Bush vetoed the bill, and an attempt to override was unsuccessful.

In 1991 and 1992, the League defended the system of public financing for presidential candidates through check-offs on income tax forms. Faced with an impending shortfall in the Presidential Election Campaign Fund, the League countered with an attack on many fronts: an appeal to taxpayers and preparers to use the check-off; testimony before the House Elections Subcommittee to increase the check-off from $1.00 to $3.00, with indexing for inflation; opposition to IRS regulations that would weaken the system; support for a House bill guaranteeing matching funds for qualified presidential primary candidates; and participation in an amicus brief that unsuccessfully challenged the US Treasury Department's regulations that subvert the language and congressional intent of the presidential public financing system. In 1993, the presidential check-off was increased to $3.00, with support from the League, assuring continued viability for the fund. Also in 1993, the League supported comprehensive campaign finance reform, which stalled in partisan wrangling.

In 1995 and 1996, the League continued its support for comprehensive reform through lobbying, testimony, grassroots action, and work with the media. League members pushed for voluntary spending limits; public benefits, such as reduced-cost broadcasting and postal services, for participating candidates; aggregate limits on the total amounts candidates could receive in PAC and large individual contributions; and closing the loopholes that allow huge amounts of special-interest money to influence the system.

The near collapse of the federal campaign finance system during the 1996 election focused national attention on the need for reform. In December 1996, LWVUS endorsed the goals of a reform proposal developed by a group of academics. The approach focused on closing gaping loopholes in the law that allow special interests, political parties, and others to channel hundreds of millions of dollars into candidates' campaigns. Among the key goals: banning "soft money" (a contribution to a political party that is not counted as going to a particular candidate, thus avoiding various legal limitations), closing the sham issue advocacy loophole, and improving disclosure and enforcement. In 1996, opponents of League-favored reforms, arguing that politics is underfunded, sought to increase the amounts of special-interest money flowing into the system by loosening many existing contribution limits. The League and its allies soundly defeated this approach in the House, but leadership prevented any action on League-supported reforms. Reformers built bipartisan support for reform outside the leadership circles.

In response to budget attacks on the FEC in the 104th Congress (1995 – 1997), the League testified and lobbied in support of the FEC's Fiscal Year 1997 budget request and against efforts to undermine the agency's core enforcement and disclosure programs through funding cuts.

Also, in this period, LWVEF launched a comprehensive program for articulating a public voice on campaign finance. The Money + Politics: People Change the Equation project brought citizens together to debate the problems in the system and discuss possible solutions.

LWVEF mounted a major advertising and grassroots education initiative calling attention to achievable campaign reforms. Working with experts from diverse political views, LWVEF published a blueprint for reform, 5 Ideas for Practical Campaign Reform. Other efforts included ads in major newspapers, a PSA featuring national news anchor Walter Cronkite, and citizen caucuses in 20 states.

An unrelenting push by LWVUS and other reform advocates succeeded in shifting the campaign-finance debate in the 105th Congress (1997 – 1999) from a deadlock over spending limits to real movement to close the most egregious loopholes. The League supported the bipartisan *McCain-Feingold* bill in the Senate and the counterpart *Shays-Meehan* bill in the House, bringing grassroots pressure to bear against efforts by congressional leaders to stonewall real reform. Leagues responded to Action Alerts and lobbied their members of Congress to defeat parliamentary maneuvers blocking votes and to support meaningful reform.

In summer 1998, reformers succeeded in forcing the speaker of the House to schedule a vote on reform bills, including *Shays-Meehan*. Despite concerted efforts to defeat it, the bill passed the House by a vote of 252-179 in August 1998. League members immediately urged senators to support a cloture vote on campaign finance reform legislation and to vote for real reform. However, in September 1998, the Senate once again failed to break the filibuster preventing a vote.

In 1998, LWVEF launched a campaign finance reform project, Strategies for Success in the Midwest, working with state Leagues in Illinois, Indiana, Iowa, Michigan, Minnesota, Ohio, and Wisconsin. Efforts focused on educating citizens on practical ways to reform campaign finance and to offer citizens an opportunity to participate in the debate. In 1999, LWVEF distributed Make the Link materials to state Leagues, drawing the connection between campaign finance and key issues such as the environment, teen smoking, and health care.

On the Hill, House leaders again worked to block the *Shays-Meehan* bill in the 106th Congress (1999 – 2001). Using a discharge petition, reformers forced the leadership to move the bill, and it passed on a strong vote. Senate passage once again proved elusive, despite citizen pressure. However, the League and other supporters were successful in achieving passage in June 2000 of so-called "527" legislation, requiring political organizations set up under Section 527 of the IRS code to disclose the identity and amounts given by their donors and how they spend the money.

As the League continued to focus on reducing the corrupting influence of big money in elections, League work at the state level contributed to real progress. Public financing, the Clean Money Option, was adopted in several states, including Arizona and Maine; other state reform efforts have made progress in Massachusetts and Vermont. Reform measures were on the 2000 ballot in Missouri and Oregon but fell short. Also, in 1999 – 2000, League members supported 90-year-old Doris Haddock, "Granny D," in her walk across the country to promote campaign finance reform.

The League and other reformers succeeded in putting campaign finance reform on the front burner of the national political agenda. In January 2000, in *Nixon v. Shrink Missouri PAC*, the US Supreme Court upheld limits on state campaign contributions that were analogous to the federal limits. LWVUS joined an amicus brief in the case. The Court's decision restated the constitutional underpinning for campaign finance reform formulated in *Buckley v. Valeo*, despite arguments by reform opponents.

The battle for meaningful campaign finance reform has been long and difficult. The Senate debated the *McCain-Feingold-Shays-Meehan* bill for more than a week in 2001. The League pushed successfully for a strengthening amendment from Senator Wellstone (MN) and to protect against a raft of weakening amendments. On the House side, the leadership once again tried to use the rules to block reform. Our allies in the House, with strong support from LWVUS, resorted to a discharge petition to force action.

LWVUS worked with the bill's sponsors and lobbied swing members of the House and Senate to achieve campaign finance reform. LWVUS conducted two rounds of phone banking, asking League members in key districts to lobby at key junctures in the congressional debate. The League participated in many press conferences and rallies to make the citizens' voice heard on campaign finance reform.

On March 27, 2002, the League's five-year campaign for the *McCain-Feingold-Shays-Meehan* bill reached fruition when President George W. Bush signed the legislation into law. The bill, which is known as the *Bipartisan Campaign Reform Act* (BCRA), closed the most significant loopholes in campaign finance regulation—the soft money loophole that allowed unlimited corporate, union, and individual contributions and the "sham issue ad" loophole that allowed undisclosed contributions to campaign advertising advocating particular candidates. The League was instrumental in developing this approach and pushing it — at the grassroots level and in Congress — to final enactment.

With the passage of BCRA, the League turned its attention to legal challenges to the law, which continue to the present day. LWVUS filed an amicus brief on sham issue ads for the US Supreme Court case *McConnell v. FEC* (2003). The brief explained why it is important that funding for attack ads in the final days of an election not be used to circumvent the soft money ban in BCRA. In September 2003, the League organized a rally at the US

Supreme Court to demonstrate public support for the law. In December, the Supreme Court upheld all the key components of BCRA in *McConnell v. FEC*, including the sham issue ad provisions briefed by the League.

In the first half of the 108th Congress (2003 – 2005), the League urged senators to cosponsor the *Our Democracy, Our Airwaves Act* introduced by Senators McCain, Feingold, and Durbin. LWVUS helped targeted Leagues organize in-district lobby visits in support of the legislation, and the LWVUS Lobby Corps lobbied select senators requesting co-sponsorship of the bill.

The League, along with partners, conducted a national public education campaign, *Our Democracy, Our Airwaves*, studying the role of television in elections, the cost of accessing these public airwaves, and the importance of strengthening public interest information coming from broadcasters. LWVUS put together organizing tools for local Leagues to use while creating educational campaigns in their communities.

In the second session of the 108th Congress (2003 – 2005), the League continued its work on improving the presidential public financing system. LWVUS sought cosponsors to legislation introduced by Senators McCain and Feingold and Representatives Shays and Meehan to fix the system. LWVUS also joined a coalition project that sought pledge commitments from the 2004 presidential candidates to support the public financing system's reform if elected. In 2003 and 2004, the League again urged taxpayers to check the box to support the Presidential Election Fund.

In 2005 and 2006, the League continued to promote campaign finance reform as well as public funding for presidential elections. In December 2005, the League president spoke at a Capitol Hill conference, The Issue of Presidential Public Financing: Its Goals, History, Current Status, and Problems. In 2006, LWVUS joined with other organizations in a letter to US representatives urging them to co-sponsor and support the *Meehan-Shays* bill that would make a series of important reforms to the presidential public financing system.

Throughout 2005, the League urged members of Congress to vote against the *Pence-Wynn* and other bills aimed at undermining existing campaign finance regulations. In December, the League joined other groups in submitting an amicus brief in the US Supreme Court case *Wisconsin Right to Life, Inc. v. Federal Election Commission*, which challenged the application of the *Bipartisan Campaign Reform Act* to the financing of television ads in Wisconsin. Through 2006, the League continued to support meaningful campaign finance reform, urging representatives to vote for a ban on leadership PACs and to support a bill that would close soft money loopholes.

In 2007 and 2008, the League endorsed legislation to fix the public financing system for President and to establish congressional public financing for the first time. During the 2008 presidential campaign, the League pressed all the candidates to support reform of the presidential public financing system. The League also supported banning leadership PACs and continued to press the courts to properly interpret and enforce campaign finance law.

In the late 2000s, LWVUS filed amicus briefs in two pivotal US Supreme Court cases: *Caperton v. Massey* and *Citizens United v. FEC*. In the latter case, the League argued that corporate spending in elections should not be equated with the First Amendment rights of individual citizens.

In 2010, the League reacted swiftly and strongly to the Court's adverse decision in the *Citizens United* case, which allowed unlimited "independent" corporate spending in candidate elections. The League president testified before the relevant House committee on the key steps that can be taken to respond, focusing on the importance of including tighter disclosure requirements. The League continues to urge passage of the *DISCLOSE Act* to counter the Court's decision and ensure that corporate and union spending in elections is fully disclosed.

With the explosion of supposedly "independent" spending by outside groups in the years since *Citizens United*, the League is pushing for tougher rules on coordination, because much of the outside spending is not independent and instead is coordinated with candidate campaigns. In addition, the League continues to push for legislation to protect and reinvigorate the presidential public financing system and to institute congressional public financing as well. The League also is working to reform the dysfunctional FEC, which has refused to enforce the law.

In early 2012, LWVUS board appointed a Campaign Finance Task Force to examine legislative and constitutional efforts to achieve campaign finance reform. Convention 2012 reaffirmed the League's commitment to campaign finance reform by passing a resolution that called for advocating strongly for campaign finance measures, including constitutional amendments.

In the summer of 2012, the League ran radio ads in Tennessee and Maine asking Senators Corker, Alexander, Snowe, and Collins to support campaign finance reform. The ads were timed in anticipation of congressional action on the *DISCLOSE Act*. The ads garnered press coverage from outlets in both states.

In the 2012 elections, significant amounts of campaign spending came from so-called independent groups, much of it from secret contributions. The League took on these issues, arguing that much of the "independent" spending was coordinated with candidate campaigns and therefore illegal. The League also pointed to the use of secret "dark money" and pushed for enhanced disclosure.

The 2014 – 2016 national program on Key Structures of Democracy focused increased attention at every level of League on Money in Politics (MIP) and included an updated study to provide additional detail to the League's position. Based on the new position statement and previous action on campaign finance reform, the four major elements of the League's MIP plan focus on disclosure, stopping Super PACs, public financing for congressional and presidential elections, and reform of the FEC to create an effective enforcement agency.

The 2016 – 2018 national program continued a focus on MIP issues as part of the Campaign for Making Democracy Work® (CMDW). Through CMDW, the League pushed for several reform measures in Congress. In the 115th Congress (2017 – 2019), the League supported legislation from Senator Tom Udall to restructure the FEC into a five-member commission with the authority to conduct investigations of campaign finance violations while also establishing a new system for enforcement. LWVUS issued Action Alerts and activated the LWVUS Lobby Corps in favor of this legislation, but it never even got through the committee process.

The FEC legislation was included in the *We the People Act*, a comprehensive reform bill that included legislation addressing money in politics, redistricting, ethics, and voting rights reforms. The LWVUS Lobby Corps lobbied select members of the US House and Senate to cosponsor this legislation. The *We the People Act* would become the precursor to legislation introduced in the 116th Congress (2019 – 2021), HR1, the *For the People Act*.

Following the 2016 presidential election and reports of foreign interference in the election, the League endorsed, lobbied, and activated grassroots action in favor of the *Honest Ads Act*. The goals of this legislation included preventing foreign interference in future elections and improving online political ad disclosure. Despite hearings on this bill with leaders of major social media and internet companies, it did not move forward. However, the interest in this bill caused the FEC to renew its interest in updating regulations on online advertisements. LWVUS participated in a comment drive with like-minded groups to urge the FEC to act. After the FEC agreed to move forward, the League submitted technical comments to the FEC on the regulations.

During the 115th Congress (2017 – 2019) the League opposed efforts to roll back the *Johnson Amendment*. This provision prohibits 501(c)(3) nonprofit organizations, like churches and universities, from endorsing or opposing political candidates. Rescinding this provision would allow these organizations to maintain their charitable status while engaging in political activities. Both the House and Senate tried several times to repeal this provision, but each time, action from the League and other organizations ensured those attempts were unsuccessful.

In 2018, the League was instrumental in finally requiring the US Senate to file campaign finance reports electronically with the FEC. Electronic filing ensures transparency and increases access for voters to determine funding for Senate candidates.

In 2018, the League signed on to various letters in support of better campaign finance regulation on the federal level. The League also sent a letter to the FEC along with 8,601 partner organizations providing comments on FEC Regulations 2011-12, relating to internet advertisements and disclosure. The League asked the FEC support the creation of regulations that require the disclosure of who is financing these ads. The League also signed onto letters endorsing key money in politics legislation, *The Anti-Corruption and Public Integrity Act*, introduced in the Senate and the House of Representatives.

After the swearing in of the 116th Congress (2019 – 2021), the League advocated for the passage of HR1, the *For the People Act*, an omnibus democracy reform bill in the House and Senate. Among other reforms, HR1 imposes new restrictions on foreign money in American elections, requires greater disclosure for online advertisements, increases IRS oversight of nonprofit organizations' activities, and creates a pilot program for public financing of congressional elections. The League also focused on several main areas of campaign finance reform, such as transparency and disclosure. The League urged Congress to allow the SEC to require publicly traded corporations to disclose their political spending. As part of its advocacy for HR1, the League also urged Congress to reject poison pill amendments that aimed to prevent the IRS from properly regulating nonprofits' political activity, limited the SEC's ability to require disclosure of corporations' political spending, and exempted federal government contractors from disclosure of political spending. Through the League and other organizations' advocacy, all three amendments failed to pass.

Leading up to the 2020 election, the League joined calls for the presidential candidates of both major parties to disclose their "bundled" donors. The identities of bundled donors, who secretly raise substantial amounts of money for candidates, were not disclosed despite the requests.

In 2022, The League testified in support of the *DISCLOSE Act of 2021* in the Senate Rules and Administration Committee's hearing on the bill. LWVUS has supported the *DISCLOSE Act* for more than a decade, as it has been introduced in the Senate in every Congress since the 111th Congress in 2010. Supporting this bill aligns with League priorities to increase transparency in election spending and resist foreign influence in federal elections.

The League's position on campaign finance reflects continuing concern for open and honest elections and for maximum citizen participation in the political process. The League's campaign finance reform strategy has two tracks: (1) achieve incremental reforms where possible in the short term and (2) build support for public financing as the best long-term solution.

Although provided under current law for presidential elections, public funding of congressional elections, which the League supports, has been an elusive goal. Current law does embody other League goals: full and timely disclosure of campaign contributions and expenditures; one central committee to coordinate, control, and report financial transactions for each candidate, party, or other committee; an independent body to monitor and enforce the law; and the encouragement of broad-based contributions from citizens.

The League continues to look for ways to limit the size and type of contributions from all sources as a means of combating undue influence in the election process. League action on this issue is built on a careful assessment of all proposed changes in campaign financing law. The League continues to assess proposals to equalize government services for challengers and incumbents so that candidates can compete more equitably. The League favors shortening the time between primaries and general elections.

🔍 SELECTION OF THE PRESIDENT

The League's Position

Statement of Position on Selection of the President, as announced by the national board, January 1970, revised March 1982, updated June 2004 and revised by the 2010 Convention:

The League of Women Voters of the United States believes that the direct-popular-vote method for electing the President and Vice President is essential to representative government. The League of Women Voters believes, therefore, that the Electoral College should be abolished. We support the use of the National Popular Vote Compact as one acceptable way to achieve the goal of the direct popular vote for election of the President until the abolition of the Electoral College is accomplished. The League also supports uniform voting qualifications and procedures for presidential elections. The League supports changes in the presidential election system— from the candidate selection process to the general election. We support efforts to provide voters with enough information about candidates and their positions, public policy issues and the selection process itself. The League supports action to ensure that the media, political parties, candidates, and all levels of government achieve these goals and provide that information.

League History

A League study of the presidential electoral process culminated in a 1970 position supporting direct election of the President by popular vote as essential to representative government. The League testified and lobbied for legislation to amend the *US Constitution* to replace the Electoral College with direct election of the President, including provisions for a national runoff election in the event no candidates for President or Vice President received 40 percent of the vote. The measure, which passed the House and nearly passed the Senate in 1971, has been revived in each Congress without success. In 1997, LWVUS again called for abolition of the Electoral College and for direct election of the President and Vice President in testimony before the House Subcommittee on the Constitution.

The League has supported national voting qualifications and procedures for presidential elections to ensure equity for voters from all states and to facilitate the electoral process.

In February 2001, LWVUS sent a memo to state and local Leagues outlining the League's position on the Electoral College under the LWVUS position on Selection of the President.

The League believes strongly that the Electoral College should be abolished and not merely reformed. One reform that the League specifically rejects is the voting by electors based on proportional representation in lieu of the present "winner-takes-all" method. Such a system would apportion the electoral votes of a state based on the popular vote in that state. Instead of making the Electoral College more representative, such proportional voting would increase the chance that no candidate would receive a majority in the Electoral College, thereby sending the election of the President to the House of Representatives, where each state, regardless of population, would receive only one vote. Election of the President by the House further removes the decision from the people and is contrary to the "one person, one vote" principle. The League also does not support reform of the Electoral College on a state-by-state basis because the League believes there should be uniformity across the nation in the systems used to elect the President.

The 2002 Convention voted to expand and update the position. The League came to concurrence on a new position in June 2004, which takes into account the entire presidential selection process and supports a process that produces the best possible candidates, informed voters, and optimum voter participation.

The 2008 Convention voted to conduct a study of the National Popular Vote Interstate Compact (NPVIC) proposal, which would establish the popular election of the President through a compact among the states governing how they would cast their votes in the Electoral College. The 2010 Convention adopted a concurrence to support the NPVIC as another method of selecting the President until the Electoral College is abolished.

Convention 2018 voted to amend and add advocacy of the NPVIC to the 2018 – 2020 Campaign for Making Democracy Work. To support this effort, in 2018 LWVUS created an online discussion group to enable members working on this issue across the country to connect and in early 2019 LWVUS created an NPVIC Task Force to assess state-level interest, evaluate the status of the effort, and recommend next steps. During the 2018 – 2020 biennium, the Task Force determined that the national office should support further education and support to states working to move the National Popular Vote. The NPVIC Task Force continued through the 2020 – 2022 biennium.

Through much analysis, discourse, and self-reflection, the 2018 – 2020 national board chose "eliminating the Electoral College through an amendment to the US Constitution" as an audacious long-term goal. In spring 2020, the League of Women Voters Board of Directors approved this organizational goal. Through this decision, the League embarked on a new North Star as part of our next 100 years — a new and audacious goal akin to achieving the 19th Amendment.

At the 2022 Convention, LWVUS announced the next big, audacious goal for the League: abolition of the electoral college. As the work begins, LWVUS will use this to build legislation to achieve our end goal and to educate League members and members of the public on the importance of this action. In addition, the membership amended the Campaign for Making Democracy Work (CMDW) to include elevating the "direct election of the President by popular vote" as a prominent, listed component. This motion includes both the National Popular Vote Interstate Compact and the Abolishment of the Electoral College by constitutional amendment.

VOTER REPRESENTATION/ELECTORAL SYSTEMS

The League's Position

Statement of Position on Voter Representation/Electoral Systems as adopted by concurrence by the 54th National Convention in June 2020:

LWVUS promotes an open governmental system that is representative, accountable, and responsive. We encourage electoral methods that provide the broadest voter representation possible and are expressive of voter choices.

Whether for single- or multiple-winner contests, the League supports electoral methods that:

- **Encourage voter participation and voter engagement.**
- **Encourage those with minority opinions to participate, including under-represented communities.**
- **Are verifiable and auditable.**
- **Promote access to voting.**
- **Maximize effective votes/minimize wasted votes.**
- **Promote sincere voting over strategic voting.**
- **Implement alternatives to plurality voting.**
- **Are compatible with acceptable ballot-casting methods, including vote-by-mail.**

The LWVUS believes in representative government. The League supports electoral systems that elect policy-making bodies--legislatures, councils, commissions, and boards — that proportionally reflect the people they represent. We support systems that inhibit political manipulation (e.g., gerrymandering).

The LWVUS supports enabling legislation to allow local jurisdictions to explore alternative electoral methods, as well as supporting state election laws allowing for more options at both the state and local levels. With the adoption of any electoral system, the League believes that education of the voting public is important and funding for startup and voter education should be available. We encourage a concerted voter education process.

League History

The League has positions on a multitude of public policy issues decided by our elected representatives, however, until the adoption of this position it did not have a position on how we elect the representatives that make those public policy decisions. Over time, 14 Leagues have conducted studies and developed positions supporting alternatives to the plurality system. This position is a compilation of positions adopted by state and Leagues in Arizona, California, Colorado, , Florida, Massachusetts, Maine, Minnesota, North Carolina, Oklahoma, Oregon, Pennsylvania, South Carolina, Vermont, and Washington, as well as Santa Monica, CA, and established LWVUS principles on representation.

This position does not support any particular election method but rather supports the LWV goals for "an open, governmental system that is representative, accountable and responsive." It allows for Leagues to use the position to evaluate or propose electoral options. This position provides us a clear but flexible base of principles to explore election method reforms and take action when appropriate for voters. Moving forward, LWVUS will work with state and local Leagues to interpret and use the position, but some basic guidelines for use include:

- The National League could use this position to support or oppose federal legislation.
- A State League can use it to support or oppose state legislation.
- Local Leagues can use it to propose or evaluate an electoral system proposed in their community.
- Local Leagues can propose or support a suitable election method as a remedy to voting rights lawsuits filed when a protected group is under-represented by the current system.

At the start of 2022, LWVUS launched a legislative office hours series to answer state/local Leagues' questions about LWVUS positions. One common theme was Ranked-Choice Voting (RCV). LWVUS has not supported legislation at the federal level to institute RCV across the board. However, LWVUS encourages state and local leagues to use the Voter Representation/Electoral Systems section of Impact on Issues — specifically, the position line that recommends informing their advocacy around state and local legislation and ballot initiatives — with regard to the use of ranked-choice voting locally.

Citizen Rights

CITIZEN'S RIGHT TO KNOW/CITIZEN PARTICIPATION

The League's Position

Statement of Position on the Citizen's Right to Know/Citizen Participation, as announced by the national board, June 1984:

The League of Women Voters of the United States believes that democratic government depends upon informed and active participation at all levels of government. The League further believes that governmental bodies must protect the citizen's right to know by giving adequate notice of proposed actions, holding open meetings, and making public records accessible.

League History

Transparency is a key tenet of the League and is often a way that LWV can weigh in on an issue, no matter how big or small. The League has worked for the public's right to know and for broad public participation in government as a necessary component of decision-making at all levels of government since its founding. League support for open meetings was first made explicit in the 1972 Congress position; in 1973, Leagues were empowered to apply that position at the state and local levels. Convention 1974 added to the League Principles the requirement that "government bodies protect the public's right to know by giving adequate notice of proposed actions, holding open meetings, and making public records accessible" and decided that Leagues could act on the Principles — with the necessary safeguards of member understanding and support. The League supported the *1976 Government in the Sunshine* law to enhance the public's access to information.

In the 1980s, the League monitored and lobbied to revamp the way federal rules and regulations are made. The League supports broad public participation at every stage of the rule-making process. LWVUS, in coalition with numerous other organizations, opposed 1983 efforts by the Office of Management and Budget (OMB) to restrict the political advocacy activities of nonprofit organizations and thereby limit public participation in federal policy making. The coalition's opposition resulted in a much less onerous OMB regulation.

As part of its concerns about the public's rights, the League supports lobbying disclosure reform to provide information on the pressures exerted on the national policy-making process and guarantee the public's access to influence the process.

Early in 1995, congressional leadership launched a broad attack on public participation in government decision making. Under the guise of regulatory reform, bills were introduced to make it much more difficult for federal agencies to promulgate regulations dealing with health, safety, and the environment. These bills were based on the premise that regulations should be judged solely on their cost to the public and private sectors and not on their benefits to society.

The League responded quickly to this major threat, lobbying both houses of Congress in opposition. Along with members of 200 other consumer, environmental, and disability rights organizations, League members met with their members of Congress and participated in media activities opposing these efforts. The opposition succeeded in stalling all regulatory reform legislation in the Senate in 1996.

The League also responded to a major congressional attack in the 104th Congress (1995 – 1996), when an amendment to severely limit the ability of nonprofits to speak out on public policy matters was added to several 1996 appropriations bills. Known as the Istook amendment after its primary sponsor, Rep. Ernest Istook of Oklahoma, it was designed to limit public participation by forcing nonprofits to choose between community service and public policy.

The League, with hundreds of other nonprofits, organized a massive campaign to educate the public and members of Congress about the serious implications of this legislation. The Istook amendment was eventually dropped from the appropriations bills, but similar efforts continued in the 104th (1995 – 1997) and 105th (1997 – 1999) Congresses. The League continues to monitor attempts to gag nonprofit organizations.

In June 2000, LWVUS urged the Federal Communications Commission (FCC) to issue requirements for broadcasters to cover local public affairs in an effort to improve the public's understanding of local governing issues.

Beginning with a grant from the Open Society Institute in 2001, LWVEF participated in the Judicial Independence Project. State and local Leagues, working in conjunction with the national office, assessed the levels of judicial independence in their state and developed citizen education campaigns to educate their communities about this important issue. A key part of this program was encouraging Leagues to include judicial candidates in their voters' guides and to organize candidate forums for judicial candidates. In 2002 and 2003, more than 200 Leagues nationwide organized 70 forums, meetings, and workshops spotlighting their state court systems and the value of an independent judiciary.

This project continued in 2004 – 2008 and evolved into Safeguarding US Democracy: Promoting an Independent Judiciary, a program that increased citizen understanding of the importance of our nation's system of separation of powers and highlighted the vital need for protecting a vibrant and independent judiciary. In 2009 and 2010, the project gained a new focus on promoting diversity at all levels of the state judiciary. In the first year of The Quest for a More Diverse Judiciary, Leagues in Kansas worked on this initiative and saw success in the new appointments that followed. In the second year, South Carolina was added and was also successful. In 2012, the State of Washington was added with a more limited scope, and in the same year the League published From Theory to Practice: A Grassroots Education Campaign, a practical guide for those wishing to create statewide education campaigns, illustrating each step of the campaign with practical information learned in Kansas, South Carolina, and Washington.

In 2002 and 2004, LWVUS participated as amicus curiae in the case of *Miller-El v. Cockrell*. The League's interest in the case focused on the use of race-based peremptory challenges to jurors as a means to block citizen participation in government. The US Supreme Court agreed with the League's position, but a lower federal court failed to carry out this interpretation, and the case was again before the US Supreme Court in late 2004. The US Supreme Court reaffirmed its earlier decision by agreeing with the League position.

In the 109th Congress (2005 – 2007), LWVUS endorsed the *Openness Promotes Effectiveness in our National Government Act* (OPEN) which expands the accessibility and accountability of the federal government by strengthening the *Freedom of Information Act* (FOIA) and making information more readily available to the public.

LWVEF has engaged in several efforts to assist Leagues in this area and to become more visible in federal transparency efforts. In 2005, the League launched Openness in Government: Looking for the Sunshine, a project to broaden public awareness about the issues involved in, and the threats related to, accountability and transparency in government. The project was continued in 2006, as Observing Your Government in Action: Protecting Your Right to Know. The League developed educational materials about federal, state, and local laws concerning citizen access; the extent and types of threats to these laws that have occurred in recent years; and data on the increasing levels of information being placed off-limits since the terrorist attacks on the United States on September 11, 2001.

Additional projects were initiated in the following years. One focused on public document audits, providing financial support to Leagues in 11 states and a toolkit, Surveying Public Documents: Protecting Your Right to Know. In 2010, work started on Sunshine 2.0, an online resource that provided criteria for assessing the transparency of local government websites and other online technologies.

At the federal level, the League was active in providing advice to the Obama administration (2009 – 2017) as it proceeded to implement its Openness in Government Directive. In so doing, the League helped several good government groups work together.

The League served as a cosponsor of the annual Sunshine Week in the mid 2000s, taking part in kickoff events in Washington, DC. Sunshine Week sponsors a nationwide live webcast to stimulate public discussion about why open government is important to everyone and why it is under challenge today. Leagues were encouraged to participate.

As we continue to push forward our general policy objectives, the League continues to make sure open meetings and open records laws are protected or expanded; state Leagues pushed for legislation to create increased transparency and public input in the redistricting process prior to the 2021 redistricting cycle.

The onset of the COVID-19 public health crisis presented new challenges to informed and active participation by citizens as states instituted shelter-in-place orders and social distancing measures and governments transitioned to virtual or closed meetings. LWVUS created Virtual Transparency Guidelines for Leagues to use to advocate for open, transparent, and accessible processes for all governmental bodies in the face of COVID-19 and to be used in future emergencies requiring the limitation of in-person contact.

The League also focused on transparency as a key tenet in redistricting processes. Together with state Leagues, we worked to urge lawmakers to codify transparency in the map-drawing process and hold redistricting commissions and elected officials accountable for the decisions they were making about the drawing of district lines.

INDIVIDUAL LIBERTIES

The League's Position

Statement of Position on Individual Liberties, as announced by the national board, March 1982:

The League of Women Voters of the United States believes in the individual liberties guaranteed by the Constitution of the United States. The League is convinced that individual rights now protected by the Constitution should not be weakened or abridged.

League History

Individual liberties, a long-standing League Principle, have been central for the League during times of national tension.

The "witch hunt" period of the early 1950s led the League to undertake a two-year Freedom Agenda community education program on issues such as freedom of speech. Next, a focused study on the federal loyalty/security programs culminated in a position that emphasized protection of individual rights.

The 1976 Convention incorporated the League's individual liberties Principle into the national Program, thus authorizing the League to act against major threats to basic constitutional rights. Subsequent Conventions reaffirmed that commitment and, in 1982, the LWVUS Board authorized a specific position statement on individual liberties.

In 2003, the League contacted members of both houses of Congress, asking them to scale back several far-reaching provisions of the *USA PATRIOT Act*, passed in October 2001. In 2004, the League lobbied on behalf of the bipartisan *Security and Freedom Ensured (SAFE) Act* , which addressed many of the *PATRIOT Act's* problems, while still allowing law enforcement officials broad authority to combat terrorism.

Late in the 108th Congress (2003 – 2005), the League lobbied against the House version of legislation to overhaul the organization of US intelligence operations because it went beyond the scope of the September 11th Commission's recommendations, expanding the government's investigative and prosecutorial powers and infringing on civil liberties. When the bill was passed in December 2004 as the *National Intelligence Reform Act*, it had been amended and a number of the troubling provisions that the League opposed were eliminated.

At the 2004 Convention, League delegates voted to make civil liberties a top priority in the next biennium. LWVUS appointed an Advisory Task Force and created an online discussion list to foster dialogue about the League's course of action.

In 2005, LWVUS also expressed concerns about reports of torture by the US military and actively supported the *McCain Amendment*, banning cruel, inhuman, or degrading treatment or punishment of anyone under custody or control of the US armed forces. The amendment passed as part of the Department of Defense appropriation.

During the 109th Congress (2005 – 2007), the League continued to lobby in support of the *SAFE Act* and in opposition to the pending reauthorization of specific provisions of the *USA PATRIOT Act*. While final reauthorization did not address many of our concerns, there was limited improvement in some critical provisions.

In 2005, LWVEF sponsored a nationwide project, Local Voices: Citizen Conversations on Civil Liberties and Secure Communities, to foster public dialogue about the balance between civil liberties and homeland security. The League sponsored public discussions in 10 ethnically, economically, and geographically diverse cities. It released the findings of these discussions and public opinion research on the issue at the US Capitol in September 2005.

In 2007 – 2008, the League fought legislation in both houses of Congress that would continue allowing the executive branch to conduct warrantless wiretapping without judicial review. The League supported legislation that would protect citizens' personal information and limit the FBI's authority to issue national security letters in lieu of judicial warrants to produce information and materials.

In 2009, the League joined other organizations in support of the *Judiciously Using Surveillance Tools in Counterterrorism Efforts (JUSTICE) Act*, legislation to amend expiring provisions of the *USA PATRIOT Act*.

Recognizing that voting is the gatekeeper for all civil rights, in 2019, the League signed on to the Leadership Conference on Civil and Human Rights' report Vision for Democracy, which lays out policy recommendations to ensure that everyone is able to fairly and equally participate in our democracy.

The League continued to defend the First Amendment as the right to protest became increasingly threatened. In 2018, the League submitted comments regarding proposed regulations pertaining to the National Park Service's protest permitting process that would have made it harder to have demonstrations at the National Mall, Memorial Parks, and President's Park. In 2020, the League condemned the use of tear gas and violence against peaceful protesters gathering to decry police brutality and the killings of unarmed Black, Latino, and immigrant people and signed onto a letter compelling the UN Human Rights Council to convene a Special Session on police violence and repression of protests in the United States.

In 2020 and 2021, the League recognized that the individual liberties of Black, Latino, and immigrant individuals are not equally protected and joined efforts calling on both houses of Congress to pass federal statutory reforms to address policing issues and legislation prohibiting the use of federal funds for police officers on K-12 school campuses, as well as for the US Department of Justice to investigate the police departments and officials that committed the horrific murders of Ahmaud Arbery, Breonna Taylor, and George Floyd for civil rights violations. The League also urged the Trump administration to take measures to protect the civil rights of Asian Americans and Pacific Islanders (AAPI) in the wake of increasing racist attacks and discrimination against the AAPI community during the COVID-19 pandemic.

From May to June 2022, the League participated in the US Department of State's Summit for Democracy Civil Society Consultations, to participate in priority-setting for the US government's upcoming Year of Action. In June 2022, the US Supreme Court ruled in *Dobbs vs. Jackson Women's Health Organization*, overturning *Roe v. Wade* and eliminating the constitutional right to abortion. Rolling back nearly 50 years of legal precedent, *Dobbs* marked the first time in history that the Court took away a fundamental right. It threatens a host of individual liberties that rely on the right of privacy as protected in the Fourteenth Amendment. These include the right to interracial marriage, certain acts of intimate conduct, same-sex marriage, and contraception. At the 2022 Convention, the League voted to adopt a position supporting the rights of women and those who can become pregnant to self-determination related to, and including, but not limited to bodily autonomy, reproductive health, and lifestyle choice. In light of the imminent threat to individual liberties, the League attended numerous related Summit for Democracy consultations on topics including racial justice, LGBTQIA+ issues, and gender, and prepared a memo for the State Department, including calling for the federal codification of the right for same-gender couples to marry under civil law.

PUBLIC POLICY ON REPRODUCTIVE CHOICES

The League's Position

Statement of Position on Public Policy on Reproductive Choices, as announced by the national board, January 1983:

The League of Women Voters of the United States believes that public policy in a pluralistic society must affirm the constitutional right of privacy of the individual to make reproductive choices.

League History

The 1982 Convention voted to develop a League position on Reproductive Choices through concurrence. That fall, League members studied the issue and agreed to concur with a statement derived from positions reached by the New Jersey and Massachusetts Leagues. LWVUS announced the position in January 1983.

In 1983, LWVUS successfully pressed for defeat of *S.J. Res. 3*, a proposed constitutional amendment that would have overturned *Roe v. Wade*, the landmark US Supreme Court decision that declared the right of privacy includes the right of a woman, or a person who can become pregnant, in consultation with their doctor, to decide to terminate a pregnancy. The League joined as an amicus in two successful lawsuits challenging proposed regulations by the US Department of Health and Human Services (HHS), thwarting attempts to implement regulations requiring parental notification by federally funded family planning centers that provide prescription contraceptives to teenagers.

The League has joined with other pro-choice organizations in continuous opposition to restrictions on the right of privacy in reproductive choices that have appeared in Congress as legislative riders to funding measures. In 1985, the League joined as an amicus in a lawsuit challenging a Pennsylvania law intended to deter women, or those who can become pregnant, from having abortions. In 1986, the US Supreme Court found the law unconstitutional, upholding the right to make reproductive choices.

In 1986, the League opposed congressional provisions to revoke the tax-exempt status of any organization that performs, finances, or provides facilities for any abortion not necessary to save the life of a pregnant person. In 1987, the League unsuccessfully opposed regulations governing Title X of the *Public Health Service Act*. The League reaffirmed that individuals have the right to make their own reproductive choices, consistent with the constitutional right of privacy, stating that the proposed rule violated this right by prohibiting counseling and referral for abortion services by clinics receiving Title X funds.

In 1988 and 1990, the League urged congressional committees to report an appropriations bill for the District of Columbia without amendments limiting abortion funding. The League also supported 1988 legislation that would have restored Medicaid funding for abortions in cases of rape or incest.

The League joined an amicus brief to uphold the right of privacy to make reproductive choices in *Webster v. Reproductive Health Services*. In July 1989, a sharply divided US Supreme Court issued a decision that severely eroded the right of privacy to choose an abortion. Although *Webster* did not deny the constitutional right to choose abortion, it effectively overruled a significant portion of the 1973 *Roe* decision by upholding a Missouri statute that prohibited the use of public facilities, employees, or funds for counseling, advising, or performing abortions and required doctors to conduct viability tests on fetuses 20 weeks or later before performing an abortion.

In the fall of 1989, the League supported the Mobilization for Women's Lives. The League also joined an amicus brief in *Turnock v. Ragsdale*, challenging an Illinois statute that would have effectively restricted access to abortions, including those in the first trimester, by imposing strict requirements on abortion clinics.

In 1990, LWVUS joined the national Pro-Choice Coalition and began work in support of the *Freedom of Choice Act*, designed to place into federal law the principles of *Roe v. Wade*.

In 1990 – 1991, the League, in *New York v. Sullivan*, opposed the HHS "gag rule regulations that prohibit abortion information, services, or referrals by family-planning programs receiving Title X public health funds." The Supreme Court upheld the regulations; Leagues nationwide responded in opposition and LWVUS urged Congress to overturn the gag rule.

The 1990 League Convention voted to work on issues dealing with the right of privacy in reproductive choice, domestic and international family planning and reproductive health care, and initiatives to decrease teen pregnancy and infant mortality (based on the International Relations and Social Policy positions). LWVUS acted on a series of pro-choice legislative initiatives. It supported the *International Family Planning Act*, which would have reversed US policy denying family planning funds to foreign organizations that provide abortion services or information. It opposed the Department of Defense policy prohibiting military personnel from obtaining abortions at military hospitals overseas and supported the right of the District of Columbia to use its own revenues to provide Medicaid abortions for women with low incomes.

In 1991 and 1992, the League continued to fight efforts to erode the constitutional right of reproductive choice by supporting the *Freedom of Choice Act* and attempts to overturn the gag rule. In coalition with 178 other groups, the

League filed an amicus brief in *Planned Parenthood of Southeastern Pennsylvania v. Casey*, arguing that constitutional rights, once recognized, should not be snatched away. In June 1992, the Court decision partially upheld the Pennsylvania regulations, further eroding the principles of *Roe*. In response, Leagues stepped up lobbying efforts for the *Freedom of Choice Act*. The 1992 LWVUS Convention voted to continue work on all domestic and international aspects of reproductive choice.

In 1993, the League continued to support legislative attempts to overturn the gag rule. In late 1993, President Clinton signed an executive order overturning it and other restrictive anti-choice policies. LWVUS continued to work for passage of the *Freedom of Choice Act* and against the *Hyde Amendment*. LWVUS supported the *Freedom of Access to Clinic Entrances (FACE) Act*, a response to escalating violence at abortion clinics. The *FACE Act* was signed into law in 1993.

During the 1993 – 1994 health care debate, the League pressed for inclusion of reproductive services, including abortion, in any health care reform package. In 1995, the League again opposed amendments denying Medicaid funding for abortions for victims of rape and incest.

In 1998, LWVUS opposed the *Child Custody Protection Act*, federal legislation designed to make it illegal for an adult other than a parent to assist a minor in obtaining an out-of-state abortion.

In spring 2000, LWVUS joined an amicus brief in *Stenberg v. Carhart*, urging the US Supreme Court to affirm a US Court of Appeals ruling that a Nebraska law criminalizing commonly used abortion procedures was unconstitutional. The Court's affirmation of the ruling in June 2000 was pivotal in further defining the right to reproductive freedom.

As Congress continued to threaten reproductive rights with legislative riders to appropriations bills, the League lobbied Congress in opposition to these back door attempts to limit reproductive choices.

In 2002, LWVUS lobbied extensively against attempts to limit funding for family planning and, in 2003, the League lobbied the House to support funding for the United Nations Population Fund, which lost by just one vote. The League strongly opposed the passage of the so-called *Partial-Birth Abortion Act* in 2003, but it was passed and signed into law under the Bush administration.

In 2004, LWVUS lobbied in opposition to the *Unborn Victims of Violence Act (UVVA)*, which conveys legal status under the federal criminal code to an embryo and fetus, but it was signed into law.

The League also cosponsored the *March for Women's Lives* in Washington, DC, for the right to make reproductive choices, which drew widespread support, including from many state and local League delegations.

In 2008, the League filed official comments with HHS voicing concern over so-called "conscience" regulations that would limit reproductive health care options for women by allowing physicians, pharmacists, and other providers to sharply limit their services according to their own views on reproductive health care.

In 2009, the League joined other groups urging rescission of the conscience regulations. HHS subsequently modified the regulations to preserve reproductive health care options and the doctor-patient relationship.

In 2012, the League successfully fought attempts in Congress to allow any employer or provider who claimed an ill-defined "religious or moral" objection to a health care service, such as reproductive health care, to be exempted from providing such coverage under the *Affordable Care Act* (ACA). The League opposed this exemption, which would undermine the very premise of the ACA that all persons, regardless of gender, should be eligible for health services under the *Affordable Care Act*, and that failure to do so is discrimination based on sex.

The League also lobbied Congress in support of fully funding the Title X Family Planning program in response to proposed cuts to *Title X*, which provides family planning and reproductive health care services to millions of individuals and families with low incomes.

In 2013, LWVUS submitted comments to HHS opposing religious exemptions for contraceptive services. This debate continued in the courts and the League joined with other concerned organizations in opposing broad religious exemptions to the requirement that all insurance plans provide access to contraception as basic care in the US Supreme Court case of *Burwell v. Hobby Lobby* Stores. The Supreme Court ruled in favor of the religious exemptions.

In the fall of 2019, LWVUS joined an amicus brief in *June Medical Services v. Russo*, a case that challenged a Louisiana law that required abortion clinics to have hospital admitting rights. The law would have closed all but one clinic providing abortion services in the state. In a 5-4 decision, the court struck down the law, protecting women, especially women of color, and retaining the three clinics across the state. The League also joined domestic and international reproductive health and women's rights partners in urging both houses of Congress to include provisions in FY2020 appropriations to repeal the reinstituted gag rule and protect the Title X program, in light of the Trump administration's new restrictive regulations on Title X-funded providers.

The League continued advocacy to protect reproductive choices and access to birth control under the ACA through 2020. The League also joined a letter to US House and Senate leadership that connected work on reproductive justice with that of the movement for racial justice following the murders of Breonna Taylor, George Floyd, and other Black Americans. The effort encouraged lawmakers to take federal action to end the use of discriminatory legislation like the Hyde Amendment, which perpetuates systems of oppression and disproportionally affects people of color.

In the fall of 2021, the League joined an amicus brief with numerous other civil rights and social justice organizations in *Dobbs vs. Jackson Women's Health Organization*, in which the Center for Reproductive Rights challenged a Mississippi 15-week abortion ban, making it the first time the US Supreme Court considered the constitutionality of a pre-viability abortion ban since *Roe v. Wade*.

In May 2022, after a draft majority opinion in *Dobbs* was leaked revealing that the Supreme Court was prepared to overturn *Roe v. Wade* and *Planned Parenthood v. Casey*, the LWVUS Board of Directors met and agreed to support filibuster reform, including elimination of the filibuster, as a targeted strategy to protect reproductive rights. The League sent a letter to the US Senate urging support of the House-passed *Women's Health Protection Act* (WHPA), which would federally codify the right to provide and receive abortion services. In May, for the second time in 2022, the WHPA was blocked in the Senate.

Then in June, the Supreme Court ruled in *Dobbs*, overturning *Roe* and *Casey*, eliminating the constitutional right to abortion, leaving it up to federal and state legislatures. LWVUS began working with state Leagues to support their state advocacy efforts to protect and expand rights and access to abortion and contraception. The decision was handed down during the 2022 LWVUS Convention, and League members immediately passed a resolution reiterating that "the League supports the rights of women and those who can become pregnant to self-determination related to, and including, but not limited to bodily autonomy, privacy, reproductive health, and lifestyle choice." Following the day's business, League members marched on the Colorado state capital in Denver to protest the decision.

The League also joined reproductive rights partners urging the administration to protect the right to abortion and ensure accessibility for all Americans. The League supported the Biden administration's executive order instructing the US Department of Justice to defend the right to abortion medication, as well as additional potential measures including declaring a public health emergency and mobilizing federal resources to support people seeking health care with associated expenses.

Evaluating Constitutional Amendment Proposals and Constitutional Conventions

CONSTITUTIONAL AMENDMENT PROPOSALS

The League's Position

Statement of Position on Evaluating Constitutional Amendment Proposals, as announced by the national board, January 2016:

The League will only support a proposed amendment to the US Constitution if it advances and conforms to an LWVUS position.

In addition, the League believes the following should be considered in identifying an appropriate and well-crafted constitutional amendment:

a. **Whether the public policy objective addresses matters of such acute and abiding importance that the fundamental charter of our nation must be changed. Amendments are changes to a document that provides stability to our system and should be undertaken to address extreme problems or long-term needs.**

b. **Whether the amendment as written would be effective in achieving its policy objective. Amendments that may be unenforceable, miss the objective, or have unintended consequences may not achieve the policy objective.**

c. **Whether the amendment would either make our political system more democratic or protect individual rights. Most adopted amendments have sought to make our system more representative or to protect the rights of minorities.**

d. **Whether the public policy objective can be achieved by a legislative or political approach that is less difficult than a constitutional amendment. In order to expend resources wisely, it is important to consider whether legislation or political action is more likely to succeed than an amendment.**

e. **Whether the public policy objective is more suited to a constitutional and general approach than to a statutory and detailed approach. It is important to consider whether the goal can best be achieved by an overall value statement, which will be interpreted by the courts, or with specific statutory detail to resolve important issues and reduce ambiguity.**

League History

Following the January 2016 meeting, the LWVUS Board announced a new position outlining considerations for evaluating constitutional amendment proposals. State Leagues can use this new position, as well as the new position calling for safeguards to govern the constitutional convention process, to address the ongoing debates in many legislatures regarding constitutional conventions, in particular as they relate to the Balanced Budget amendment.

The League continues to use this position to evaluate the Constitutional amendments proposed to overturn the Supreme Court's *Citizens United* decision. In 2019, as part of the *For the People Act*, the Democracy for All amendment was introduced within the bill and as stand-alone legislation. The League declined to endorse the legislation, but continues to look for opportunities to overturn the *Citizens United* decision through the promotion of other legislation that would remedy the issues it raised.

Another important topic during the 116th Congress (2019 – 2021) was the abolition of the Electoral College. Several amendments were introduced to abolish the Electoral College. Moving forward, the LWVUS will use the criteria highlighted above as well as the Selection of the President position to analyze additional proposals.

CONSTITUTIONAL CONVENTIONS

The League's Position

Statement of Position on Constitutional Conventions under Article V of the US Constitution, as announced by the national board, January 2016:

The League is concerned that there are many unresolved questions about the powers and processes of an Article V Constitutional Convention. The League believes such a convention should be called only if the following conditions are in place:

a. **The Constitutional Convention must be transparent and not conducted in secret. The public has a right to know what is being debated and voted on.**

b. **Representation at the Constitutional Convention must be based on population rather than one-state, one-vote, and delegates should be elected rather than appointed. The delegates represent citizens, should be elected by them, and must be distributed by US population.**

c. **Voting at the Constitutional Convention must be by delegate, not by state. Delegates from one state can have varying views and should be able to express them by individual votes.**

d. **The Constitutional Convention must be limited to a specific topic. It is important to guard against a "runaway convention," which considers multiple issues or topics that were not initiated by the states.**

e. Only state resolutions on a single topic count when determining if a Constitutional Convention should be called. Counting state requests by topic ensures that there is sufficient interest in a particular subject to call a Convention and enhances citizen interest and participation in the process.

f. The validity of state calls for an Article V Constitutional Convention must be determined by the most recent action of the state. If a state has enacted a rescission of its call, that rescission must be respected by Congress.

League History

Following the January 2016 meeting, the LWVUS Board announced a new position calling for safeguards to govern the constitutional convention process. State Leagues can use this position, as well as the position outlining considerations for evaluating constitutional amendment proposals, to address the ongoing debates in many legislatures regarding constitutional conventions, in particular as they relate to the balanced budget amendment.

In the summer of 2016, LWVUS joined a coalition of groups working to address a wave of resolutions introduced in state legislatures calling for constitutional conventions under *Article V* of the US Constitution. At that time, 28 of the needed 34 states had passed resolutions calling for a convention. Proponents of a constitutional convention include the American Legislative Exchange Council (ALEC) and the tea party. The coalition believes that without a clear construct, a US constitutional convention would throw the country into turmoil, creating legal and political battles of great consequence to the nation's future. This is a power grab that would put control of our country's future into the hands of politicians and special interests. Many constitutional scholars also support this position.

As efforts to call for a Constitutional Convention continued in the most recent biennium, LWVUS worked with state Leagues to activate League members to contact their legislators, testify at hearings against these resolutions, and generate attention on social media and with traditional press. LWVUS continues to work with these coalition partners by monitoring activities around this issue, attending steering committee meetings of the national coalition, and engaging state Leagues in on-the-ground coalitions to fight these resolutions in their own legislatures.

Congress and the Presidency

CONGRESS

The League's Position

Statement of Position on Congress, as announced by the national board, April 1972 and revised March 1982:

The League of Women Voters of the United States believes that structures and practices of the US Congress must be characterized by openness, accountability, representativeness, decision-making capability, and effective performance. Responsive legislative processes must meet these criteria:

Accountability

A Congress responsive to citizens and able to hold its own leaders, committees, and members responsible for their actions and decisions.

Representativeness

A Congress whose leaders, committees, and members represent the nation as a whole, as well as their own districts and states.

Decision-making Capability

A Congress with the knowledge, resources, and power to make decisions that meet national needs and reconcile conflicting interests and priorities.

Effective Performance

A Congress able to function in an efficient manner with a minimum of conflict, wasted time, and duplication of effort.

Open Government

A Congress whose proceedings in committee as well as on the floor are open to the fullest extent possible.

League History

Congress has been a part of the League agenda for many decades. In 1944, the League adopted as a Program focus: "Strengthening governmental procedures to improve the legislative process and relationship between Congress and the Executive." In 1946, LWVUS worked successfully for passage of the *Legislative Reorganization Act*. In 1954, the League unsuccessfully called on Congress to coordinate and simplify its budgetary procedures.

In 1970, the League undertook a comprehensive study of Congress, leading to a 1972 position on specific changes to make Congress more responsive to citizen needs. League members urged Congress to open the doors to its committee and hearing rooms, free up access to leadership positions, and coordinate its budgetary processes.

League support of procedural changes and the *1974 Budget Reform and Impoundment Control Act* led to many improvements:

- New committee procedures that modified the seniority system and made committee membership more representative of diverse interests.
- Rule changes for more adequate staffing.
- Electronic voting.
- Modification of the Senate cloture rule.
- Moves to open all committee meetings and proceedings to the public, except when matters of national security are involved.
- Reorganization of the budget process, so that Congress can establish priorities and evaluate the budget package as a whole.

The League has continued to assess proposals for additional procedural changes in Congress. In 1986, the League urged the Senate to provide for radio broadcast and trial closed-circuit television coverage. In 1989, LWVUS successfully urged the House to enact an ethics reform package that included limits on honoraria and outside income. In 1998, the League joined 13 national groups in urging the Senate Majority Leader to eliminate the use of "secret holds" in the Senate. The League and 52 other groups endorsed draft legislation to put Congressional Research Service reports and products online.

In 1991, the League announced its opposition to term limits for members of the US Congress on the grounds that such limits would adversely affect the accountability, representativeness, and effective performance of Congress and, by decreasing the power of Congress, upset the balance of power between Congress and an already powerful presidency. The 1992 Convention reaffirmed opposition to term limits and authorized state and local Leagues to use national positions to take action on term limits for state and local offices.

In 1993 – 1994, the Leagues of Washington and Arkansas participated in suits challenging state term limit laws based on the US Constitution. In 1995, after hearing the Arkansas case, the US Supreme Court agreed that term limits imposed by states on the US House and Senate are unconstitutional. Proposals to amend the Constitution to allow or set federal term limits failed to receive the necessary two-thirds majority in both houses. The League vigorously opposed the proposed amendment through testimony, lobbying, and grassroots action. In 1997, the League again successfully lobbied House members on this issue.

In 1999, LWVUS and the LWV of Missouri filed an amicus brief in the US Court of Appeals in *Cook v. Gralike*, challenging a Missouri law requiring the phrase "disregarded voters' instruction on term limits" to appear on the ballot next to the name of any candidate who had not taken certain actions related to term limits. The law was struck down by the Appeals Court, both because it was a backdoor attempt to impose term limits and because it burdened the election process. The state LWV and LWVUS subsequently filed amicus briefs with the US Supreme Court when the case was considered on appeal.

In 2007 and 2008, the League responded directly to congressional scandals that demonstrated a failure in the mechanisms that regulated ethics and lobbying. The League pushed Congress to enact lobbying reform measures to set fundraising limits on lobbyists and lobbying firms; change the gift, travel, and employment relationships among members of Congress, lobbyists, and lobbying firms; and institute new, more-effective enforcement mechanisms.

In 2008, the House passed new ethics procedures, including new ethics rules, disclosure requirements for campaign contributions bundled by lobbyists, and a new ethics enforcement process. The League also supported strengthening the investigative powers of the new Office of Congressional Ethics by providing access to subpoena power so investigators would be able to compel cooperation from outside entities and individuals, congressional staff, and Members.

In 2010, and again in 2012 and 2014, the League and coalition partners sent a letter to the Speaker urging him to preserve and strengthen House ethics rules and standards of conduct.

In 2018 and 2020, as the US Senate considered the nominations of two Supreme Court justices, the LWVUS contacted senators reminding them of their duty and responsibility to conduct the confirmation process in such a way as to build trust in our systems of government and ensure the longstanding independence of the judicial branch. This follows on the League's actions in 1991, when the League urged the Senate Judiciary Committee to extend time for additional testimony on a Supreme Court nominee to let all voices be heard. This is in keeping with the League of Women Voters principle that all powers of the US government should be exercised within the constitutional framework of a balance among the three branches of government: legislative, executive, and judicial.

In 2021 and 2022, the League called on the US Senate to "fix or nix" the filibuster rule that continues to stand in the way of progress for the American people. After the draft Supreme Court decision to overturn *Roe* and *Casey* was leaked, LWVUS Board members voted to urge the Senate to pass the *Women's Health and Protection Act* by any means necessary, including by amending or eliminating the filibuster.

THE PRESIDENCY

The League's Position

Statement of Position on the Presidency, as announced by the national board, January 1976, and revised March 1982:

The League of Women Voters of the United States believes that presidential power should be exercised within the constitutional framework of a dynamic balance between the executive and legislative branches. Accountability and responsibility to the people require that unnecessary secrecy between the President and Congress be eliminated. Therefore, the League supports the following measures:

Executive Agreements

Presidential authority to negotiate international executive agreements should be preserved. Accountability to the public requires that the President report to Congress the text of all such agreements and that Congress review them periodically.

War Powers

The President should be required to seek the advice of the Congress before introducing US armed forces into situations where hostilities are imminent, to report promptly to Congress any action taken, and to obtain within a specified time congressional approval for continued military activity.

Emergency Powers

Presidential authority to declare a state of national emergency should be subject to periodic congressional review. The President should transmit to Congress yearly notice of all existing national emergencies and significant orders issued under each. Congress should review the emergencies and significant orders issued under each. Congress should review the emergencies every six months and should have the power to terminate them at any time by concurrent resolution. (All states of emergency now in existence should be terminated after a grace period for adjustment.)

Fiscal Powers

The President should exercise executive responsibility for sound management of public funds in a manner consistent with the programs and priorities established by Congress. This requires procedures for congressional consideration of the budget as a whole and measures for congressional disapproval of presidential impoundment of funds.

Succession and Tenure

The League of Women Voters of the United States supports the succession procedures spelled out in the 25th Amendment. However, the League favors a limit on the amount of time Congress may take to confirm the Vice President.

The League also favors retention of a two-term limitation on presidential terms of office.

League History

In view of growing public concern about presidential powers, the 1974 Convention adopted a two-year study of the executive branch with emphasis on presidential powers, succession, and tenure. The 1976 position tied closely to earlier positions on Congress and enabled the League to act to promote a dynamic balance between the powers of the President and those of Congress. Such a balance, according to member agreement, requires elimination of unnecessary secrecy between the branches, periodic congressional reviews of executive agreements and states of national emergency, and proper use of the procedures spelled out in the War Powers Resolution. LWVUS support of anti-impoundment measures in 1973 was consistent with the emphasis on the balance of power between the two branches.

In 1985, the League opposed the *Gramm-Rudman-Hollings Balanced Budget and Emergency Deficit Control Act* as a threat to this balance of power. In 1986, the US Supreme Court declared unconstitutional the key part of the law that provided for automatic budget cuts to be decided by the Comptroller-General if deficit targets were missed. A revision of the law met the separation-of-powers objection of the Court.

Privatization

The League's Position

Statement of Position on Privatization as announced by the national board in June 2012:

The League of Women Voters of the United States believes that when governmental entities consider the transfer of governmental services, assets, and/or functions to the private sector, the community impact and goals of such transfers must be identified and considered. Further, the League believes that transparency, accountability, and preservation of the common good must be ensured.

The League believes that some government-provided services could be delivered more efficiently by private entities; however, privatization is not appropriate in all circumstances. Privatization is not appropriate when the provision of services by the government is necessary to preserve the common good, to protect national or local security or to meet the needs of the most vulnerable members of society. While the League recognizes that the definition of core government services will vary by level of government and community values, services fundamental to the governance of a democratic society should not be privatized in their entirety. These services include the electoral process, justice system, military, public safety, public health, education, transportation, environmental protection, and programs that protect and provide basic human needs.

The decision to privatize a public service should be made only after an informed, transparent planning process and thorough analysis of the implications of privatizing service delivery. While specific criteria will vary by service and local conditions, the League believes the following considerations apply to most decisions to transfer public services, assets, and functions to the private sector:

- Ongoing and timely communication with stakeholders and the public.
- Statement of the circumstances as they exist and what is to be gained.
- Definition of the quality, level, and cost of service expected.
- Assessment of the private market— whether there are providers to assure competitive pricing and delivery (in some cases there may not be multiple providers if a service is so specialized (e.g., high-tech, airports).
- Cost-benefit analyses evaluating short- and long-term costs of privatization, including the ongoing costs of contract administration and oversight.
- An understanding of the impact on customers, the broader community, environment, and public employees.
- An open, competitive bidding process with clearly defined criteria to be used in selecting a contractor.
- A provision and process to ensure the services or assets will be returned to the government if a contractor fails to perform.
- A data-driven selection of private entities whose goals, purposes, and means are not incompatible with the public well-being.
- The careful negotiation and drafting of the controlling privatization contract.
- Adequate oversight and periodic performance monitoring of the privatized services by the government entity to ensure that the private entity is complying with all relevant laws and regulations, contract terms and conditions, and ethical standards, including public disclosure and comment.

The League believes that the enactment of state laws and issuance of regulations to control the process and delivery of privatization within a state's jurisdiction is often appropriate and desirable. Best practices for government regulation of the privatization process should include the following requirements:

- An open process that allows for citizen input and oversight in a timely manner.
- A reasonable feasibility study and project evaluation appropriate to the size and scope of the project.
- The establishment of carefully crafted criteria for selection of the private entity (beyond the lowest-cost bid).
- Additional consideration for local bidders in order to support the local economy.
- The retention of liability and responsibility with the government entity.
- Allowance for and promotion of opportunities for innovation and collaboration.
- Provision for employment, benefits, and training plans on behalf of employees displaced as a result of privatization.

League History

Convention 2010 delegates voted to undertake a study of the issue of privatization. Local and state Leagues across the country participated in the study and the League announced its position in June 2012.

Digital Equity

The League's Position

Statement of Position on Digital Equity as adopted by concurrence by delegates to Convention in June 2022:

The League of Women Voters believes that high-speed affordable internet access is an essential service that should be readily available to all US residents and businesses. National, state, and local government policies should support broadband, wireless, and other means of high-speed internet deployment throughout the nation. Efficient, high-speed, affordable access to the internet for all US residents in their homes, schools, and workplaces — regardless of geographic location or neighborhood demographics — is a necessity for assuring equal access to local and state government, maintaining openness and transparency in government activities, communicating with legislative leaders, engaging in political discourse, competing in the global marketplace, and assuring that voters receive the information they need to participate in our democracy.

The League of Women Voters supports making high-speed internet access available to all residents of the United States, without charge, through schools, libraries, and other secure public buildings.

Community Access and Public Affairs Media

The League of Women Voters believes that community access media – for public, educational, and governmental programming (PEG) – must be adequately protected, promoted, and funded, regardless of the provider of media services. Statewide public affairs programming must be adequately protected, promoted, and funded by state legislatures and available to all residents, regardless of the provider of media services. Government should provide opportunities for citizen participation in decisions regarding community access, or PEG media.

Access to public affairs programming through modern media communication is essential to the public interest and to the League of Women Voters' mission and purpose — to protect civil liberties, ensure open, transparent government, and promote the public's right to know. To protect the public interest, high-quality PEG transmission and PEG availability on basic service tiers and on the internet are essential.

League History

The 2022 convention voted to include this position in Impact on Issues and the national office will track the League's engagement and work around this issue for the next biennium. Convention 2022 adopted the LWV Connecticut position by concurrence.

IMPACT ON ISSUES

International Relations

LWV

Promote peace in an interdependent world by working cooperatively with other nations and strengthening international organizations.

A commitment to international cooperation as an essential path to world peace is deeply rooted in League history. Founded just after World War I, the League rejected a policy of isolationism as "neither wise nor possible for this nation." The League's commitment has taken many forms. Action to support free trade began during the Depression and support for aid to developing countries in the 1950s. As World War II ended, the League launched a nationwide campaign to build public understanding of the agreements setting up the United Nations and was proud to be one of the nongovernmental organizations (NGO) first affiliated with the UN, a relationship that continues today.

In the 1960s, the League played an important role in educating citizens and creating the climate for normalization of US relations with the People's Republic of China. Also in the 1960s, after a reappraisal of trade policy, the League acted to reduce trade barriers while supporting assistance for economic adjustment in the United States. Throughout the 1970s, the League was active on trade issues, working for the history-making multilateral process that built a new structure for international trade.

In the 1980s, positions on Arms Control and on Military Policy and Defense Spending added new dimensions to the League's international relations efforts. With these positions, the League supported international negotiations and agreements to reduce the risk of war and prevent the development and deployment of nuclear weapons and worked against the costly, technologically suspect, and destabilizing national missile defense program.

Adoption of a US Relations with Developing Countries position in 1986 provided further definition to the League's efforts to promote peace, with special emphasis on human rights, sound management of natural resources, and economic development.

In the 1990s, the League launched training and education projects to build political participation in emerging democracies. Beginning in nations from Eastern Europe and the former Soviet Union and extending to Africa and the Americas, the League experience has proved invaluable in developing the potential for citizen participation and NGOs in democratic systems, especially for women leaders.

In the 2000s, the League expanded its global democracy program and updated its positions on the United Nations and International Trade. The League continued its strong support for the UN, added its support for the International Criminal Court and endorsed enhanced peace operations. The League reiterated its support for measures to expand international trade, while recognizing the importance of protecting environmental, labor, and political values.

UNITED NATIONS

The League's Position

Statement of Position on the United Nations, as announced by the national board, June 1977, and updated, June 2002:

The League of Women Voters of the United States supports a strong, effective United Nations and endorses the full and active participation of the United States in the UN system. The League supports UN efforts to:

- **Promote international peace and security.**

- Advance the social and economic well-being of the world's people.
- Ensure respect for human rights and fundamental freedoms.
- Foster trust and cooperation among nations by encouraging adherence to conventions, treaties, and other international agreements.
- Protect the integrity of the world environment.
- Achieve the full and equal participation of women in all aspects of civil and political life.

The United Nations should be an important component of US foreign policy. The League supports US policies that strengthen the UN's capacity to solve global problems and promote prosperity throughout the world. The United States should work actively and constructively within the UN system, exercising diplomatic leadership in advance of decision-making. The United States should not place conditions on its participation in the United Nations, except in the most extreme cases, such as flagrant violations of the Charter.

The League supports UN leadership in a comprehensive, multi-faceted approach to promoting world peace and security that includes ongoing efforts to eliminate the underlying causes of conflict. UN peace operations should include such strategies as:

- An increased emphasis on preventive diplomacy and the use of such techniques as an early warning system to identify possible threats to peace and mediation to help resolve disputes.
- Preventive deployment of UN peacekeepers to forestall the outbreak of hostilities.
- Enhanced capacity to respond rapidly and effectively to contain conflict and establish a just and stable peace.
- UN peacekeeping operations that have strong political and financial support from the world community and the consent of the local parties.
- Military intervention, as a last resort, to halt genocide and other crimes against humanity and to prevent the spread of conflict.
- Protection of civilian populations, including protection of displaced persons.
- Long-term commitment, both pre- and post-conflict, to establishing the institutions and conditions needed for real economic and social development.
- Enhanced capacity at UN headquarters to plan, manage, and support UN peace operations.

The United States should support all aspects of UN peace operations. Non-governmental organizations (NGOs) have an important role to play in peace operations, including participating in behind-the-scenes diplomatic efforts and providing humanitarian aid.

The League strongly supports the central role of the United Nations in addressing the social, economic, and humanitarian needs of all people. The advancement and empowerment of women is fundamental to achieving peace and prosperity and should be a high priority for UN programs. Other areas for emphasis include:

- Eradicating poverty and hunger.
- Improving basic living standards worldwide.
- Promoting the well-being and potential of children, with special attention to the girl child.
- Promoting human and political rights.
- Ensuring access to a basic education for all.
- Ensuring a basic level of health care for all.
- Protecting the environment and the world's natural resources.

The League supports efforts to strengthen the development and humanitarian work of the United Nations through greater coordination among agencies, more efficient use of resources, additional funding as required, and more partnerships with NGOs and other non-state actors. UN-sponsored world conferences are valuable forums for building international consensus and developing practical plans of action to solve global problems.

The United States should provide strong leadership and financial support to the UN specialized agencies, participate constructively in international conferences, and fulfill all agreed-upon commitments.

The League believes that world peace and progress rest in part on a body of international law developed through conventions, covenants, and treaties and on the judgments of international courts. Disputes between nations should be considered and settled in the International Court of Justice, and its judicial decisions should be honored.

The League supports the creation of a permanent international tribunal, such as the International Criminal Court, to try individuals charged with crimes of genocide, war crimes, and other systematic crimes against humanity.

All court procedures must meet the highest judicial standards, including guarantees of due process protections and the integrity and impartiality of the courts' officials.

The League supports full US participation in the international judicial system and US ratification and observance of international treaties and conventions consistent with LWVUS principles and positions.

The League supports the basic principles of the UN Charter. The League supports one-nation, one-vote in the General Assembly, the veto power in the Security Council, and a strong, effective office of the Secretary-General. The League supports measures to make the Security Council a more representative body that better reflects the diverse interests of UN member nations and the world's people. The United States should work to encourage member nations to consider the needs of the world and avoid divisive politicization of issues.

Member nations have the collective responsibility to provide the resources necessary for the UN to carry out its mandates, with each providing financial contributions commensurate with its ability to pay. The United States should meet its financial obligations to the UN on time, in full, and without conditions.

League History

At the first League Convention in 1920, delegates called for "adhesion of the United States to the League of Nations with least possible delay," in recognition of the need for a mechanism to facilitate settlement of international disputes. When the issue of US participation in the League of Nations turned into a bitter partisan battle, active League support did not materialize until 1932.

During World War II, the League, conscious of its earlier hesitancy, began to study "US participation in the making and execution of plans for worldwide reconstruction and for a postwar organization for peace to eventually include all peoples, regardless of race, religion, or political persuasion." In 1944, the League supported "US membership in an international organization for the peaceful settlement of disputes, with the machinery to handle economic, social, and political problems."

Even before the United Nations was formally established, the League launched an unprecedented nationwide campaign to help build public understanding of the Dumbarton Oaks and Bretton Woods agreements to establish the United Nations, the World Bank, and the International Monetary Fund. The League trained more than 5,000 speakers and distributed more than a million brochures during a six-month period. At the UN Charter Conference in 1945, the League was one of 42 NGOs invited by President Truman to serve as consultants to the US delegation. Since then, the League has maintained a presence at the United Nations through its UN Observers; working with UN agencies, member states, and other NGOs to advance LWVUS positions; and by periodically hosting League Day at the UN for League members.

The League's UN position evolved through continued study. By 1948, the League called for strengthening the United Nations and its specialized agencies through increased use, adequate financial contributions, and improved procedures. It also supported the UN's peacekeeping functions. In 1962, the League evaluated "means of strengthening the UN under present conditions," most notably heightened antagonism between the United States and the Soviet Union.

In 1976, the League reexamined the UN system "with emphasis on relations between developed and developing countries and their implications for US policy." Members studied how world issues had changed alignments at the United Nations from a primarily East-West to an increasingly rich-nation/poor-nation focus and its effect on US participation in the UN system. The result was a resounding reaffirmation of support for a strengthened UN system and agreement that the United States should work constructively within the UN to further our foreign policy goals.

The League consistently monitors US actions at the UN, engaging in programs at the US Mission and providing support for mutually held policies. The League continues to urge adequate funding for the UN, by regular assessments and voluntary contributions, full payment of US financial obligations to the UN, and full US participation in the UN system.

In addition to supporting increased use and strength of the UN peacekeeping machinery under the UN position in support of "continuing efforts to reduce the risk of war," the League has lobbied for Senate ratification of certain disarmament measures, notably the UN-negotiated nuclear nonproliferation treaty. Leagues' efforts in their communities to develop public understanding and awareness of UN accomplishments, limitations, and potential took on special significance in 1995 when the League celebrated its 75th anniversary and the United Nations its 50th.

In 1995, the League participated in the UN 4th World Conference on Women and the NGO Forum on Women in Beijing, sponsoring workshops on Organizing Candidate Debates and Making Democracy Work®: Strategies for Grassroots Organization, Education, and Advocacy. This was followed in 1999 with a League co-sponsored regional conference of the President's Interagency Council on Women, Women 2000: Beijing Plus Five, to prepare for the Special Session of the General Assembly, Women 2000, Gender Equality, Development, and Peace for the Twenty-First Century, which LWVUS UN Observers were accredited to attend in 2000.

In 1997, the League was granted Special Consultative Status with the United Nations Economic and Social Council, which provides the opportunity to intervene on issues the League supports. We joined other NGOs in submitting an official statement on behalf of the girl child that was presented at the UN Commission on the Status of Women meeting in March 2000. As a result of interventions, the League has successfully launched and supported the Working Group on Girls (WGG), a coalition of 80+ NGOs dedicated to focusing governments on the plight of girls throughout the world. The International Day of the Girl is also celebrated around the world as a result of League and WGG efforts. Women in Saudi Arabia enjoy the right to vote after the League provided an intervention that linked women's enfranchisement with GDP.

League activity on women- and girl-related issues continued in the 2000s. In 2002, LWVUS submitted testimony to the Senate Foreign Relations Committee in support of Senate ratification of the UN Convention for the Elimination of All Forms of Discrimination Against Women (CEDAW). The League joined other NGOs in official statements to the UN Commission on the Status of Women: advocating protection of girls' rights in a lifecycle approach to gender issues in 2004; emphasizing that financing for girls' equality and the empowerment of girls is a basic and sound strategy for the implementation of all human rights in 2008. The League also joined the United Nation's campaign UNITE to End Violence against Women, 2008 – 2015, whose overall objective is raising public awareness and increasing political will and resources for preventing and responding to all forms of violence against women and girls worldwide. In 2011, as the move to ratify CEDAW continued, LWVUS submitted testimony to the Senate Judiciary Committee on Civil and Constitutional Rights.

Since then, the League, in coordination with WGG, developed a comprehensive strategy to prevent sexual human trafficking at major events. This strategy was adopted by the Special Representative to the UN Secretary General to Prevent Violence Against Children in her work with member states on preventing violence. It was also adopted by Brazil and implemented at its 2014 World Cup and Mardi Gras, as well as by the New Jersey Attorney General for the 2014 Super Bowl. The United States included components of the strategy in its 2014 Trafficking in Persons Report.

In 2002, the League urged President George W. Bush to work with the UN to develop clear policy goals and actions regarding the US's possible intervention in Iraq. On initiation of combat operations, the League's Board issued a statement saying that continued diplomatic efforts through the UN would have better served international unity and military force should have been used only as a tool of last resort.

Leagues nationwide work to realize the United Nations' Millennium Goals outlined by UN Secretary General Kofi Annan at the September 2000 Millennium Summit and adopted by 191 states. In 2005, the League urged the administration to support the goals of the UN's 2005 World Summit Outcome Document, an historic effort to end global poverty, promote peace, and strengthen the UN, and urged Congress to reject the *United Nations Reform Act.*

In June 2014, the League formally adopted a position opposing human trafficking. As a result of that position, the LWVUS UN Observers are focusing efforts in the areas of demand and labor trafficking.

In 2015, League members had the opportunity to directly voice their opinions and witness UN conferences through the use of technology. By voting on the Goals We Want, LWV members had an opportunity to encourage the adoption of post-2015 goals seeking to eliminate severe world poverty, encourage mandatory education for girls and boys at the primary and secondary levels, and improve women's economic and political empowerment.

In recent years, the LWVUS UN Observer team's work has centered on aligning the domestic and international policy portfolios around the Campaign for Making Democracy Work and the United Nations Sustainable Development Goals (SDG). In particular, the Observer team has focused on SDG3 (Health & Well-Being), SDG5

(Gender Equality), SDG13 (Climate Action) and SDG16 (Peace, Justice, and Strong Institutions) by working to personify the lessons learned at the UN (thinking globally) with League vision (acting locally).

During the summer of 2019, the UN Observer Corps worked to align its objectives and goals with the LWVUS national program agenda. The UN Observer Corps Objectives included two pillars under the campaign for Making Democracy Work®: Improving Elections and Voting Rights, and its work also focused on several policy positions including Climate Change, Health Care, and Violence Prevention.

In fall 2019, the UN Observers partnered with the Inter-Parliamentary Union to host an event on violence against women at the nation's capital. Several Members of Parliament attended, including representatives from Mexico, Kenya, and Iceland. The event was sponsored by Representatives Debbie Lesko, Jackie Speier, and Dan Kildee, and was moderated by Reuters. Both Board President Chris Carson and LWVUS Chief Executive Officer Virginia Kase Solomón attended the program. The program centered on the increasing instances of violence aimed at female politicians and their overall impact on female leaders around the world. Several members of Congress also attended: Representatives Debbie Lesko, Barbara Lee, and Bonnie Watson Coleman. Each representative spoke on the importance of continuing to elevate this issue and the importance of female political leaders.

In the 2020 – 2022 biennium, the global COVID-19 pandemic put many activities on pause internationally and the work moved to more virtual spaces. In 2021, LWVUS introduced a rigorous new recruitment and application process that resulted in a new LWVUS UN Chief Observer, Connie Sobón Sensor, installed four new members to the UN Observer team with two continuing members, and were assigned two board liaisons. Each member serves a three-year renewable term. The team also sent 12 individuals to the COP26 conference in Glasgow. The LWVUS Observer team hosted a side event. For the first time, due to a generous donor, two participants received scholarships to attend.

The newly installed LWVUS UN Observer team spent its first year (2021) participating in a variety of committees and activities dealing with global issues of climate change, human trafficking, and women's economic and political empowerment. For Women's Equality Day, the UN Observers took time to honor all women and girls working towards liberty and equality despite the Afghanistan conflict. The UN Chief was elected to the Global NGO Executive Committee, which works to build a closer relationship between UN and NGOs. The LWVUS UN Observer group also signed on to several collective statements, including the No Climate Justice without Debt Justice Campaign; International Alliance of Women focused on UN CW66, which was a statement focused on elevating the need for policies and programs to protect the rights and well-being of women around the world; and the Women Gender Constituencies Key Demands for COP16. The group also moderated a side event at COP26 on Disabilities and Climate where the ambassador of Finland, Human Rights Watch, McGill University, and Global Action on Disability Network provided remarks. LWVUS also openly supported the US rejoining the Paris Agreement. In spring of 2022, the LWVUS UN Observer team organized and sponsored an event during the 66th session of the UN Commission on the Status of Women (CSW66) entitled Climate Change Threats to Democratic Elections: Preparing for the Worst featuring a panel of experts. In prior years the team hosted We Have Your Back — Ending the cycle of online violence against women and girl leaders with Inter-Parliamentary Union, UN Women, Trinidad & Tobago, Canada, Albania, and other NGOs. To close out the biennium, Chief LWVUS UN Observer Sensor, in her role as co-chair of the Global NGO Executive Committee Programs and Briefings Committee, organized and moderated a communication workshop in collaboration with the UN Department of Global Communications Civil Society Unit, which was open to the global NGO community.

TRADE

The League's Positions

Statement of Position on Liberal Trade Policies announced by the national board, June 1973 and updated, April 2002:

The League of Women Voters of the United States supports a liberal US trade policy aimed at reducing trade barriers and expanding international trade. Such a policy helps foster international cooperation, democratic values, and economic prosperity at home and abroad as well as benefiting consumers through lowered prices, expanded choice, and improved products and services. The League believes that US trade policy should be based on the long-term public interest, not on special interests, and should advance the achievement of other important policy goals, including:

- **Improvement of basic living standards worldwide; reduction of inequalities within and among nations.**
- **Protection of the environment and global natural resources.**
- **Respect for human, labor, religious, and political rights.**
- **Improvement of labor conditions around the world.**

The League endorses the worldwide systematic reduction of tariffs, subsidies, and quotas. The League also supports the reduction of non-tariff barriers to trade consistent with the goals and strategies set forth in this position statement. Administrative and customs procedures should be efficient and flexible.

The League supports US participation in an international trade organization aimed at promoting worldwide economic growth via an open trading system. This organization should have the power to hold nations accountable for commitments made in multilateral trade treaties and should recognize the legitimacy of international agreements in the areas of the environment, labor, and human rights. Its proceedings should be open to scrutiny by the public, the press, and non-governmental organizations. The public should have timely access to a wide range of its documents, and its dispute settlement process should allow friend-of-the-court briefs.

The organization should recognize the legitimacy of a country's measures in the areas of the environment, health, labor, and human rights that are more stringent than international standards or than those of its trading partners. These measures should not discriminate between domestic products and imports and should not be used as a pretext for restricting the flow of trade. The League believes that trade agreements should be negotiated multilaterally in the broadest possible international forum. Regional and bilateral trade agreements can be useful steppingstones to broader trade liberalization but should not be allowed to block progress in multilateral negotiations nor to marginalize poor countries.

The League believes that the US trade policy-making process should be open, transparent, and efficient and should advance League trade policy goals. The President should be given the authority to negotiate trade agreements within prior guidelines and conditions set by Congress. Congress should have an adequate but limited time period to debate and accept or reject the resulting proposed agreements, without amendment.

Congress should take an active part in the policy-making process, establishing trade priorities and negotiating objectives and observing and monitoring trade negotiations. Congress should have the resources and staff expertise necessary to fulfill its trade responsibilities. The trade policy-making processes of both Congress and the executive branch should include meaningful opportunities for input from a broad range of public interest perspectives, as well as from business interests, and should include timely assessment of the impact of proposed trade agreements.

The League supports a variety of trade-related strategies to protect the environment and promote labor, political, religious, and human rights, including:

- Trade negotiations and trade agreements that lead to progress on environmental and social objectives.
- Monitoring and reporting of countries' practices and performance in these areas.
- Recognition of the legitimacy of multilateral environmental agreements.
- Strengthening the International Labor Organization and promoting ratification of ILO core labor rights.
- Promoting ratification of the Universal Declaration of Human Rights and similar international agreements.
- International sanctions aimed at ending egregious violations of human rights.
- Legitimate labeling and certification programs (e.g., eco-labeling).
- Protection of endangered species.
- Elimination of environmentally and economically harmful subsidies and incentives (e.g., for fishing, timber, agriculture).
- Codes of conduct to encourage responsible business practices in these areas (e.g., guarding against abusive child labor).
- Domestic regulations and practices that advance environmental and social goals and that are not a pretext for restricting trade.
- Aid to developing countries to improve their ability to create and enforce national laws protecting the environment and human and labor rights.

The League supports trade and related policies that address the special needs of developing countries, with emphasis on economic growth and improving income distribution. The League supports such measures as:

- Priority elimination of tariffs and quotas on exports of developing countries.
- Longer adjustment periods and financial and technical assistance for implementation of trade commitments.
- Special measures to ensure access to essential medicines.
- Financial and technical assistance to enable developing countries to participate effectively in the world trading system.
- Financial aid for infrastructure improvements.
- Policies that recognize the special circumstances of developing countries in the areas of food security and transition to the world trading system.

The League supports strong US leadership in, and financial support of, international institutions and programs that reduce poverty and address the special needs of developing countries in the areas of the environment and human and labor rights.

The League supports measures to address the adverse impact of international trade on domestic workers, firms, and industries. Training, education, and safety net programs — such as cash assistance, relocation assistance, and health care — should be enhanced and made easily available to dislocated workers, whether or not a trade connection can be made. Portability of health care coverage, pension rights, and other fringe benefits should also be assured. The League supports temporary trade barriers consistent with international trade rules to permit firms seriously injured by surging import competition to adjust to changed conditions.

League History

The League's longstanding interest in world trade has its origins in a 1920 study of high postwar prices. This study and another on the economic causes of war convinced the League that high tariffs and restrictive trade practices add to consumer prices, reduce competition in the marketplace, and cause friction among nations. The Depression accentuated the impact of high tariffs and moved the League to act for the first time on trade matters. The League was involved with every major piece of trade legislation until 2010, always strongly supporting measures that expand rather than restrict trade.

After an extensive reappraisal in the early 1960s, the League urged that the United States systematically reduce trade barriers; delegate long-term, flexible negotiating authority to the executive; and use trade adjustment assistance as a positive alternative to import restrictions. In 1965, the League added another dimension — support for measures to relax restrictions on trade with Eastern Europe and the Soviet Union. The 1972 Convention, during a time of dollar devaluation and balance-of-trade deficits, asked Leagues to reexamine trade policies to find new ways to help the economy adjust to changing trade patterns, especially measures to counter rising protectionist sentiment. The revised 1973 position in support of liberal trade policies placed a new emphasis on expanding and improving adjustment assistance programs.

The League vigorously supported the *Trade Act of 1974*, which led to US participation in the Tokyo Round of tariff negotiations under the auspices of the *General Agreement on Tariffs and Trade* (GATT). In 1979, the League mounted a major lobbying effort to assure implementation of the Tokyo Round of multilateral trade negotiations agreements designed to establish a fair, open, and disciplined trading structure for the next decade. Throughout the five years of negotiations, the League worked to deflect protectionist efforts in Congress to block the negotiations. Through its efforts, the League helped assure overwhelming passage of the *Trade Agreements Act of 1979*, the largest single trade bill in US history. Attempts to undermine the trade agreements have been vigorously opposed by the League.

The League also has been instrumental in promoting measures to improve trade opportunities for developing countries and in defeating protectionist amendments to foreign assistance appropriation bills. The League strongly supported the *Trade and International Economic Policy Reform Act of 1987* and worked to defeat restrictive amendments.

In 2002, the League voiced its opposition to providing President George W. Bush with new negotiating authority for trade agreements because the proposed authority did not adequately provide for protecting environmental, labor, and political values as part of trade agreements.

In response to the COVID-19 pandemic the League sent a letter to the Biden administration asking him to allow low- and middle-income countries access to COVID-19 vaccines by waiving intellectual property rights provided for in World Trade Organization rules. This action is based in LWVUS past work on trade policy. The League also joined housing justice coalitions in urging the Consumer Financial Protection Bureau and the Federal Trade Commission to use their authority to enforce the eviction moratorium and protect renters and homeowners. This housing justice coalition letter urged the Consumer Financial Protection Bureau and the Federal Trade Commission to use their authority to enforce the eviction moratorium and protect renters and homeowners. This ask came in addition to advocacy in Congress and with President Biden for a more robust and expansive eviction moratorium. in addition to advocacy in Congress and with President Biden for a more robust and expansive eviction moratorium.

US RELATIONS WITH DEVELOPING COUNTRIES

The League's Positions

Statement of Position on US Relations with Developing Countries, as announced by the national board, April 1986:

The League of Women Voters of the United States believes that US interests in developing countries should reflect the reality of global interdependence. Paramount among these interests are reducing the risk of military conflict, promoting the sound management of global resources, protecting human rights, stimulating economic growth, and improving the quality of life in developing countries. US policies toward developing countries should not be based on maintaining US preeminence.

LWVUS strongly believes that development assistance, which is designed to meet the long-term social and economic needs of developing countries, is the most effective means of promoting legitimate US interests. Military assistance and the direct military involvement of US forces are not appropriate means to further the League's stated paramount interests in developing countries.

Developing countries should not be the pawns or the playing fields for geopolitical competition. The relationship between the superpowers should not be an important factor in determining US policies toward developing countries. LWVUS supports efforts to reduce international competition in developing countries, including:

- **Enhancing the role of the United Nations and other multilateral organizations.**
- **Supporting regional approaches to conflict resolution.**
- **Encouraging cooperative efforts to promote the sound management of global resources and improve the quality of life.**
- **Promoting measures to reduce tensions and increase communication, including scientific and cultural exchanges and other cooperative programs.**

Statement of Position on International Development Assistance, as announced by the national board, April 1970, and revised, April 1986:

The League of Women Voters of the United States believes that long-term requirements for world peace, humanitarian obligations, and long-range national interests demand US policies that help developing countries reach self-sustaining economic growth.

League members understand that the development process encompasses more than economic growth and urge that the focus be on the human concerns of development and on an improved quality of life for the people of developing countries. US development assistance policies should enhance human dignity and fulfill basic human

needs. The policies should be coordinated with other development efforts, and they should respect cultural differences. The League favors greater participation by the recipient nations in the planning and execution of development programs. The development effort should be one of a partnership between developed and developing countries. Development programs should be long-range, adequately financed, and effectively coordinated and administered.

League members recognize that population pressures affect all other aspects of the development process. The League supports US efforts to assist other nations in their population planning programs, in accordance with the culture and mores of each country. The League also emphasizes strongly the importance of programs for nutrition, health, employment, and education.

The League advocates that the proportion of US assistance given through multilateral channels should be substantially increased, with concurrent efforts being made to strengthen the multilateral agencies where necessary.

The League deems it essential that the trend of reduced aid be reversed and that US contributions for development assistance be increased.

League members believe that aid alone is not enough to meet the needs of developing countries. Measures other than direct grants and loans must be utilized. The League advocates such measures as reduced tied aid, prevention and relief of debt burdens, and changed patterns of trade. The US government must ensure that its trade, monetary, political, and military policies do not subvert the goals of its development policies. The League also urges active participation in the development process by the private sector.

The League recognizes the gross disparity in trading positions between developed and developing countries. The exports of developing countries must be expanded if they are to broaden their economic base and improve their people's standard of living. Because of their need for greater access to US and other industrialized countries' markets, the League favors generalized, temporary preferential tariff treatment and certain commodity arrangements for developing countries. The principle of reciprocity in trade agreements, which the League supports, should be waived in order to make special trade concessions to developing countries.

Statement of Position on Private Investment and Commodity Arrangements, as announced by the national board, April 1964 and revised, April 1970:

The League of Women Voters of the United States believes that private investment of US capital in developing countries can be an important supplemental means of helping these countries reach self-sustaining economic growth. In order to facilitate the flow of private capital to those developing countries that most need it and that can use it most advantageously, appropriate safeguards are necessary against risks for both the investor and the developing countries. In order to protect outside investors against risks, the League favors continuation of governmental assistance, such as pre-investment surveys, investment guarantees, and investment loans.

The League believes that tax credits on funds invested in developing countries could provide additional encouragement. In order to guard against risks for the developing country, the League believes that investors should be encouraged to engage in joint-venture-type investments with local businesses, to seek matching investment funds within the country, to employ and train as high a proportion of local personnel as possible for responsible positions, and to send to these countries carefully chosen, well-briefed US representatives. The League welcomes continued efforts by developing countries to encourage their citizens to invest more in their own countries' development efforts and to create a more favorable climate for public and private investment through appropriate internal reforms.

International commodity arrangements serve as a short-term supplement to long-run efforts to promote self-sustaining growth in developing countries.

Insofar as commodity arrangements can help moderate sharp fluctuations in the price of primary products and help stabilize the export income of developing countries, they can serve a useful, though necessarily short-term, purpose.

Each commodity arrangement should be evaluated on its own merit. Such arrangements should be flexible and open to renegotiation within a reasonable period of time.

Each arrangement needs careful supervision and regular review in order not to inhibit diversification within these countries of land, labor, and capital or to distort international patterns of trade. These arrangements might include such compensatory financing efforts as those initiated under the International Monetary Fund.

If any commodity arrangement is to bear fruit, primary-product countries should be encouraged through technical and financial assistance to diversify both their primary-product and industrial position. If diversification efforts are not to be frustrated, the developed countries, including the United States, need to open their export doors wider, to a broader range of imports — whether raw materials, semiprocessed, or finished goods. In order to help the United States meet new competition, greater use might be made of trade adjustment assistance to affected US industries and workers.

The League recognizes that continuation of freer trade policies and reduction of various trade barriers are essential to improve the terms of trade of developing countries.

League History

The League's work on development issues began in the 1920s, when members studied the economic and social work of various international organizations. In 1940, the League studied proposals for closer economic and cultural relations between the United States and other American republics, including possible financial and technical cooperation. After World War II, the League supported the implementation of the Marshall Plan and President Truman's Point Four Program as part of its commitment to international efforts to support the poor and emerging nations of Asia, Africa, the Middle East, and Latin America.

The League's position on Development Assistance evolved through two restudies in 1964 and 1970. The latter reiterated the need for separating development from military aid. The League supported the "basic needs" approach mandated by Congress in 1973 and adopted by the Agency for International Development (AID).

In the 1980s, the League's Development Assistance position was revised to reflect the results of the study of US Relations with Developing Countries. Members reviewed current trends in trade, development assistance, and the United Nations. They also examined US commitments to developing countries, criteria for evaluating development and military assistance, and the role of US-Soviet relations in determining US policies toward developing countries.

The resulting 1986 position emphasizes development assistance over military assistance as the most effective means of meeting the long-term social and economic needs of developing countries and downplays the role of international competition in determining US policies toward developing countries. In 1986, the League urged Congress to reject aid that included military assistance to Nicaraguan counter-revolutionaries ("contras") and address the region's long-term social and economic needs. In 1987, the League pressured Congress to increase development and humanitarian aid in the foreign aid budget.

In the 1990s, LWVEF began a series of global outreach projects that led to the current Global Democracy Program. Thinking Globally was designed to educate Americans about the links between their communities and the developing world.

Outreach in Europe in the 1990s led to the Global Community Dialogue program in 1992 with the Building Political Participation in Poland initiative and subsequent citizen exchange projects to share grassroots skills with people in Hungary, Russia, Ukraine, the American Republics, and Africa.

In 1996, LWVEF opened a US coordination office for absentee voting in the post-war elections in Bosnia and Herzegovina. In an unprecedented effort to enfranchise Bosnian refugees and displaced persons residing in 55 countries for elections in 1996, 1997, and 1998, the League worked with the Organization for Security and Cooperation in Europe on the Bosnian Citizen Get-Out-the-Vote Campaign. LWVEF formed a partnership with the League of Women Voters' in Bosnia and Herzegovina to help women take an effective role in the post-war reconstruction process.

Beginning in 2005, the League participated in The Open World Leadership Center's Civic Hosting Program, first introducing Russian leaders to US democracy and subsequently hosting visitors from Ukraine and Central Asia.

Outreach in Africa started in the late 1990s when LWVEF joined Civitas Africa to share methodologies, tools, and experiences with civic education groups. A citizen exchange program in Sub-Saharan Africa with grassroots organizations and activists, Woman Power in Politics: Building Grassroots Democracy in Africa, was initiated with League members traveling to Africa as co-trainers in democracy-building skills until 2002. The League also worked with four nongovernmental organizations in Malawi to train thousands of poll monitors as civil society observers on Election Day 2004. It joined with the National Council of Women of Kenya to sponsor Kenyans Working Together for Good Governance: Civil Society, Government, and Members of Parliament in 2006, including an exchange program between Kenyan citizens and League staff.

In early 2012, citing the League's outstanding record of nonpartisanship in advocating and promoting informed political participation in government, the US government selected the League to serve as its nongovernmental partner in the 2012 G8 Broader Middle East and North Africa Initiative (BMENA).

The year-long initiative had as its ultimate goal to achieve agreement among the G8 and regions' foreign ministers on the language of the final declaration of the 9th Forum for the Future, the culminating meeting of the initiative. The second goal was to achieve civil society and private sector agreement on the recommendations forwarded to the governments. Both goals were achieved due to a steady building of trust among the participants as a result of the hard work of the League, the US government, the Republic of Tunisia, and the three NGO participants.

Outreach in the Americas began with Making Democracy Work in the Americas, at the Vital Voices of the Americas conference in 1998, followed by the League hosting women civic leaders and officials from Latin America in 1999.

In the 2000s, the League completed a successful program in Brazil called Women in Political Leadership, was invited by the International Foundation for Election Systems (IFES) to join a team of international election observers for Paraguayan elections, sponsored Women in the Americas: Paths to Political Power, and participated in the State Department-sponsored exchange Connecting Civil Society and Future Legislators from Colombia and Brazil.

Between 2010 – 2012, the League attended an international conference in La Havana, Cuba, organized by the Gender Department of the University of La Havana, titled Women in the XXI Century. The League also accepted invitations to work with women in democratic transitions in Tunisia and Egypt in North Africa; in Antananarivo, Madagascar, in Africa; in Dhaka, Bangladesh, in South Asia; and in Belgrade, Serbia, in Southeast Europe.

In 2019, the United Nations continued its work to raise the visibility of the UN's Sustainable Development Goals 16 (SDG) around peace, justice, and strong institutions by organizing a discussion during the UN's Commission on the Status of Women (CSW63) alongside several partners, including Inter-Parliamentary Union, UN Women, Trinidad & Tobago, Canada, Albania, and other NGOs to discuss Critical Mass to Gender Parity—Women in Decision-Making DO Make a Difference. The UN Observers focus their work around three of the SDGs: Gender Equality, Climate Action, and Think Globally, Act Locally.

ARMS CONTROL

The League's Position

Statement of Position on Arms Control, as announced by the national board, December 1983 and updated by the 2010 Convention:

The League of Women Voters of the United States believes that arms-control measures are essential to reduce the risk of war and increase global stability.

Toward that end, the US government should give the highest level of importance to arms control efforts that:

- **Limit or reduce the quantity of weapons.**
- **Limit proliferation and prohibit first use of nuclear weapons.**
- **Prohibit first use and possession of chemical, biological, and radiological weapons.**
- **Prohibit explosive testing of nuclear weapons.**
- **Reduce tensions in order to prevent situations in which weapons might be used.**

While these objectives should receive the highest level of attention, the US government should also negotiate measures that inhibit the development and improvement of weapons, particularly nuclear weapons that increase incentives to attack first in a period of crisis.

As a goal of international negotiations, the League supports the worldwide elimination of nuclear weapons.

The League of Women Voters recognizes that peace in an interdependent world is a product of cooperation among nations and therefore strongly favors multilateral negotiations. Leadership by the United States in advancing arms control measures through negotiations and periodic review is encouraged.

Given the potential for worldwide proliferation of nuclear technology, efforts involving all countries are essential to limit the spread of nuclear weapons and to protect commonly held nuclear weapons-free regions such as the seabed and outer space. Multilateral efforts are appropriate as well to achieve bans on the possession of chemical, biological, and radiological weapons; and to achieve limitations on the transfer or trade of all weapons.

The League of Women Voters also supports bilateral arms control efforts which may be especially appropriate in negotiations to limit, safeguard, and reduce quantities of weapons. The League believes that unilateral initiatives are not the most appropriate means to achieve arms control.

The League does not support tying progress in arms control to other issues. The League believes that arms control is too important in and of itself and too crucial to all nations to be linked to other foreign and military policy goals.

The League of Women Voters believes that arms control measures should be evaluated in terms of the following factors:

Equity

The terms should be mutually beneficial, and each nation's security and interests should be adequately protected, as should the security of all nations. Equity does not necessarily require equality in numbers of weapons but may be achieved through a relative balance in capabilities.

Verifiability

Each party should be able to ensure that other parties comply with the terms of the agreement, whether using national technical means (such as satellites, seismic sensors, and electronic monitors) or on-site inspection. The League recognizes the role that multilateral and international institutions can play in assisting verification efforts and believes it is extremely important to ensure compliance, acknowledging that absolute certainty is unattainable.

Equity and verifiability are critical in efforts to limit and reduce quantities of weapons and to prohibit the possession and spread of nuclear weapons.

Confidence-Building

Each party should be assured of the political or military intentions of other parties. Fostering confidence is vital in efforts to stem the development and proliferation of weapons and prohibit their first use, and to reduce tensions.

Widespread Agreement

All appropriate parties should participate in and approve the results of the negotiating process. However, the League recognizes that, in specific cases, progress can be achieved even though some key parties do not participate.

Environmental Protection

The quality of the earth's environment should be protected from the effects of weapons testing or use. Environmental protection has special significance in negotiations regarding all weapons of mass destruction as well as conventional weapons that have residual effects.

Continuity

Negotiations should build on past agreements and should be directed toward future negotiations whenever feasible. Innovative thinking and new approaches should, however, be encouraged when appropriate.

Further Guidelines

League support of arms control measures includes actions on proposals, negotiations, and agreements.

The League supports efforts to achieve quantitative limits or reductions that focus on nuclear warheads, non-nuclear weapons of mass destruction, missiles and other delivery systems, antiballistic missiles, conventional weapons, or troop levels.

The League advocates limits on the spread or proliferation of weapons, nuclear technology, and fissile materials. The League opposes the proliferation of weapons, nuclear technology, and fissile materials to non-state actors or to commonly held areas such as the seabed or outer space. The League supports establishing effective international monitoring, accounting, and control of such transfers.

The League's pursuit of bans on the possession or use of weapons may apply to existing weapons or those not yet developed.

The League seeks to reduce tensions through better means of communication, exchange of information, or prior notification of military tests and maneuvers in order to avoid the risks of miscalculation or accident. Other League-supported measures to reduce tensions and create a climate of trust among nations include scientific and cultural exchanges, conflict resolution training, and strengthening the United Nations and its supporting agencies. Efforts are encouraged to mediate regional issues and arrive at negotiated settlements to minimize arms build-ups and avoid conflicts. The United States should keep lines of communication open.

The League supports efforts to inhibit the development and improvement of weapons through qualitative limits, including limits on testing of weapons. These constraints may be selective or comprehensive in their application.

Efforts to improve the arms control regime of international laws, oversight bodies, and verification modalities are also supported, and US engagement and leadership in this regard is encouraged. The League supports diligence by the United States in meeting the terms of ratified arms control agreements and in reviewing their effectiveness over time.

League History

The League's 1982 – 1984 national security study was intended to add focus and direction to existing support for "efforts to reduce the risk of war, including negotiations on disarmament and arms control" under the UN position. Once the 1983 position was reached, League action in support of arms control measures was immediate and effective, particularly on the issues of the Strategic Defense Initiative (SDI) — a missile defense plan that undermines the 1972 Anti-Ballistic Missile (ABM) Treaty — and anti-satellite weapons. The League has continued to play a key role in legislative efforts to limit funding for unworkable and destabilizing missile defense systems and to uphold the traditional interpretation of the ABM Treaty.

Other arms control measures supported by the League included negotiation of a bilateral, mutually verifiable freeze on the testing, production, and deployment of nuclear weapons to be followed by reductions; a comprehensive test ban treaty; and the Chemical Weapons Convention.

In 1988, the League was successful in lobbying for Senate ratification of the Intermediate Nuclear Forces Treaty (INF), an unprecedented agreement between the United States and the Soviet Union to eliminate an entire class of nuclear weapons. In October 1991, the League urged the Senate to ratify the Conventional Forces in Europe Treaty.

The League lobbied for ratification of the Comprehensive Test Ban Treaty (CTBT) from 1997 until October 1999, when Senate arms control opponents brought the treaty up without full hearings and the Senate rejected the resolution of ratification.

In 2000, the League again worked in support of the ABM Treaty and in opposition to deployment of a planned national missile defense (NMD) system.

After extensive review by a Board-appointed task force, the League's position was updated at Convention 2010 by concurrence of League delegates. In 2010, LWVUS successfully lobbied for the new START Treaty between the United States and Russia. In 2011, the Treaty, which includes new verification requirements for deployed strategic warheads as well as delivery vehicles, was ratified and signed by President Obama.

MILITARY POLICY AND DEFENSE SPENDING

The League's Position

Statement of Position on Military Policy and Defense Spending, as Announced by national board, April 1984 and Revised, April 1986:

The League of Women Voters of the United States believes that the US government should seek to protect its interests at home and abroad through the use of nonmilitary measures, including diplomacy, mediation, and multilateral cooperation. These measures reflect the importance that the League attaches to US efforts to strengthen international organizations, reduce tensions among nations, and minimize the risk of conflict worldwide.

The League believes that military force should be viewed as a tool of last resort. Unquestionably, defense of the homeland is an appropriate military objective. In this context, conventional weapons are clearly preferable to nuclear weapons. Any decision to defend another nation militarily should be in support of clear foreign policy goals and tailored to specific circumstances. Military assistance and the direct military involvement of US forces are not appropriate means to further the League's stated paramount interests in developing countries.

The League believes that nuclear weapons should serve only a limited and specific function — that of deterring nuclear attack on the United States — until such time as these weapons are eliminated through arms control and disarmament agreements. The goal of US military policy, however, should be to ensure that nuclear weapons are never used.

Nuclear Deterrence

The League believes that the United States should vigorously pursue arms control negotiations in order to ensure that all nations reduce and eventually eliminate their stockpiles of strategic nuclear weapons. The League does not support unilateral elimination of any leg of the strategic nuclear triad of intercontinental ballistic missiles (ICBMs), submarine-launched ballistic missiles (SLBMs), and long-range bombers. However, the League does not support any modernization of the land leg that would result in weapons systems that are vulnerable or increase incentives to attack first.

North Atlantic Treaty Organization

The League believes that the defense of NATO allies should continue to be a shared responsibility. The League supports the United States' commitment to defend NATO allies with conventional forces. The League urges continued efforts to negotiate mutual and balanced reductions in conventional forces in Europe.

The League believes there is no appropriate role for US nuclear weapons in the defense of NATO allies. The League strongly opposes the policy of threatening to introduce nuclear weapons into a conventional conflict in Europe, a policy commonly referred to as "first use." Consistent with these views, the League opposes the deployment of US nuclear weapons on European soil.

Other Commitments

The League supports the US commitment to defend Japan with conventional forces. Conventional forces are also appropriate for defending other allies. The League rejects any nuclear role in defending Japan and other allies, in protecting access to vital resources, or in responding to military conflicts around the world.

Defense Spending

The League believes that defense spending should be examined in the same way as spending for other national needs. Within any given level of defense funding, the United States should move toward emphasizing readiness over investment. Preference should be given to operations and maintenance expenditures and military pay as opposed to research and development, procurement of new weapons, and construction of military facilities. The League believes that savings in the defense budget can be achieved through increased efficiency and improved accountability.

In summary, the League believes that national security has many dimensions and cannot be limited to military policy alone. It can be defined as ensuring domestic tranquility, providing for the common defense, and promoting the general welfare. Key elements include the country's ability to implement social and environmental programs and to maintain cooperative relationships with other nations. Other important components are effective political leadership and a strong economy. Therefore, in decisions about the federal budget, political leaders should assess the impact of US military spending on the nation's economy and on the government's ability to meet social and environmental needs.

League History

The second part of the League's 1982 – 1984 national security study focused on military policy objectives and defense spending, including spending priorities and links between defense and domestic spending in the federal budget. League members first evaluated US military missions, then scrutinized military forces and defense budget priorities. This comprehensive approach stemmed from the principle that weapons systems should reflect a nation's military policy, which in turn should be developed from basic military purposes or missions. The resulting April 1984 statement related military policy and defense spending.

League action focused on congressional efforts to limit deployment of the MX missile and oppose funding for a rail garrison basing system. The League also strongly opposed funding for the Strategic Defense Initiative. Since the mid-1980s the League has called on Congress and the President to focus on defense spending when making budget cuts for deficit reduction.

As a result of the 1984 – 1986 study of US relations with developing countries, the Military Policy and Defense Spending position was revised to emphasize that "Military assistance and the direct military involvement of US forces are not appropriate means to further the League's stated paramount interests in developing countries."

Natural Resources

Promote an environment beneficial to life through the protection and wise management of natural resources in the public interest.

The League's Position

Statement of Position on Natural Resources, as affirmed by the 1986 Convention, based on positions reached from 1958 through 1986:

The League of Women Voters of the United States believes that natural resources should be managed as interrelated parts of life-supporting ecosystems. Resources should be conserved and protected to assure their future availability. Pollution of these resources should be controlled in order to preserve the physical, chemical, and biological integrity of ecosystems and to protect public health.

League History

League members became concerned about depletion and conservation of natural resources as far back as the 1920s and 1930s, when the League studied flood control, erosion, and the creation of the Tennessee Valley Authority (TVA). Water resources were the focus of activities in the 1950s, and with the nascent environmental movement in the 1970s, the League built a broad national program focused on protecting and managing the interrelated aspects of air, water, land use, energy, and waste management. Since then, the League has been in the forefront of the environmental protection movement, helping to frame landmark legislation and seeking to preserve and protect life-supporting ecosystems and public health. Fighting to improve opportunities for public participation on natural resource issues has always been a League theme, in addition to the substantive concerns that the League has pushed.

The League's citizen activists helped pass the landmark *Clean Water Act* in the early 1970s and worked to protect, expand, and strengthen it through the 1990s. Water issues, from groundwater protection to agricultural runoff to the *Safe Drinking Water Act*, have energized League leaders, especially at the local level, for decades. Solid and hazardous waste issues and recycling also have been the focus of strong state and local action, and the federal legislative fights for the *Resource Conservation and Recovery Act* and Superfund focused on those issues as well.

The League has been a leader in fighting efforts to gut the *Clean Air Act* from the early 1980s to the present. It pushed for acid rain and toxic air pollutant controls as the act was reauthorized in 1990, building on the successful work of the previous decade in controlling the worst air pollution from automobiles and industrial sources. In the 2000s, the League not only fought to protect the *Clean Air Act*, but also turned attention to combatting global climate change.

With its work on energy policy beginning in the late 1970s, the League began a decades-long push for energy conservation and the use of renewable resources. As global climate change emerged as a key environmental and international issue in the late 1990s, energy conservation, renewable resources, and air pollution controls took on new significance and the League's interrelated approach to natural resource issues proved farsighted. Understanding the need for global solutions to many environmental problems, LWVUS has urged full US participation in international efforts.

In the late 2000s, the League lobbied vigorously for comprehensive legislation to control global climate change by setting a cap on greenhouse gas pollution and encouraging conservation and renewable energy. As part of an education and advocacy project on climate change, six state Leagues held forums with trips by the League president to speak at public events and meet with key senators and staff. In early 2010, the LWVUS president was honored by Oxfam America with a Sisters on the Planet Climate Leader Award for the League's grassroots work on climate change.

In 2011, the League launched the Clean Air Promise Campaign to raise awareness of the dangers of harmful pollutants like industrial carbon, mercury, and other toxic air pollutants that created a growing threat to the health of our children and seniors. Seven state Leagues engaged in the project and raised awareness in their local communities and at the state and local levels of their governments while generating media attention around the growing problem of climate change caused by industrial carbon pollution. LWVUS released television ads in Massachusetts and Missouri that called out votes taken by Senators Brown and McCaskill that would have blocked new air pollution standards for carbon. By demonstrating the political salience of the climate change issue — and the effects on human health — the ads succeeded in discouraging the Senate from taking up legislation that would undermine efforts to address climate change.

The League continued its strong advocacy on climate issues by supporting President Obama's Climate Action Plan and New Source Pollution Standard. The cornerstone of the plan controls carbon pollution from new and existing power plants, which are the largest source of industrial carbon pollution in the United States. In addition, the League voiced support for putting a price on carbon to compliment the regulatory effort.

In the 2014 – 2016 biennium, the League continued work to fight climate change by supporting regulations from the Environmental Protection Agency, fighting legislation to stop or hurt progress on climate initiatives, and pushing for the full rejection of the Keystone XL pipeline. The League continued support for the EPA's Clean Power Plan and New Source Pollution Standard by participating in field hearings across the country and collecting comments from grassroots supporters in support of the regulations, all while working to fight legislation to overturn and weaken the regulations in Congress. The League strongly supported the People's Climate March in New York City and the UN Paris Agreement, which was a historic international agreement that established a commitment to reduce carbon pollution and fight climate change. The League also endorsed regulations from EPA to reduce the levels of ozone in the atmosphere and regulate methane in the oil and gas sector.

In the 115th Congress (2017 – 2019), the League worked to stand against regulations overturning the Obama administration's pro-environment, anti-pollution standards. The League unsuccessfully opposed the use of the *Congressional Review Act* to repeal regulations. It also opposed the *Regulations from the Executive in Need of Scrutiny Act* (REINS), which was an extreme measure that would effectively make it impossible to protect the public by shutting down the entire regulatory system.

In the 116th Congress (2019 – 2021), the League joined progressive climate groups to support the momentum behind the idea of a "Green New Deal. Through this work, the League urged Congress to consider the instituting principles that harnessed the full power of the *Clean Air Act*, ensured climate justice in communities and with workers across the country, and transitioned the United States into a renewable economy. While the League did not endorse specific legislation, the principles endorsed were consistent with League positions and allowed the League to advocate for a bold agenda addressing climate change, clean air, and other environmental factors necessary to protect our country and our planet.

Resource Management

The League's Position

Resource management decisions must be based on a thorough assessment of population growth and of current and future needs. The inherent characteristics and carrying capacities of each area's natural resources must be considered in the planning process. Policy makers must take into account the ramifications of their decisions on the nation as a whole as well as on other nations.

To assure the future availability of essential resources, government policies must promote stewardship of natural resources. Policies that promote resource conservation are a fundamental part of such stewardship. Resources such as water and soil should be protected. Consumption of nonrenewable resources should be minimized. Beneficiaries should pay the costs for water, land, and energy development projects. Reclamation and reuse of natural resources should be encouraged.

The League believes that protection and management of natural resources are responsibilities shared by all levels of government. The federal government should provide leadership, guidance, and financial assistance to encourage regional planning and decision making to enhance local and state capabilities for resource management.

The League supports comprehensive long-range planning and believes that wise decision-making requires:

- Adequate data and a framework within which alternatives may be weighed and intelligent decisions made.
- Consideration of environmental, public health, social, and economic impacts of proposed plans and actions.
- Protection of private property rights commensurate with overall consideration of public health and environmental protection.
- Coordination of the federal government's responsibilities and activities.
- Resolution of inconsistencies and conflicts in basic policy among governmental agencies at all levels.
- Regional, interregional, and/or international cooperation when appropriate.
- Mechanisms appropriate to each region that will provide coordinated planning and administration among units of government, governmental agencies, and the private sector.
- Procedures for resolving disputes.
- Procedures for mitigation of adverse impacts.
- Special responsibility by each level of government for those lands and resources entrusted to them.
- Special consideration for the protection of areas of critical environmental concern, natural hazards, historical importance, and aesthetic value.
- Special attention to maintaining and improving the environmental quality of urban communities.

League History

The League's 1956 – 1958 water resources study was the basis for action on a broad range of resource management issues. By 1958, the League had taken a position that, as rephrased and expanded in 1960, has formed one of two foundations for League action on water ever since. The key concept is a strong federal role in formulating national policies and procedures.

The issue of water management led the League toward later interrelated positions on air pollution, solid waste disposal, and land use — all focused on management policies to protect natural resources.

In 1970, the League recognized the need for federal control of air pollution and adopted a position for control of air emissions. The 1970 Convention also authorized a study of solid waste disposal, which focused League attention on reuse and recycling.

In 1972, Convention delegates voted to "evaluate land-use policies and procedures and their relationship to human needs, population trends, and ecological and socioeconomic factors." The three-year land-use study focused on achieving optimum balance between human needs and environmental quality. Members agreed in 1975 that land ownership implies responsibilities of stewardship and consideration of public and private rights. They concluded that every level of government should share responsibility for land planning and management and that federal policies should enhance the capabilities of other levels.

Although efforts in 1975 to pass comprehensive land-use legislation failed, the League has successfully supported more-specialized land-use laws — notably, coastal-zone planning and strip-mining controls.

Since 1982, most action on land-use issues has been at the state and local levels. Many Leagues work on such issues as floodplain management, coastal-zone management, wetlands protection, open-space preservation, facility siting, transportation, wilderness designations, and offshore energy development.

In the 1980s, LWVUS lobbied for reauthorization and strengthening of the Coastal Zone Management (CZM) program, which provides federal funds for planning at the state level. The League also supports the Coastal Barrier Resources System, legislation that would eliminate federal flood insurance subsidies to barrier islands and other coastal areas subject to frequent storm action.

In 1990, the League provided testimony on federal reclamation policy in support of legislation to eliminate abuses and close loopholes in the *Reclamation Reform Act of 1982*. Specifically, the League supported action to ensure compliance with the acreage limitations of the act and to reduce water subsidies that are uneconomical and environmentally destructive. In 1992, the League supported broad reform of the National Flood Insurance Program to increase enrollment and encourage risk management practices to reduce future losses.

League work on energy began in the early 1970s; in 1975 LWVUS adopted a position supporting energy conservation as national policy. In 1976, the LWVUS Board approved guidelines to implement the position. Since then, the League has made conservation the crux of its energy agenda, recognizing that the conservation of energy guarantees major long-term benefits — environmental, economic, and strategic — to individuals, the country, and the world.

The 1976 Convention authorized a study to "evaluate sources of energy and the government's role in meeting future needs," which resulted in a broad 1978 position on energy policies and sources (including conservation) that is the basis for action on a wide variety of energy issues at all government levels. The 1979 Council recommended that the LWVUS Board review application of the energy position to nuclear energy; it subsequently determined that the League would work to minimize reliance on nuclear fission.

The League advocates a national energy policy emphasizing increased fuel-efficiency standards for automobiles, opposition to oil drilling in environmentally sensitive areas including the Arctic National Wildlife Refuge (ANWR), and support for government action in the development and use of energy conservation and renewable energy sources.

Worldwide recognition of the global nature of environmental problems and the need for sustainable development came to the forefront with the United Nations Conference on Environment and Development (UNCED) in Rio de Janeiro in 1992. Leagues across the country hosted meetings to funnel citizen input into the UNCED agenda, and LWVUS urged support for the summit's recommendations on global cooperation.

The League opposed efforts in the 104th Congress (1995 – 1997) to pass eminent domain legislation that would seriously undermine environmental protections in the name of private property rights. While an extreme bill passed the House early in 1995, there was no Senate action. The League supported stewardship of critical resources, opposing congressional measures to transfer coastal lands from public to private hands.

In 2005, the League urged Congress to oppose energy legislation that would have wrongfully used the devastation of Hurricane Katrina and other disasters as a pretext for undermining important environmental protections.

Throughout the 2000s, the League continued its opposition to repeated efforts to drill for oil in ANWR. In 2006, the League submitted comments to the *National Environmental Policy Act* (NEPA) task force, urging its members to uphold the integrity of the original landmark legislation.

Early in 2012, the League declared its opposition to the proposed Keystone XL (KXL) pipeline because of the need to put the United States on a path of emissions reductions, protect against climate change, and ensure safe drinking water for all Americans. Later that year, the League commended President Obama's decision to delay the approval of the pipeline until appropriate study and consideration could be taken. The League also worked to encourage the President to veto legislation from Congress in 2015 that would have forced the approval of the KXL pipeline. The League celebrated when the pipeline project was finally fully rejected. In 2021, the LWVUS urged President Biden to immediately shut down the Dakota Access Pipeline (DAPL). Later that year, we joined with other organizations to urge the President to cancel the Gulf of Mexico Outer Continental Shelf Oil and Gas Lease Sale 257.

LWVUS submitted comments in support of full restoration of NEPA to its essential form following modifications made by the Trump administration.

The League continues to lobby against legislation that would undermine clean air standards, make global climate change worse, and fail to provide for needed energy conservation measures.

Environmental Protection and Pollution Control

The League's Position

The League supports the preservation of the physical, chemical, and biological integrity of the ecosystem and maximum protection of public health and the environment. The League's approach to environmental protection and pollution control is one of problem solving. The interrelationships of air, water, and land resources should be recognized in designing environmental safeguards. The League's environmental protection and anti-pollution goals aim to prevent ecological degradation and to reduce and control pollutants before they go down the sewer, up the chimney, or into the landfill.

The League believes that although environmental protection and pollution control are responsibilities shared by all levels of government, it is essential that the federal government provide leadership and technical and financial assistance.

The federal government should have the major role in setting standards for environmental protection and pollution control. Other levels of government should have the right to set more stringent standards. Enforcement should be carried out at the lower levels of government, but the federal government should enforce standards if other levels of government do not meet this responsibility. Standards must be enforced in a timely, consistent, and equitable manner for all violators in all parts of society, including governmental units, industry, business, and individuals.

Environmental protection and pollution control, including waste management, should be considered a cost of providing a product or service. Consumers, taxpayers and ratepayers must expect to pay some of the costs. The League supports policies that accelerate pollution control, including federal financial assistance for state and local programs.

The League supports:

- Regulation of pollution sources by control and penalties.
- Inspection and monitoring.
- Full disclosure of pollution data.
- Incentives to accelerate pollution control.
- Vigorous enforcement mechanisms, including sanctions for states and localities that do not comply with federal standards and substantial fines for noncompliance.

Further Guidelines and Criteria

Air Quality

The League supports:

- Measures to reduce vehicular pollution, including inspection and maintenance of emission controls, changes in engine design and fuel types and development of more energy-efficient transportation systems.

- Regulation and reduction of pollution from stationary sources.
- Regulation and reduction of ambient toxic air pollutants.
- Measures to reduce transboundary air pollutants, such as ozone and those that cause acid deposition.

Energy

The League supports:

- Energy goals and policies that acknowledge the United States as a responsible member of the world community.
- Reduction of energy growth rates.
- Use of a variety of energy sources, with emphasis on conserving energy and using energy-efficient technologies.
- The environmentally sound use of energy resources, with consideration of the entire cycle of energy production.
- Predominant reliance on renewable resources.
- Policies that limit reliance on nuclear fission.
- Action by appropriate levels of government to encourage the use of renewable resources and energy conservation through funding for research and development, financial incentives, rate-setting policies, and mandatory standards.
- Mandatory energy-conservation measures, including thermal standards for building efficiency, new appliance standards, and standards for new automobiles with no relaxation of auto-emission control requirements.
- Policies to reduce energy demand and minimize the need for new generating capacity through techniques such as marginal cost or peak-load pricing or demand-management programs.
- Maintaining deregulation of oil and natural gas prices.
- Assistance for low-income individuals when energy policies bear unduly on the poor.

Land Use

The League supports:

- Management of land as a finite resource not as a commodity, since land ownership, whether public or private, carries responsibility for stewardship.
- Land-use planning that reflects conservation and wise management of resources.
- Identification and regulation of areas of critical concern:
    - Fragile or historical lands, where development could result in irreversible damage (such as shore-lands of rivers, lakes, streams, estuaries, and bays; rare or valuable ecosystems and geological formations; significant wildlife habitats; unique scenic or historic areas; wetlands; deserts).
    - Renewable resource lands, where development could result in the loss of productivity (such as watersheds, aquifers and aquifer-recharge areas, significant agricultural and grazing lands, forest lands).
    - Natural hazard lands, where development could endanger life and property (such as floodplains, areas with high seismic or volcanic activity, areas of unstable geologic, ice or snow formations).
- Reclamation of lands damaged by surface mining, waste disposal, overgrazing, timber harvesting, farming, and other activities.
- Acquisition of land for public use.

- Identification and regulation of areas impacted by public or private investment where siting results in secondary environmental, and socioeconomic impacts.
- Review of environmental, social and economic impacts of major public and private developments.
- Review of federally funded projects by all government levels:
  - Conformance of federal land resource activities with approved state programs, particularly where state standards are more stringent than federal standards.

Water Resources

The League supports:

- Water resource programs and policies that reflect the interrelationships of water quality, water quantity, groundwater, and surface water and that address the potential depletion or pollution of water supplies.
- Measures to reduce water pollution from direct point-source discharges and from indirect nonpoint sources.
- Policies to achieve water quality essential for maintaining species populations and diversity, including measures to protect lakes, estuaries, wetlands, and in-stream flows.
- Stringent controls to protect the quality of current and potential drinking-water supplies, including protection of watersheds for surface supplies and of recharge areas for groundwater.

Proposed Interbasin Water Transfers

Interstate and inter-basin transfers are not new or unusual. Water transfers have served municipal supplies, industry, energy development, and agriculture.

Construction costs of large-scale water transfers are high, and economic losses in the basin of origin also may be high. Environmental costs of water transfers may include quantitative and qualitative changes in wetlands and related fisheries and wildlife, diminished aquifer recharge, and reduced stream flows. Lowered water tables also may affect groundwater quality and cause land subsidence.

As we look to the future, water transfer decisions will need to incorporate the high costs of moving water, the limited availability of unallocated water, and our still-limited knowledge of impacts on the affected ecosystems.

To develop member understanding and agreement on proposals for large-scale water transfer projects, state and local Leagues need to work together. The following guidelines are designed to help Leagues jointly evaluate new proposals for large-scale water transfers.

The process for evaluating the suitability of new proposed inter-basin water transfers should include:

- Ample and effective opportunities for informed public participation in the formulation and analysis of proposed projects.
- Evaluation of economic, social, and environmental impacts in the basin of origin; the receiving area; and any area through which the diversion must pass, so that decision-makers and the public have adequate information on which to base a decision.
- Examination of all short- and long-term economic costs including, but not limited to, construction, delivery, operation, maintenance, and market interest rate.
- Examination of alternative supply options, such as water conservation, water pricing, and reclamation.
- Participation and review by all affected governments.

- Procedures for resolution of inter-governmental conflicts.
- Accord with international treaties.
- Provisions to ensure that responsibility for funding is borne primarily by the user with no federal subsidy, loan guarantees, or use of the borrowing authority of the federal government, unless the proposal is determined by all affected levels of the League to be in the national interest.

Waste Management

The League supports:

- Policies to reduce the generation and promote the reuse and recycling of solid and hazardous wastes.
- Policies to ensure safe treatment, transportation, storage, and disposal of solid and hazardous wastes in order to protect public health and air, water, and land resources.
- Planning and decision-making processes that recognize suitable solid and hazardous wastes as potential resources.
- Policies for the management of civilian and military high- and low-level radioactive wastes to protect public health and air, water, and land resources.
- The establishment of processes for effective involvement of state and local governments and citizens in siting proposals for treatment, storage, disposal, and transportation of radioactive wastes.
- Full environmental review of treatment, storage, and disposal facilities for radioactive wastes.
- Safe transport, storage, and disposal of radioactive wastes.

Criteria For Siting Waste Disposal Facilities

The following criteria are derived from the League's Natural Resources positions. They were developed to assist state and local Leagues in reviewing specific waste disposal sites and to help state and local Leagues evaluate both the process employed in site selection and the suitability of a proposed site or hazardous and radioactive waste treatment, storage, and disposal facilities. This decision-making process should provide for:

- Ample and effective opportunities for public participation, including funding to conduct such participation.
- Evaluation of economic, social, and environmental impacts so that decision-makers and the public have adequate information on which to base a decision. In addition to the actual site, secondary land use impacts (e.g., buffer areas, adequacy of roads, sewers, water) should be considered.
- Examination of alternative sites and methods of treatment and disposal. Comparison of costs must include short- and long-term costs, such as liability insurance, postclosure maintenance, monitoring of ground and surface waters and air before and after closure, and potential loss of land or water resources due to contamination.
- Participation and review by all government levels to assure conformance with all adopted comprehensive plans at each level of government.
- Procedures for resolution of inter-governmental conflicts.
- Hazardous and radioactive waste treatment, storage, or disposal facilities should be sited in areas that pose the least amount of risk to the public and to sensitive environmental areas. They should be located away from areas of critical concern such as:
  - Natural hazard areas subject to flooding, earthquakes, volcanoes, hurricanes, or subsidence.
  - Drinking-water supply sources, such as reservoirs, lakes, and rivers and their watersheds, and aquifers and their recharge areas.
  - Fragile land areas, such as shorelines of rivers, lakes, streams, oceans, estuaries, bays, or wetlands.

- Rare or valuable ecosystems or geologic formations, significant wildlife habitat, or unique scenic or historic areas.
- Areas with significant renewable resource value, such as prime agricultural lands or grazing and forest lands that would be destroyed as a result of the siting of hazardous waste facilities.
- Residential areas, parks, and schools.

Nuclear Issues

The League's approach to nuclear issues is one of problem solving. The League's aim is to work constructively for the maximum protection of public health and safety and the environment and for citizen participation in the decision-making process at all levels of government.

The League opposes increased reliance on nuclear fission but recognizes its place in the nation's energy mix. To achieve this objective:

- State and local Leagues may oppose licensing for construction of nuclear power plants based on the national position.
- State and local Leagues may oppose licensing for operation of these plants now under construction on a case-by-case basis, after careful consideration of the need for power and of available alternatives and after notifying the national board.
- State and local Leagues may support licensing for construction and operation of nuclear power plants only in special cases and only with prior permission from the national board.
- State and local Leagues may call for the closing of operating nuclear power plants because of specific non-generic health and safety problems, but only with prior permission from LWVUS.

Siting/Storage of High-Level Wastes (HLWs)

The disposal of HLWs is a national concern, and national policy should govern selection of any facilities constructed, whether an Away-From-Reactor (AFR) interim storage facility, a Monitored Retrievable System (MRS) facility, or a permanent geological repository. The *Nuclear Waste Policy Act of 1982* sets forth a program for selection, authorization, and licensing of permanent repository sites and outlines programs for possible MRS and AFR facilities. In taking any action on this issue, LWVUS will work to ensure that HLWs are disposed of in a manner that protects public health and safety and the environment.

During the 1981 – 1982 congressional debate over disposal of nuclear wastes, LWVUS made several statements regarding storage and disposal. The League testified that the storage of HLWs from commercial reactors should be maximized at reactor sites; the League would support a utility-financed AFR facility if one were needed to prevent nuclear power plants from being forced to cease operations because of spent-fuel buildup. In addition, the League supports an active state role in the HLWs decision-making process. These concerns, in addition to LWVUS positions on the process and criteria for siting and storage of HLWs, provide the foundation for LWVUS action.

While only a limited number of facilities will probably be built, LWVUS recognizes that Leagues located in states or communities under consideration as potential sites for such facilities may wish to act based on national positions. In that event, the state League, or a local League working in concert with the state League, must consult with LWVUS before taking any action. In making any action determinations on HLWs, LWVUS will consider three questions: 1) Is the proposed facility needed at this time? 2) Is the site suitable? and 3) Did the selection process provide ample and effective opportunities for public participation? Leagues requesting LWVUS clearance for action should address these questions, particularly the assessment of the suitability of a specific site.

State Leagues also should be alert to action opportunities relating to the process of state consultation and concurrence in the proposed sites.

Siting/Storage of Low-Level Wastes (LLWs)

The *Low-Level Radioactive Waste Policy Act of 1980* makes states responsible for the disposal of LLWs generated at commercial facilities within their borders. The act authorizes states to form regional compacts to establish disposal sites, and it allows states to refuse wastes from other states outside their compact region after January 1, 1986. State legislatures must approve a state's membership in a regional compact, but a compact does not become operational and legally binding until Congress consents to the agreement.

Appropriate State League Action

Some state Leagues are participating in state-level or regional-level discussions/negotiations over regional compacts and are seeking agreement on the compacts. LWVUS believes it is important for all state Leagues within a proposed compact region to work together to resolve any differences and establish agreement. Clearly, that agreement must be in accord with national positions. Because this is a national concern, LWVUS must review and approve any agreement reached among state Leagues in a compact region before state Leagues can take any action.

A state League in the proposed compact region that does not support the League agreement cannot act in opposition to that agreement. For example, if a state League disagrees with the approved League agreement, that state League can only lobby its state legislature either to withdraw from the proposed regional compact, i.e., "go it alone," or to join another compact region. A state League also may request LWVUS permission to contact its US senators and representatives at the time Congress considers ratification of the regional compact to lobby them to withdraw the state from the proposed compact. Some individual state Leagues have undertaken studies of proposed compacts for their regions and have reached consensus on a proposed regional compact. Again, that consensus must be in accord with national positions. In addition, before taking any action, the state League must obtain clearance from other state League boards in the proposed compact region because any action would involve government jurisdictions beyond that League. The state League also should consult LWVUS before acting.

A state League or a local League working with the state League can act on a proposed LLW disposal site based on the public participation process if it concludes the process was inadequate or based on a study of the environmental safety/suitability of the proposed disposal site (see Siting Criteria). If potential environmental impacts of a proposed site affect more than one League, clearance must be obtained from the relevant League boards before any action can be taken. If any unresolved differences develop among Leagues, LWVUS will decide the appropriate course of action.

Transportation of Nuclear Wastes

The League recognizes that transporting nuclear wastes increases the likelihood of accidents that could endanger public health. The League also recognizes that transportation is less risky than allowing these wastes to accumulate at an environmentally unsafe facility.

State and local Leagues can work to improve the regulation of transportation of nuclear wastes, but they cannot support blanket bans on transporting nuclear wastes through a region or city. There may be instances, however, in which a carefully thought-out ban, based on extensive League study, would be appropriate for a specific area. Such a study should include the overall subject of transporting and managing nuclear wastes, including regulation of types of wastes; packaging; escort; notification of routes to local and state authorities; effective emergency response; and the designating of routes that minimize health, safety, and environmental risks. The study should not be confined to one aspect of the transportation issue, such as routes.

If after a study of the wide-ranging issues involved, a League concludes that wastes should not be transported through an area, that League must discuss the results of the study and obtain clearance for any contemplated action from all appropriate levels of the League.

Defense Wastes

In managing high-level nuclear wastes, the League supports equivalent treatment of civilian and military wastes. The League supports the state consultation and concurrence process, consideration of environmental impacts of proposed sites, and NRC licensing for defense waste facilities, as well as for civilian waste facilities. The League's position on equivalent treatment of all wastes includes transportation of defense wastes. Low-level defense wastes include wastes from military medical programs, naval shipyards that maintain nuclear-powered naval vessels, and research facilities. The treatment of low-level defense wastes, however, is not spelled out in the *Low-level Waste Policy Act of 1980*. Most low-level defense wastes are disposed of in special federal facilities; however, some are disposed of in existing commercial sites.

Leagues may take the same action on transporting, siting, and storing defense wastes as on civilian wastes. Action on defense wastes should be in accordance with any relevant future National Security position(s) developed by the League.

Inter-League Cooperation

Leagues contemplating action on nuclear waste issues should keep in mind that any action almost invariably will affect areas beyond their jurisdiction. Thus, in all cases, local Leagues should clear action with the state League and the League boards at the appropriate jurisdictional levels.

One example of necessary inter-League action on a regional level is the low-level radioactive waste compacting process. The League believes this is an important national, state, and local concern aimed at responsible management and disposal of low-level wastes. Many state Leagues are actively participating in their regional processes, and some are taking consensus on the issue.

League History

Since the 1960s, the League has been at the forefront of efforts to protect air, land, and water resources. Since the enactment of the *Clean Air Act*, the *Clean Water Act*, the *Safe Drinking Water Act*, and the *Resource Conservation and Recovery Act* (RCRA), the League has worked for effective regulatory programs.

The League's pioneering focus on the interrelationships among air and water management issues forms the basis of efforts to ensure that government decision-making recognizes that environmental protection must be a seamless web. The evolution continues as the League's efforts go beyond fighting for pollution control and waste management strategies to demanding pollution prevention and waste reduction.

During the 1980s, the League fought hard to thwart attempts to weaken environmental protections through legislative and regulatory channels and severe federal budget cuts. League members pushed for strong environmental safeguards in the reauthorization of the *Clean Air Act* and the *Clean Water Act*. A League-endorsed reauthorization of the Superfund program proved a major step toward continuing the clean-up of the nation's hazardous waste sites. The 1990s and 2000s brought continued pressure to weaken environmental legislation and underfund programs. The League has continued to push for strong laws and full program funding for EPA, as well as for the defeat of across-the-board regulatory reform proposals that would weaken environmental protections.

Air Quality

After beginning its study of air pollution in 1970, the League reached its 1971 position in support of federal air pollution controls on industrial production, government installations, fuels, and vehicles. The position opened the way for League action at the federal, state, regional, and local levels.

Ever since, the League has pressed for full implementation of the *Clean Air Act of 1970* and for strengthening amendments, while fighting against attempts to weaken it. Early on, the League opposed the continued extension of deadlines for meeting ambient air quality standards and auto emission standards and supported visibility protection for national parks and the prevention of significant deterioration program to protect air in areas with relatively clean air.

In the 1980s, the *Clean Air Act* came under strong attack, and the League helped lead the effort to protect and strengthen it. Finally, in 1990, League environmentalists were rewarded with passage of the 1990 *Clean Air Act*, which included major improvements to combat acid rain and smog and to cut emissions of toxic air pollutants. The legislation mandated major reductions in sulfur and nitrogen oxide emissions using the best available technology and energy efficiency. It attacked both stationary and mobile sources of pollutants. The Act set national standards and helped cities and states deal with local problems. The League at all levels worked to ensure full implementation of the revised Act.

The League has also worked for tighter fuel efficiency standards (Corporate Average Fuel Economy or CAFE standards) for automobiles to improve energy efficiency and reduce pollution.

In the 1990s, antiregulatory legislation gave Congress unprecedented authority to reject new regulations issued by federal agencies by passing a resolution of disapproval. League members strenuously urged their members of Congress to oppose efforts to reject strengthened standards and LWVUS strongly supported the EPA's issuance of new National Ambient Air Quality Standards (NAAQS) for ground-level ozone and fine particulate matter to protect public health. The League worked successfully to defeat amendments to the *Intermodal Surface Transportation Efficiency Act* (ISTEA) that would have allowed designated air quality funds to be spent on highway programs.

Following the December 1997 treaty negotiations in Kyoto on the Framework Convention on Climate Change, also known as the Kyoto Protocol, the League applauded the President's initiative to make the United States a world leader in combating global climate change and to seek negotiated, fair reductions and meaningful participation from developing countries in reducing greenhouse gases. League members lobbied against Senate passage of a resolution to oppose the Kyoto Protocol, which called for nations to reduce their greenhouse gases, and they lobbied their senators to reject any actions that undermine international negotiations to stop climate change.

EPA instituted major new initiatives to clean up the air in 1998 – 2000, and the League worked to see them promulgated. The League commented on EPA's proposed new emissions standards for sport utility vehicles (SUV) and heavy vehicles, arguing for the importance of controlling the mobile sources of air pollution that had largely gone unregulated.

In 1999 – 2000, while Congress fought to a standstill over clean air issues, the League produced a Q&A on global warming, a valuable resource for citizens on this key issue. LWVUS believes that climate change is a serious problem that requires immediate international action. The League believes the US government should move ahead immediately, without waiting for other nations, on initiatives to reduce emissions of heat-trapping gases; such actions will reduce the threat of global climate change, combat air pollution, increase energy security, and create new jobs.

In the 2000s, energy legislation became the primary vehicle for attempts to weaken the *Clean Air Act*. The League worked throughout the 2000s to block these efforts. In the later 2000s, LWVUS significantly increased its advocacy concerning global climate change legislation. In 2006, the League and other concerned organizations submitted a statement to EPA urging strengthened air quality standards consistent with the *Clean Air Act*. Later that year, the League joined other groups in issuing a statement of principles on the importance of reducing climate change. The League also created a Climate Change Task Force.

In 2008, the League called on Congress to enact legislation to significantly cut the greenhouse gas emissions that cause global climate change and supported increased energy efficiency and a shift to clean, renewable energy. The League called for a moratorium on the building of new coal-fired electric power plants and supported requirements for utilities to produce a significant percentage of electricity from renewable resources.

The League supported the *Climate Security Act of 2008*, as well as amendments to strengthen the bill. This legislation provided for a cap-and-trade system, which would have cut greenhouse gas emissions from electric power, transportation, and manufacturing sources. The emissions cap would be reduced over time to meet pollution reduction goals based on the best-available scientific information. These emissions reductions could be traded on a market set up by the legislation, allowing polluters to buy, sell, borrow, and trade emission allowances to ensure economic efficiency in the program. The League also urged elected officials to extend clean energy tax incentives. Though it passed the House, the legislation was sidetracked in the Senate by special interests.

In December 2009, the League was thrilled to participate on the international stage, sending an official NGO delegation to Copenhagen for the UN Framework Convention on Climate Change. In March 2010, 19 League leaders from as many states went to Washington to lobby congressional leaders on strong climate change legislation. In addition, the Climate Change Task Force developed and promoted the Toolkit for Climate Action to assist Leagues and League members throughout the country in the fight to combat global climate change.

In 2012, when the EPA proposed the first-ever standards to control industrial carbon pollution from power plants, which causes global climate change and increases health problems, the League joined with its environmental and social justice allies in collecting the largest number of comments ever submitted in a review of an EPA regulation. More than three million comments were submitted in support of the proposed rules for new and existing power plants and urging EPA to take the next step and set carbon standards for existing plants.

In 2012, with Congress unable or unwilling to act on climate change, the League launched an initiative to urge the President to use his executive authority under the *Clean Air Act* to control carbon pollution from both new and existing power plants, which are the largest source of industrial carbon pollution in the United States. The League strongly urged the President to lead the world in the right direction in the face of the greatest environmental challenge of our generation: climate change. With the proposed rules on new power plants in limbo and standards for new plants not yet proposed, the League used paid advertising, action alerts, and new media tools to urge the President to get the job done.

Efforts by the 115th Congress (2017 – 2019) were primarily focused on repealing, replacing, and modifying many of the regulations that the League supported and acted on during the previous decade. The League opposed efforts by Congress to use the *Congressional Review Act* to roll back the Clean Power Plan, Mercury and Air Toxics Standard (MATS), and the Clean Cars Rule. The League submitted comments to the EPA opposing each of these moves and joined with coalition partners to draw attention to the dangers that the repeal of such regulations would have on public health and the environment.

Water Resources

Passage of an expanded *Safe Drinking Water Act* in 1986 and the *Clean Water Act* of 1987 marked important milestones in the League's effort to ensure safe drinking water for all Americans and safeguards against nonpoint pollution.

Groundwater, virtually unprotected by national legislation, became the focus of state and local League efforts in 1990, when LWVEF undertook a project to increase citizen awareness of the importance of protecting groundwater supplies, the source of 50 percent of the nation's drinking water. Leagues in 17 states sponsored public forums, conferences, action guides, educational videos, "water-watcher" teams, and media outreach. The local efforts were documented in a citizen handbook: Protect Your Groundwater: Educating for Action. In 1994, LWVEF sponsored a national videoconference on groundwater protection with more than 140 downlink sites nationwide. The education efforts were complemented with LWVUS lobbying to address groundwater concerns in the renewal of the *Clean Water Act of 1994*.

Leagues across the country conducted surveys of local drinking water officials and held educational forums under the LWVEF Safe Drinking Water Project.

The project's publications, Safety on Tap and Crosscurrents, were used widely by Leagues and other citizen groups. In 1994 and 1995, the League opposed amendments to the *Safe Drinking Water Act* that would require EPA to conduct formal cost-benefit analyses with comparative risk analyses for every regulatory action and urged Congress to restore funding and adopt improvements to the act.

In 1997, LWVEF sponsored a second videoconference, Tools for Drinking Water Protection, featuring protection strategies and mechanisms at work in diverse communities around the United States. It was downlinked to more than 750 sites in the United States (including Puerto Rico and the US Virgin Islands), Canada, and Brazil, and allowed citizens, officials, business leaders, and NGOs to share information. It won the 1997 award for "Most Outstanding Broadcast for the Public Good" from the teleconferencing industry. In 1998, LWVEF published Strategies for Effective Public Involvement in Drinking Water Source Assessment and Protection, a handbook to facilitate the public involvement required by the Safe Drinking Water Act amendments of 1996.

The League also focused education efforts on wetlands protection. In 1996, LWVEF held a Wetlands Protection Workshop, bringing together members from 23 states, national environmental specialists, and local leaders to explore the value of coastal and freshwater wetlands, highlight measures and programs geared toward wetlands protection, and examine methods for effective communication of wetlands information in local communities. In 1997 – 98, LWVEF provided pass-through grants to 11 Leagues to educate their communities on wetlands. In 1998, LWVUS supported the President's proposed action plan to crack down on polluted runoff and to restore and protect wetlands. In related action, the League submitted comments to the Army Corps of Engineers urging revocation of Nationwide Permit 26 (NWP 26), which sanctions the loss of thousands of acres of wetlands every year.

In May 2000, LWVEF sponsored The Ech$_2$O Workshop: An Introduction to the Watershed Approach, where League activists learned how to take leadership in protecting their local watersheds and educating the public about watershed protection.

In February 2003, LWVUS submitted comments to the EPA on attempts to redefine and limit the jurisdictional focus of the Clean Water Act, noting that the Act covers all waters. "Whether large or small, they function as an interconnected system; excision of parts of the system [from regulation] will impair health and optimal functioning of the whole." The League fought the threat to streams and rivers from mountaintop removal, a coal-mining technique that can bury those water bodies. In 2005, the League urged senators to protect women and children from toxic mercury by supporting a bipartisan resolution to reject EPA's rule to delay reductions in mercury emissions from power plants.

Delegates at the 2010 Convention shared information about hydraulic fracturing, commonly referred to as "fracking," a process by which high pressure water, sand, and chemicals are pumped underground to fracture geologic formations to release natural gas. This process, as well as other fossil fuel extraction, poses a threat to water and other natural resources. State Leagues, using LWVUS positions on natural resources — particularly clean water and drinking water — worked to reduce the environmental impact of mining processes that contaminate and pollute.

In 2012, LWVUS made its voice heard to several regulatory authorities of the federal government in relation to fracking. Comments went to the EPA, the Bureau of Land Management (BLM), and the Federal Energy Regulatory Commission (FERC). In 2015, the League supported a set of five bills referred to as the Frack Pack. The legislation would help protect the environment and public health from the risks of hydraulic fracturing by ending exemptions for oil and gas production from major environmental laws such as the Safe Drinking Water Act.

State and local Leagues were active in the development of the Waters of the United States regulation. This regulation would define the waterways, rivers, streams, and tributaries protected by the *Clean Water Act*. State and local Leagues sent in comments, participated in hearings, and worked with partners on the ground during the development of the regulation. They also worked to defend it when it was repealed by the Trump administration.

Together with coalition partners, the League participated in a final effort to push President Obama to permanently protect designated parts of the Atlantic and Arctic Oceans from offshore oil drilling. The League was successful in its efforts and President Obama designated certain areas off-limits to oil and gas leasing. The League continues to battle the Department of the Interior and BLM on this issue while engaging in this fight with our partners as the decisions of the previous administration are reversed. The League continued advocacy to prevent coastal oil and gas leases by fighting rulemaking by the National Oceanic and Atmospheric Administration (NOAA) that would make procedural changes to the *Coastal Zone Management Act* (CZMA). If promulgated, this rule would weaken the federal review process of oil and gas leasing, reduce the amount of time for states affected to communicate about concerns, and endanger the well-being of citizens.

In the 116th Congress (2019 – 2021), the League worked to ensure that funding for the EPA's Nonpoint Source Management Program was increased. Adding funding to this program under Section 319 of the *Clean Water Act* ensured that the primary federal program with a nationwide reach and a mission of cleaning up waterways impaired by nonpoint source pollution protects streams, rivers, and other tributaries across the country. In the 117th Congress (2021 – 2023), the LWVUS joined with LWV Utah in urging the Department of Interior to preserve the Red Cliffs National Conservation Area.

Solid Waste

Work on solid waste began in 1971, when Leagues studied solid waste disposal in their home communities and then turned their attention to national policies on reuse, reclamation, and recycling. By April 1973, members had reached an agreement that solid waste should be regarded as a resource and that although the major responsibility should be at the state and local levels, the federal government should play a greater role in managing solid waste. Diminishing landfill capacity and a growing awareness of the pollution hazards of incineration brought concerns about interstate commerce in waste and renewed enthusiasm for recycling in the late 1980s. Leagues continue to support national and state recycling efforts, waste reduction measures, and household hazardous waste collection programs.

By the late 1970s, League attention to hazardous waste resulted in two major victories at the federal level. *The Resource Conservation and Recovery Act of 1976* (RCRA) provided for hazardous waste management programs, grants to states and localities for solid waste planning and implementation programs, and the *Toxic Substance Control Act of 1976* (TSCA) regulated products that pose an unreasonable risk to human health or the environment. During the 1980s, the League continued to support the reauthorization of these laws.

The League closely monitored RCRA implementation, commenting on proposed regulations and working for effective state programs. The League was a leader in efforts to pass legislation prohibiting the injection of toxic wastes into and above underground sources of drinking water; set location standards for siting waste treatment, storage, and disposal facilities; and permit land disposal of untreated hazardous waste only as a last resort for selected substances.

In the 1991 – 1994 battle over the reauthorization of RCRA, the League strongly supported the "reduce, reuse, recycle" hierarchy. The League pushed for mandatory recycling measures, including minimum recycled-content standards, a national bottle bill, and a pause in the construction of municipal incinerators. The League urged the Clinton Administration to issue executive orders to promote recycling.

In 1992, LWVEF published Recycling Is More Than Collections, a grassroots investigation of recycling conducted by League volunteers across the country. LWVEF continued its educational work with the publication of The Garbage Primer and The Plastic Waste Primer in 1993 and with citizen training programs.

The League also supported pollution prevention and community access to information on emissions, as well as measures to enable state and EPA regulators to compel federal facilities to comply with RCRA standards.

In 1980 the League helped pass the *Comprehensive Environmental Response, Compensation, and Liability Act* (CERCLA), known as Superfund. The act authorized $1.6 billion over five years for the clean-up of the nation's toxic waste sites. Over the years since then, the League repeatedly has gone to Congress to ensure that a reauthorized Superfund contains adequate funding and safeguards to continue the job.

In the 116th Congress (2019 – 2021), LWVUS supported legislation designed to reduce the production and use of certain single-use plastic products and packaging; improve the responsibility of producers in the design, collection, reuse, recycling, and disposal of their consumer products and packaging; prevent pollution from consumer products and packaging from entering into animal and human food chains and waterways; and other purposes.

Nuclear Waste

The League pushed for congressional passage of the *Low-Level Waste Policy Act* in 1980 and the *Nuclear Waste Policy Act* in 1982 to ensure a national policy that incorporates adequate environmental safeguards with a strong role for public participation in nuclear-waste repository siting decisions. Leagues across the country have used League positions to support their involvement in the siting of low-level nuclear waste sites, high-level waste sites, and nuclear power plants. LWVEF has published a wide range of materials, including the acclaimed Nuclear Waste Primer. Following the passage of the *Nuclear Waste Policy Act of 1985*, LWVEF sponsored a public policy training program and published The Nuclear Waste Digest.

In 1992, LWVEF signed a five-year cooperative agreement with the Department of Energy (DOE) to publish a third edition of The Nuclear Waste Primer (1993) and conduct civic education programs on nuclear waste. In 1995, LWVEF launched a second five-year cooperative agreement with DOE to focus educational and community involvement efforts on defense waste management issues. In June 1998, LWVEF held two regional discussions on nuclear material and waste and issued a report to DOE.

In 1995, LWVUS opposed congressional efforts to designate Yucca Mountain, Nevada, as a permanent or temporary repository for nuclear waste prior to studies verifying suitability. The League urged Congress to oppose the *Nuclear Waste Policy Act of 1997*, which mandated an interim storage site at Yucca Mountain.

For many years, the League worked in opposition to making Yucca Mountain a permanent repository site for nuclear waste. The organization has also participated in helping to educate members of the Senate Energy Committee about the dangers of transporting materials to new sites and consolidating storage facilities. State Leagues have also advocated against the use of temporary storage facilities in Texas and New Mexico and opposed the transportation of hazardous materials through communities in their states.

Transfer of Federal Public Lands

The League's Position

Statement of Position as adopted by concurrence at the 54th LWVUS National Convention in June 2020:

The League believes that federal public lands should benefit all Americans. The lands should remain under the jurisdiction of the federal government with Forest Service and Bureau of Land Management lands and be managed according to the Multiple-Use Sustained-Yield policy. We support improvements in management and regulation. Federal law allows for the sale or exchange of federal lands if it is in the public interest. Prior to any transfer, a comprehensive assessment that covers the following issues should be performed:

- **Environmental analysis, including air and water quality, biodiversity, endangered and threatened species**
- **Health impacts**
- **Environmental justice**
- **Suitability of proposed land use**
- **Subsurface resources**
- **Financial and economic impacts**
- **Cultural resources**
- **Public access**
- **Management for fire and other natural disasters**
- **Consultation with tribal governments**

The League is opposed to the sale of federal lands to private entities except for small tracts surrounded by nonfederal lands. The League is opposed to the transfer of subsurface rights to the state or other entities. Any development of subsurface rights on federal land should benefit all Americans.

League History

Convention 2020 delegates voted to adopt a concurrence on the Transfer of Federal Public Lands. The position was derived from a LWV New Mexico-initiated study of the transfer of federal public lands in 2017 in response to legislation discussed in several Western states. Specifically, Utah had passed legislation in 2012 demanding transfer of selected federal public lands to the state. Although no transfers occurred as a result, LWVNM believed it was necessary to have a position that could be used for advocacy if or when such legislation was proposed in New Mexico. Federal government, as defined in the position, includes the US Forest Service and the Bureau of Land Management.

The federal government owns 28% of land in the United States, which is managed by three different agencies. There are numerous issues at the federal level in relation to land ownership, acquisition, and the balance between protection and use. As a result, LWV believes there is significant risk that transfer of public lands may be a fast-moving issue in any state with federal public lands. The proportion of lands held by the federal government varies significantly by state, with the largest shares in the West, but the transfer of public lands could affect all states.

Climate Change

The League's Position

Statement of Position on Climate Change Policy, as announced by the national board, January 2019:

The League believes that climate change is a serious threat facing our nation and our planet.

The League believes that an interrelated approach to combating climate change — including through energy conservation, air pollution controls, building resilience, and promotion of renewable resources — is necessary to protect public health and defend the overall integrity of the global ecosystem. The League support climate goals and policies that are consistent with the best-available climate science and that will ensure a stable climate system for future generations. Individuals, communities, and governments must continue to address this issue, while considering the ramifications of their decision at all levels — local, state, regional, national, and global.

League History

In the later 2000s, LWVUS significantly increased its advocacy concerning global climate change. LWVUS believes that climate change is a serious problem that requires immediate domestic and international action. The League believes the US government should move ahead immediately, without waiting for other nations, on initiatives to reduce emissions of heat-trapping gases like carbon, methane, and other toxic air pollutants. Such actions will reduce the threat of global climate change, combat air pollution, increase energy security, and create new jobs.

In late 2006, the League joined other groups in issuing a statement of principles on the importance of reducing climate change. The League also created a Climate Change Task Force to provide information and assistance to the national board and staff on issues pertaining to climate change. The Task Force also works to develop materials for use by League members at the local, state, and national levels.

In 2008, the League called on Congress to enact legislation to significantly cut the greenhouse gas emissions that cause global climate change and supported increased energy efficiency and a shift to clean, renewable energy. The League called for a moratorium on the building of new coal-fired electric power plants and supported requirements for utilities to produce a significant percentage of electricity from renewable resources.

The League supported the *Climate Security Act of 2008*, as well as amendments to strengthen the bill. This legislation provided for a cap-and-trade system, which would have cut greenhouse gas emission from electric power, transportation, and manufacturing sources. The emissions cap would be reduced over time to meet pollution-reduction goals based on the best-available scientific information. These emissions reductions could be traded on a market set up by the legislation, allowing polluters to buy, sell, borrow, and trade emission allowances to ensure economic efficiency in the program. The League also urged elected officials to extend clean energy tax incentives. Though it passed the US House of Representatives, the legislation was sidetracked in the US Senate by special interests.

In December 2009, the League was thrilled to participate on the international stage, sending an official NGO delegation to Copenhagen for the UN Framework Convention on Climate Change. In March 2010, 19 League leaders from as many states went to Washington to lobby congressional leaders on strong climate change legislation. In addition, the Climate Change Task Force developed and promoted the Toolkit for Climate Action to assist Leagues and League members throughout the country in the fight to combat global climate change.

In the late 2000s, the League lobbied vigorously for comprehensive legislation to control global climate change by setting a cap on greenhouse gas pollution and encouraging conservation and renewable energy. As part of an education and advocacy project on climate change, six state Leagues held forums with trips by the League president to speak at public events and meet with key senators and staff. In early 2010, the LWVUS president was honored by Oxfam America with a Sisters on the Planet Climate Leader Award for the League's grassroots work on climate change.

In 2012, when EPA proposed the first-ever standards to control industrial carbon pollution from power plants, which causes global climate change and increases health problems, the League joined with its environmental and social justice allies in collecting the largest number of comments ever submitted in review of an EPA regulation. More than three million comments were submitted in support of the proposed rules for new power plants urging the EPA to take the next step and set carbon standards for existing plants.

In 2012, with Congress unable or unwilling to act on climate change, the League launched an initiative to urge President Obama to use his executive authority under the *Clean Air Act* to control carbon pollution from both new and existing power plants, which are the largest source of industrial carbon pollution in the United States. The League strongly urged the president to lead the world in the right direction in the face of the greatest environmental challenge of our generation: climate change. With the proposed rules on new power plants in limbo and standards for new plants not yet proposed, the League used paid advertising, action alerts, and new media tools to urge the president to get the job done.

The League continued its strong advocacy on climate issues by supporting President Obama's Climate Action Plan. In addition, the League voiced support for putting a price on carbon to complement the regulatory effort. By demonstrating the political salience of the climate change issue — and the effects on public health — League ads succeeded in discouraging the Senate from taking up legislation that would undermine efforts to address climate change.

In the 2014 – 2016 biennium, the League continued work to fight climate change by supporting regulations from the EPA, fighting legislation to stop or hurt progress on climate initiatives, and pushing for the full rejection of the Keystone XL pipeline. The League continued support for the EPA's Clean Power Plan and New Source Pollution Standard by participating in field hearings across the country and collecting comments from grassroots supporters in support of the regulations, all while working to fight legislation to overturn or weaken the regulations in Congress. The League strongly supported the People's Climate March in New York City and the UN Paris Agreement, which was a historic international agreement that established a commitment to reduce carbon pollution and fight climate change. The League also endorsed regulations from EPA to reduce the levels of ozone in the atmosphere and regulate methane in the oil and gas sector.

In 2017 and 2018, the League opposed efforts by the 115th Congress and the Trump administration to roll back key agreements and regulations to combat climate change. This included the withdrawal of the United States from the Paris Climate Agreement, the plan to gut the Clean Power Plan, the rollback of the clean cars standards and methane regulation, and the approval of the Keystone XL pipeline.

In 2016, LWVUS joined with LWVOR to file an amicus brief in the US District Court for the District of Oregon in the case of *Juliana et al v. United States*. Together, the brief reiterates the Leagues' support for the 21 young people from across the United States who have filed a landmark constitutional climate change lawsuit against the federal government, via Our Children's Trust, based in Eugene, Oregon. In 2018, the Justice Department filed a motion to dismiss the case but allowed the President to be removed as a named party to the case. In 2019, there was a flurry of activity as LWVUS and LWVOR filed another joint amicus brief with the Ninth Circuit Court arguing that the case is unique and timely because plaintiffs have no other mechanism to resolve their issues. However, in January 2020, the Ninth Circuit dismissed the case. Following on this, the League advocated for passage of the Children's Fundamental Rights and Climate Recovery Resolution in the 116th Congress.

In the 116th Congress (2019 – 2021) the League supported the passage of the *Climate Action Now Act*, legislation to keep the United States in the Paris Climate Agreement and reinforce national resolve to meet America's climate action commitments. The League also endorsed bicameral legislation, the *Climate Risk Disclosure Act of 2019*. This legislation took steps to ensure that shareholders have the information needed to adequately mitigate financial, physical, and legal climate related risks to their investments and accelerate the transition from fossil fuels to cleaner, more-efficient energy standards. In the 117th Congress, LWVUS support for addressing the climate change crisis continued with Senate lobbying in support of legislation and executive orders from the Biden administration that establish climate change as a major priority for the nation. In 2022, the League urged Congress to support the *National Climate Adaptation and Resilience Strategy Act*, which would require the federal government to create a national strategy to prepare for climate hazard.

Public Participation

The League's Position

Statement of Position on Public Participation as announced 1986 – 88:

The League believes that public understanding and cooperation are essential to the responsible and responsive management of our nation's natural resources. The public has a right to know about pollution levels, dangers to health and the environment, and proposed resource management policies and options. The public has a right to participate in decision-making at each phase in the process and at each level of government involvement.

Officials should make a special effort to develop readily understandable procedures for public involvement and to ensure that the public has adequate information to participate effectively. Public records should be readily accessible at all governmental levels. Adequate funding is needed to ensure opportunities for public education and effective public participation in all aspects of the decision-making process.

The appropriate level of government should publicize, in an extensive and timely manner and in readily available sources, information about pollution levels, pollution-abatement programs, and resource management policies and options. Hearings should be held in easily accessible locations, at convenient times and, when possible, in the area concerned. The hearing procedures and other opportunities for public comment should actively encourage citizen participation in decision-making.

The League supports public education that provides a basic understanding of the environment and the social, economic, and environmental costs and benefits of environmental protection, pollution control, and conservation.

Mechanisms for citizen appeal must be guaranteed, including access to the courts. Due process rights for the affected public and private parties must be assured.

League History

While fighting for a broad range of environmental legislation, the League has stressed citizen participation as a necessary component of decision-making at all levels of government.

In pressing for full implementation of the *Clean Air Act of 1970*, the League fought for greater citizen access to state plans for achieving national ambient air-quality standards. League efforts to educate and involve the public in waste management issues at the state and local levels have included support for mandatory beverage container deposit legislation, known as "bottle bills," to promote recycling and reuse. In supporting the *Nuclear Waste Policy Act of 1982*, Leagues pushed for adequate state consultation and concurrence in nuclear-waste repository siting decisions. In statements to the nuclear regulatory community, state Leagues emphasized the need for citizen participation in nuclear power decisions.

League efforts to promote household-hazardous-waste collection across the country, to ensure safe drinking water for all, and to protect groundwater also are part of a continuing focus on heightening citizen awareness and participation in decision making.

Passage of the *Emergency Planning and Community Right-to-Know Act of 1986* (SARA Title III) gave Leagues a new tool to combat pollution. This act gives communities access to information from chemical facilities on releases and spills, allows "regulation by information," and encourages the development of emergency response plans and strong pollution prevention measures by industry. During the 1990s, the League continued the fight, advocating expansion of community right-to-know provisions in the renewal of the *Resource Conservation and Recovery Act* (RCRA). It was also successful in defeating congressional efforts to pass regulatory reform legislation aimed at crippling the adoption and enforcement of environmental protection regulations.

In 1996, the League joined 24 public interest organizations in supporting the President's move to phase out the use of methyl bromide, an extremely toxic pesticide. Also, LWVUS and 84 national, international, and local organizations jointly urged Congress to cosponsor the *Children's Environmental Protection Act of 1997* (CEPA), which sought to ensure a citizen's right to know if there are harmful toxins in the environment.

In 1996, the Department of Energy asked LWVEF to help develop a National Dialogue on Nuclear Materials and Waste Management. Pilot field workshops were held in 1997, but the Dialogue was opposed by some environmentalists and state officials. LWVEF held two discussions in San Diego and Chicago on nuclear material and waste in 1998 and issued a report.

The League continued activism in the 2010s by joining millions of activists at the largest climate rallies in history. In 2013, the League joined environmental groups, women's groups, and social justice groups as a sponsor of the Forward on Climate rally in Washington, DC. In 2014, the League became a sponsor of the People's Climate March, which brought together the largest group of activists working on meaningful action on climate change. Leagues joined the main march in New York City and also sister marches in cities around the country and the world to help show lawmakers and administration officials that there is strong public support for policies that promote solutions to climate change.

In 2002, the LWVUS submitted comments in support of the Securities and Exchange Commission's (SEC) proposed amendment to rules under the *Securities Act of 1933* and *Securities Exchange Act of 1934* to require corporations to release climate-risk information to its shareholders.

Federal Agriculture Policies

The League's Positions

Statement of Position on Federal Agriculture Policy, as announced by the national board, October 1988 and updated, May 2014:

LWVUS believes that federal agriculture policies should promote adequate supplies of food and fiber at reasonable prices to consumers, farms that are economically viable, farm practices that are environmentally sound, and increased reliance on the free market to determine prices.

Sustainable Agriculture

Federal policy should encourage a system of sustainable, regenerative agricultural production that moves toward an environmentally sound agricultural sector. This includes promoting stewardship to preserve and protect the country's human and natural agricultural resources.

Research and Development

Agricultural research, development, and technical assistance should continue to be a major federal function. Resources should be targeted to developing sustainable agricultural practices and addressing the needs of mid-size farms.

Agricultural Prices

LWVUS supports an increasing reliance on the free market to determine the price of agricultural commodities and the production decisions of farmers, in preference to traditional price support mechanisms.

Agriculture and Trade

US efforts should be directed toward expanding export markets for our agricultural products while minimizing negative effects on developing nations' economies. Consistent with the League's trade position, multilateral trade negotiations should be used to reduce other countries' barriers and/or subsidies protecting their agricultural products.

Farm Credit

Farmers should have access to credit with reasonable terms and conditions. Federally provided farm credit is essential to maintaining the viability of farm operations when the private sector is unable or unwilling to provide the credit farmers need.

Of these policies, the League believes the most essential for the future of agriculture are encouraging sustainable agriculture; providing research, information, and technical assistance to agricultural producers; and increasing reliance on the free market to determine prices.

The League believes that government should provide financial support for agriculture that includes disaster assistance, crop insurance, need-based loans, and incentives to adopt best management practices. Support should be extended to specialty crops (such as fruits, vegetables, and nuts), new production methods (such as organic, hydroponic, and urban practices), and farms that supply local and regional markets.

Subsidized crop yield insurance should be linked to implementation of best management practices with the subsidy denied for marginal or environmentally sensitive land. The premium subsidy for crop insurance should be available for a wide range of crops, such as fruits, vegetables, and specialty crops. Government should limit the amount of the premium subsidy received by larger farms.

The League supports policies that increase competition in agricultural markets. Antitrust laws should be enforced to ensure competitive agricultural markets. Alternative marketing systems such as regional hub markets, farmers' markets, and farmer cooperatives should be promoted.

Clean air and water regulations should apply to all animal and aquaculture production and processing facilities, and not just to the very large confined animal feeding operations (CAFO). Such regulations should be designed in a manner that takes into account environmentally sound technologies and the scale of the operation being regulated. Small-size operations should not be granted automatic exemption from regulation.

The League believes that government regulatory agencies dealing with animal and aquaculture production should have adequate authority and funding to 1) enforce regulations and 2) gather information that supports monitoring the impacts of all animal feeding and aquaculture operations on human and animal health and the environment.

Government should fund basic research related to agriculture. Government-funded research should also address the impact of new technologies on human health and the environment prior to widespread adoption of products developed with such technologies. Assessment of products developed with new technologies should be conducted as transparently as possible, while respecting intellectual property rights. Research should be funded to support the continuation of diversified and sustainable agricultural systems, such as seed banking and promoting and preserving genetic diversity.

To provide adequate safety of our food supply, the government should:

- Clarify and enforce pre-market testing requirements for foods and food additives developed using any new chemical technology, such as genetic engineering or nanotechnology.
- Require developers to monitor all such new food products developed after releasing to the market.
- Require developers of such new food products to provide data and other materials to independent third parties for pre- and post-marketing safety assessment.
- Fund independent third-party risk assessment examining how long-term and multiple exposures to such new foods affect human health and the environment.
- Withdraw marketing approval and require recall if such products are shown to be unsafe.
- Require post-market monitoring of human health and environmental impacts for pharmaceutical applications used in animal and aquaculture production.
- Limit use of antibiotics in animal production to the treatment of disease.
- Promote crop management practices that decrease dependency on added chemicals.
- Fund, employ, and train sufficient personnel for assessment and compliance functions of regulatory agencies.

The League supports government developing and requiring more informative and standardized definitions on product labeling. Food labeling and advertising should display only approved health and safety claims and an accurate representation of the required ingredient and nutrition lists. The League supports consumer education about labeling of foods developed using any new technology.

League History

In 1986, the League undertook a two-year study and member agreement process on the role of the federal government in US agriculture policy, examining elements of federal farm policy, and its contemporary setting and policy alternatives. The resulting 1988 position on agriculture policy supports policies for sustainable agriculture and action to reduce the use of toxic chemicals on farms. A second position on federal agriculture policies was adopted in 2014. The League also supports targeting research programs and technological assistance to mid-size farms and to sustainable agriculture. While many of the programs the League supports — farm credit at reasonable terms and conditions and programs to enable farmers to use sustainable agriculture — may benefit family or mid-size farms, the League supports these programs for all farms, regardless of size.

The position supports "decoupling" (moving away from direct payments based on production) as consistent with the strong League consensus in favor of greater reliance on the free market to determine prices. Reliance on the free market for price determination can also support a gradual reduction in loan rates. The League does not envision total reliance on the free market to determine agriculture prices. In assessing programs that move agriculture toward greater reliance on the free market, consideration would include problems peculiar to agriculture, such as severe climate or natural disasters.

The League supports federally provided farm credit but believes the federal government should be the lender of last resort. The League position does not address supply controls, capping payments to farmers, protecting farm income, or any particular commodity program. It supports the conservation reserve program and opposes the removal of lands prematurely from the conservation reserve.

In 1989, the League opposed legislation that would have preempted stricter state laws on the regulation of pesticides. In 1990, it urged the House to pass a farm bill that would protect land and water resources, reduce the use of toxic chemicals, and target research and technical assistance to developing environmentally sound agriculture practices. The League called for measures to strengthen conservation provisions, continue the conservation reserve, and permit retention of base payments and deficiency payments when farmers file and implement an approved plan for farming with environmentally beneficial practices. The League also called for national standards of organic production and opposed the export of pesticides that are illegal in the United States. In 1988 – 1991, LWVEF worked with Public Voice for Food and Health Policy and state and local Leagues on a citizen education project on agricultural issues, including pesticide residues in food and water, sustainable agriculture, and research and technology.

At Convention 2012, delegates voted to review and update the LWV Agriculture position. A study committee was appointed and in 2014, Leagues reached member agreement on a new position, which was announced in May 2014. As part of that study, League members were unable to come to consensus on genetically modified organisms (GMO).

In the 115th Congress (2017 – 2019), the League worked with partners to urge conferees on the Farm Bill in Congress to include provisions that protected and strengthened the Supplemental Nutrition Assistance Program (SNAP). The joint advocacy of the League and others pushed for policies that addressed the complex realities of the lives of women with low incomes and their families, who seek to meet their basic human needs — including health, well-being, and economic security. During the COVID-19 pandemic, LWVUS contacted Congress to urge support for increased SNAP benefits in the relief package.

Social
Policy

LWV

Secure equal rights and equal opportunity for all. Promote social and economic justice, and the health and safety of all Americans.

From its inception, the League has worked for equal rights and social reforms. In the early years, the League was one of the first organizations to address such issues as child welfare, maternal and child health programs, child labor protection, and laws that discriminated against women.

In the 1960s, with the nation's unrest over civil rights, the League began building a foundation of support for equal access to education, employment, and housing. The fight against discrimination broadened in the 1970s and 1980s, and the League supported the Equal Rights Amendment (ERA) in 1972, fighting hard for ratification by the states. As that effort fell short, support for the ERA undergirded action on issues from pay equity to Title IX, which requires equal educational opportunity for women.

Based on 1970s work to combat poverty and discrimination, a two-year study evaluating public and private responsibilities for providing food, shelter, and a basic income level ended in 1988, culminating in a position on Meeting Basic Human Needs. Programs to increase the availability and quality of child care and protect children at risk remained a concern.

In the 1980s, fiscal issues, from tax reform to entitlement programs and deficit reduction, were at the forefront of the League program. The League was a major force in the tax-reform effort to cut loopholes and promote fairness. It sought deficit reduction while protecting federal old-age, survivors, disability, and health insurance.

In the late 1980s and early 1990s, the League worked to increase the availability of high-quality child care and adopted a position in favor of community and government programs to help children reach their full potential, including early childhood education.

Leagues nationwide also worked hard on transportation issues, focusing on environmental protection and ensuring the availability of public transportation for access to employment and housing.

In the 1990s, concern for violence prevention spurred a new League position and brought strong support for commonsense measures to control gun violence. The League supported the Brady bill and sought to close loopholes that undermine consumer safety.

The 2006 Convention voted to undertake a study on immigration. After study and consensus, the new position was finalized in 2008 and sent to Capitol Hill.

Given the growing crisis in health care delivery and financing in the 1990s, the League developed a comprehensive position supporting a health care system that provides access to affordable, quality health care for all Americans and protects patients' rights. In 2010, the League's efforts saw success — the *Affordable Care Act* (ACA) was signed into law. Since 2010, the League continues to defend the ACA from challenges in Congress and the courts.

At Convention 2010, delegates voted to study the role of the federal government in public education and in March 2012, the Board announced a new position. Delegates to Convention 2012 adopted by concurrence a new position on Sentencing Equality.

The League's position on Human Trafficking was adopted by concurrence at Convention 2014 and Behavioral Health was added to the Health Care position at Convention 2016.

At Convention 2022, delegates passed a new position on Criminal Justice and an update of the Health Care position by concurrence with existing state positions.

Criminal Justice

The League's Position

Statement of Position on Criminal Justice as adopted by concurrence by delegates to 55th LWVUS Convention 2022:

- **A criminal justice system that is just, effective, equitable, transparent, and that fosters public trust at all stages, including policing practices, pre-trial procedures, sentencing, incarceration, and re-entry.**
- **The elimination of systemic bias, including the disproportionate policing and incarceration of marginalized communities.**
- **Policing practices that promote safety for both law enforcement officers and the communities they serve.**
- **Collaboration between government and community throughout every stage of the criminal justice system.**
- **A focus on humane treatment and rehabilitation with the goal of promoting the successful reentry into communities of those who have been incarcerated.**
- **Reliance on evidence-based research in decision-making about law enforcement programs and policies (including scheduled, periodic audits of program and policy effectiveness)**

Policing Practices — constitutional policies and procedures established by law enforcement with input from the communities they serve

- **Ensure that crime prevention and promotion of public safety are the primary roles of state and local law enforcement agencies.**
- **Build public trust and positive community relationships through police engagement with community members.**
- **Encourage community participation in the development of policing policy.**
- **Provide police accountability via independent citizen oversight of law enforcement and publicly available data on officer conduct.**
- **Disseminate information to the public about policing policies, recruitment, procedures for complaint/ commendation, and the rights and responsibilities of citizens and officers in interactions with each other.**
- **Provide sufficient psychological services and counseling to meet stress-related needs of police personnel.**
- **Staff police departments to reflect the diversity of the communities they serve and establish recruitment efforts that reflect this principle.**
- **Train police to identify individuals with mental health conditions, disabilities, or substance abuse/ addiction, so that officers will request support from appropriate medical and mental health professionals, with the goal of diverting those individuals into treatment instead of jail.**
- **Require all officers to render first aid to people who have been injured as a result of police action.**

- Conduct comprehensive background checks, to include such history as PTSD, domestic violence, sex offenses, and affiliations with domestic terrorist groups, for all applicants to law enforcement positions.
- Establish de-escalation (the use of time, distance, communications and available resources whenever it is safe to do so) and anti-bias training and ensure that all staff are provided with this training.
- Authorize minimal use of force during police encounters with the public and consider deadly force only when necessary to prevent imminent death or serious bodily injury.

Pre-trial Procedures — actions taken after an individual has been arrested, which embody the constitutional presumption of innocence

- Ensure no person suffers discrimination before the law due to their economic status nor should they be subject to risk assessment tools that can produce biased outcomes.
- Provide adequate numbers of public defenders to defend indigent accused.
- Provide prosecutors, defense attorneys, court counselors, and judges with regular training on alternatives to incarceration, including pre-trial diversion and restorative justice practices.
- Recognize that mental health conditions and substance abuse/addictions are public health issues, not crimes.
- Implement the use of specialty courts, e.g. drug treatment courts and restorative justice programs.
- Consider community-based treatment programs and other alternatives to incarceration when appropriate.

Sentencing — judgment made after an individual has been declared to be guilty

- Consider the individual circumstances of the person charged and nature of the crime, rather than mandatory minimum sentences.
- Consider split sentencing and/or alternatives to incarceration when appropriate.

Incarceration — policies and procedures that apply to employees of and incarcerated individuals in local jails and state prisons

- Ensure that all correctional systems provide humane, dignified, non-discriminatory treatment of incarcerated people and personnel, including appropriate health care and access to community-based rehabilitation programs.
- Eliminate the practice of solitary confinement.
- Ensure that incarcerated people and corrections officers have clear, safe, and accessible ways to report abuse.
- Address recidivism by instituting programs that focus on rehabilitation, education, mental health treatment, substance abuse recovery, and transitional programs.
- Adapt case management services to match education, behavior, job training, work, and mental health programs with the needs of incarcerated individuals.
- Provide sufficient psychological services, including training and evaluation, to meet the needs of corrections officers.
- Encourage family and community visitations and ways to maintain contact.
- Eliminate private prisons. Until space in public prisons is available, ensure that private prisons comply with all of the standards for state-run jails and prisons.

Re-entry — programs in place during and after incarceration to help individuals become successful members of their communities

- Collaborate with community-based organizations to facilitate reintegration of people released from prison.
- Provide pre- and post-release programs, inclusive of probation services, to prepare as well as assess and address the needs of people re-entering the community.
- Remove technical violations of parole as a reason to return an individual to prison.

General — statements that apply to some or all of the above categories

- Standardize data and setting up systems so that information can be easily shared among criminal justice agencies.
- Rely on evidence-based research in decision-making about criminal justice programs and policies.

League History

The Criminal Justice position was adopted by delegates at Convention 2022.

Equality of Opportunity

The League's Position

Statement of Position on Equality of Opportunity, as revised by the national board in January 1989, based on positions announced by the national board in January 1969, adopted by the 1972 Convention, expanded by the 1980 Convention and the 2010 Convention:

The League of Women Voters of the United States believes that the federal government shares with other levels of government the responsibility to provide equality of opportunity for education, employment, and housing for all persons in the United States regardless of their race, color, gender, religion, national origin, age, sexual orientation, or disability. Employment opportunities in modern, technological societies are closely related to education; therefore, the League supports federal programs to increase the education and training of disadvantaged people. The League supports federal efforts to prevent and/or remove discrimination in education, employment, and housing and to help communities bring about racial integration of their school systems.

The League of Women Voters of the United States supports equal rights for all regardless of sex. The League supports action to bring laws into compliance with the ERA: a) to eliminate or amend those laws that have the effect of discriminating on the basis of sex; b) to promote laws that support the goals of the ERA; c) to strengthen the enforcement of such existing laws.

The League of Women Voters of the United States supports equal rights for all under state and federal law. LWVUS supports legislation to equalize the legal rights, obligations, and benefits available to same-gender couples with those available to heterosexual couples. LWVUS supports legislation to permit same-gender couples to marry under civil law. The League believes that the civil status of marriage is already clearly distinguished from the religious institution of marriage and that religious rights will be preserved.

Further Guidelines and Criteria

In more specific terms, the kinds of programs the League supports include:

- Programs in basic education, occupational education, and retraining when needed at any point of an individual's working career.
- Expanded opportunities in apprenticeship and on-the-job training programs.
- Child-care centers for preschool children to give parents the opportunity for employment.
- Greatly increased educational opportunity through compensatory programs for disadvantaged groups beginning at the preschool level and extending through secondary education.
- Federal financial aid to help needy students remain in high school and to take advantage of post-high school training and education.
- A regional approach to problems of economically depressed areas that cuts across state lines. This approach can be handled administratively by such means as interstate cooperation or more formal interstate compacts, or commissions made up of representatives of state and federal governments. Development programs should reflect the needs of the particular area and can include such measures as provision of education and training for available jobs, encouragement of new industry in the area, development and conservation of natural resources, and the building of public facilities.
- Programs that would inform individuals of their civil rights in education, employment, and housing, and of the opportunities open to them.
- Full use of mediation and conciliation in efforts to bring about integration of minority groups into full participation in community life.
- A federal clearinghouse for the exchange of information on solutions communities have found to problems of integration in employment, education, and housing.
- Programs to bring about effective integration of schools through federal technical assistance such as training programs and institutes for teachers and school administrators.
- Withholding federal funds from school districts that fail to meet realistic and effective guidelines and standards for school integration.
- Withholding government contracts from businesses and industries that discriminate in employment.
- An effective federal fair employment practices agency.

Education and Employment Criteria

In evaluating federal programs that have been, or will be, established to provide equality of opportunity for education and employment, the League will support those programs that largely fulfill the following criteria:

- The nationwide effort to achieve equality of opportunity in education and employment should include participation of government at all levels and encourage the participation of private institutions.
- Programs should be carefully tailored to the educational or employment needs of the people they are intended to reach.
- People for whom community action programs are designed should be involved in the planning and implementation of those programs.
- The programs should be carried out by personnel competent to meet the specific requirements of their jobs.
- Programs should assist people to become self-supporting, contributing members of society.
- The programs should be nondiscriminatory with provisions for enforcement.

- Research, pilot projects, and continuing evaluation should be encouraged and, where feasible, built into programs.
- Programs may be closely related but should avoid unnecessary duplication.
- State and local governments should contribute to the extent their resources permit; at the same time, adequate federal funds for the establishment and continuation of programs should be available if necessary.

Fair Housing Criteria

The following criteria should be applied to programs and policies to provide equal opportunity for access to housing without discrimination:

- Opportunities for purchase or renting of homes, and for borrowing money for housing should not be restricted because of discriminatory reasons such as race, color, sex, religion, or national origin.
- Responsibility in the nationwide effort to achieve equality of opportunity for access to housing resides with government at all levels and with the private sector — builders, lending institutions, realtors, labor unions, business and industry, news media, civic organizations, educational institutions, churches, and private citizens.
- The continued existence of patterns of discrimination depends on the covert support of community leaders, institutions, and residents. Award or withdrawal of federal contracts and placement of federal installations should be used as levers to change this covert support.
- After positive steps such as mediation and conciliation have been exhausted, the federal government should have the option for selective withholding of federal funds where patterns of discrimination in access to housing occur. In applying the option to withhold funds, the federal government should weigh the effects of its actions on the welfare of lower-income and minority groups.
- Federal programs should include provisions to guarantee equal opportunity for access to housing. Federal funds should not be used to perpetuate discrimination.
- In the enforcement of fair-housing laws, speedy resolution should be ensured. Administrative procedures and responsibilities should be clearly defined and widely publicized.
- Mediation and legal redress should be readily available. The process should ensure every possible protection for both complainant and persons or institutions against whom complaints are lodged. Avenues for mediation and legal redress should be widely publicized and should be easily accessible.
- Funding should be adequate to provide trained, competent staff for public education to inform citizens of the provisions of fair-housing legislation, of their fair-housing rights, and of procedures to be followed in securing them. Adequate funding should also be available for mediation and for all aspects of speedy enforcement.
- There should be continued evaluation to provide a basis for revision and strengthening of all procedures so that equality of opportunity for access to housing can be accomplished.

League History

By 1966, the League had reached its first position on combatting poverty and discrimination: support of policies and programs to provide equal opportunity for all in education and employment. The position described general criteria and specific kinds of programs to further these goals.

"An evaluation of equality of opportunity for housing" was in the proposed program slated for 1968 Convention consideration. Two events that spring caused delegates to alter the normal sequence of study/consensus/position:

the shock waves in cities following the assassination of Dr. Martin Luther King, Jr. and the passage of a new civil rights bill that included fair housing.

Convinced that League members knew where they stood on fair housing, delegates amended the existing position at Convention, adding support for equality of opportunity for housing, and they redirected the study from an evaluation of the concept to an evaluation of the means to achieve the goal. By December 1969, members had endorsed criteria for ensuring fair housing and adequate housing supply.

The League has consistently supported federal programs aimed at combating poverty and discrimination and has worked at the community level for successful implementation. The list is long — starting with programs initiated under the long-defunct Office of Economic Opportunity (OEO), legal services, community action agencies, Job Corps, urban renewal, Model Cities, and others designed to provide equal access to housing, employment, and education.

When the federal government combined many categorical grant programs into block grants, the League found new ways to work for the goals and policies it supports. In 1973, the League began monitoring the impact of the General Revenue Sharing (GRS) program on poverty and discrimination. This resulted in reforms incorporated into the 1976 GRS amendments that tightened weak antidiscrimination provisions and expanded citizen participation and accountability requirements, but efforts to direct more funds to jurisdictions in greatest need failed.

Since the late 1970s, threats to League goals and policies have taken the form of frequent legislative and executive attempts to drastically reduce federal funding of League-supported programs, as well as persistent moves to dilute existing civil rights laws and policies. The League has actively opposed tuition tax credits, budget cuts in social welfare programs, and large, untargeted block grants, while supporting strengthened fair-housing legislation and civil rights legislation to reaffirm congressional intent in passing Title IX of the *Education Amendments of 1972* that the law be broadly interpreted and applied.

The League's Social Policy positions were revised in 1989. The Equal Access to Education, Employment, and Housing position was combined with Equal Rights into one Equality of Opportunity position.

The 1992 Convention added language to the Equality of Opportunity position, stating that it referred to "all persons, regardless of their race, color, gender, religion, national origin, age, sexual orientation or disability." In July 1992, LWVUS joined the National Endorsement Campaign in calling for the extension of existing civil rights laws by local, state, and federal legislation to prohibit discrimination against lesbians and gay men in jobs, housing, and public accommodations. In the 106th Congress (1999-2001), LWVUS supported federal legislation targeting hate crimes. Convention 2010 added language to the Equality of Opportunity position to equalize the rights of same-gender couples to those of heterosexual couples.

EMPLOYMENT

The League has supported federal job training programs and is on record in favor of a full employment policy, i.e., the concept of assuring a job for all those able and seeking to work. In 1978, the League supported passage of the *Humphrey-Hawkins* bill to promote full employment.

The League supported the public service employment (PSE) component of the Comprehensive Employment and Training Program (CETA) during the 1970s and worked for the passage of emergency jobs legislation in 1983, spearheading a Call to Action for Jobs for Women that resulted in more funding for the types of public-service jobs that women traditionally perform. In 1994, the League unsuccessfully supported passage of the *Infrastructure Jobs Act* and the *Full Employment Opportunity Act*, both targeted specifically toward urban areas.

FAIR HOUSING

The League made passage of the Fair Housing Amendments a priority in 1980, which passed the House but was filibustered in the Senate. Another attempt in 1983 – 84 was put on hold in light of more-pressing civil rights issues.

In addition to the League supporting the reauthorization of the *Home Mortgage Disclosure Act* (HMDA) in 1982, LWVEF's participation in a Department of Housing and Urban Development (HUD)-funded project in 1979 – 81 enabled local Leagues to promote the entry of women into the mortgage credit market. This involvement also sparked interest in the problems of single-headed households, displaced homemakers, and discrimination against families with children, which LWV supported prohibitions against throughout the 80s.

In 2005, the League urged Congress to create the Affordable Housing Fund, a long-overdue step toward addressing the housing crisis that confronts families with low and extremely low incomes. It also urged House members to protect activities of the nonprofit groups providing the bulk of housing services for our poorest communities. In June 2020 during the COVID-19 pandemic, LWVUS signed on to a coalition letter authored by The Leadership Conference and the National Community Reinvestment Coalition calling on congressional representatives to vote in favor of *H.J. Res. 90*, a *Congressional Review Act* resolution of disapproval to nullify rulemaking by the Office of the Comptroller of Currency. Changing the rules would have undermined the *Community Reinvestment Act of 1977* by allowing for large investments where the largest rewards could be made, rather than requiring smaller targeted investments in underserved neighborhoods.

Nondiscrimination & Affirmative Action

Through legislative and regulatory approaches, as well as litigation, the League advocates affirmative action programs for minorities and women. Action has included a lawsuit to compel the US Department of Labor (DOL) to issue goals and timetables governing the employment of women in nontraditional jobs and apprenticeship programs and prodding to ensure enforcement. The League has worked to combat administrative initiatives to restrict the enforcement authority of DOL's Office of Federal Contract Compliance Programs (OFCCP) and the Equal Employment Opportunity Commission (EEOC). Since 1977, the League has supported measures to combat employment discrimination in Congress itself.

The League has been outspoken in supporting affirmative action programs and policies. That support has included filing amicus briefs in key affirmative action lawsuits, including *Kaiser Aluminum and Chemical Corp. v. Weber* in 1979, *Boston Firefighters Union, Local 718 v. Boston Chapter NAACP* in 1983, *Firefighters Local Union No. 1784 v. Stotts* in 1984, and *Williams v. City of New Orleans* in 1983. The League has actively opposed attempts by OFCCP to weaken regulations that govern the federal contract compliance program. During the 1985 – 86 Supreme Court term, the League filed amicus briefs in three key affirmative action cases: *Local 28 Sheet Metal Workers v. EEOC, Local*

93 *International Association of Firefighters v. City of Cleveland*, and *Wygant v. Jackson Board of Education*. The Court reaffirmed the validity of voluntary race-based affirmative action in these cases.

In 1986, LWVUS signed on to another amicus brief filed in the US Supreme Court, *Johnson v. Transportation Agency*. In 1987, the Court held that public employers may adopt voluntary affirmative action plans to attain workforce balances in traditionally segregated job categories, the first instance in which the Supreme Court upheld a gender-based affirmative action plan.

In 1988, the League participated in a Supreme Court amicus brief in *Patterson v. McLean Credit Union*. In its 1989 decision, the Court reaffirmed that Section 1981 of the *Civil Rights Act of 1986*, which prohibits racial discrimination in contracts, applies to private acts of discrimination. However, the Court also held that Section 1981 does not apply to racial harassment or other discriminatory working conditions that arise after an employment contract has been entered.

Between 1984 and 1988, the League was an active player in successfully urging Congress to pass the *Civil Rights Restoration Act*, which restored four anti-discrimination laws that were narrowed by the Supreme Court's 1984 *Grove City v. Bell* decision. Subsequently, the League endorsed the *Civil Rights Act*, which reversed a series of 1989 Supreme Court decisions that seriously weakened federal employment discrimination laws and strengthened protections under federal civil rights laws. In 1990, the bill passed both houses of Congress but was vetoed by the President. In 1991 a compromise bill was passed by Congress and signed by the President. The League did not actively support this bill, in part because it placed a monetary limit on damages for sex discrimination, including sexual harassment. In 1992, the League joined other groups in supporting the *Equal Remedies Act*, which would remove the monetary limit on damages in civil rights laws.

In response to continued congressional attacks, the League joined other concerned organizations in the Leadership Conference on Civil and Human Rights to reaffirm strong support for affirmative action programs.

In 2008, the League joined other organizations in support of the *Americans with Disabilities Act* (ADA) *Amendments Act of 2008* (ADAAA), designed to restore the ADA to its original intent and ensure coverage for Americans with disabilities in all aspects of society. The bill was passed and signed into law. In 2012, the League joined an amicus brief in *Fisher v. University of Texas*, an affirmative action case before the Supreme Court, urging the Court to recognize that diversity in higher education is crucial for the success of our multi-racial democracy.

The League continued to support this line of cases and in 2019 joined a group of social justice organizations in support of *Bostock v. Clayton County, et al*, a trio of cases challenging whether anti-LGBTQ discrimination is a form of sex discrimination in order to demonstrate to the court the importance of this issue to civil rights litigation nationwide. In addition, the League has condemned discrimination and hate, speaking out against white supremacists in Charlottesville, asking Congress to demilitarize our immigration enforcement, and not build a border wall. The League also urged Congress to support the *No Hate Act*, legislation establishing grants for state and local governments to combat hate crimes while authorizing additional penalties for hate crime offenses.

Delegates to Convention 2020 passed a resolution around social justice reform. The resolution states:
We Resolve First, That the League advocates against systemic racism in the justice system and, at a minimum,

for preventing excessive force and brutality by law enforcement. We also call for prompt actions by all League members to advocate within every level of government to eradicate systemic racism, and the harm that it causes;

We Resolve Second, That the League help our elected officials and all Americans recognize these truths to be self-evident; that Black, Indigenous, and all people of color (BIPOC) deserve equal protection under the law; and that we demand solutions for the terrible wrongs done, so that regardless of race, ethnicity, religion, disability, and gender identity or sexual orientation, we may truly become a nation "indivisible, with liberty and justice for all."

Pay Equity

The League's work on pay equity (equal pay for jobs of comparable worth) stemmed from member concern over the feminization of poverty. The League played a key role at the national level through its work with the broad-based National Committee on Pay Equity in the 1980s. In 1986, LWVEF participated in an amicus brief before the US Supreme Court in the pay equity case *Bazemore v. Friday*. The Court ruled a state agency may be held liable for disparities in salaries between Black and white employees, even if the disparities were caused by racial discrimination that occurred before the 1964 *Civil Rights Act*.

State and local Leagues have also endorsed legislative efforts to undertake job evaluation studies, as well as efforts to implement pay equity for public and private employees and prohibit questions about salary history.

Equal Rights for Women

In 1972, shortly after congressional passage of the Equal Rights Amendment (ERA), the national Convention overwhelmingly approved support of "equal rights for all regardless of sex" as a necessary extension of the League's long-term support for equal opportunity for all. Delegates also voted to support the ERA. With this decisive action, the League came full circle in giving priority support once again to equal rights for women and men.

The foremothers of the women's movement, in their 1848 Conventions at Seneca Falls and Rochester, New York, rooted the movement in a demand for women's equality before the law. The right to vote came to be seen as the key that would unlock the door to the other rights. This vision sustained the National American Woman Suffrage Association (NAWSA), the forerunner of the League.

When the 19th Amendment was passed in 1920, suffrage leaders divided on strategy. Some founded the National Woman's Party, which sponsored the first ERA, introduced in Congress in 1923. Others — the founders of the League among them — decided not to push for an ERA. While it's hard to imagine a time in which the League opposed the ERA., delegates at the League's 1921 Convention decided that an ERA might adversely affect new, hard-won state labor legislation, which offered some protection to tens of thousands of women working in nonunionized and similar jobs.

Moreover, though it was an organization of women, the early LWV wanted to affirm strongly that its interests and lobbying activities were not confined to women's issues. In the 1920s and 1930s, the League set the stage for future program development by focusing on a broad range of social issues. Many were of obvious concern for women: the *Sheppard-Towner Act*, which provided federal funds for infant and maternity care; the removal of discrimination against women in immigration and naturalization laws; equality for women in the *Civil Service Classification Act*; and equal pay for equal work. During the same period, local and state Leagues worked to eliminate sex discrimination affecting jury duty, property rights, the treatment of women offenders, and a number of other issues.

Through the 1940s, the national League program included "removal of legal and administrative discriminations against women," but retained its statement in opposition to an ERA until 1954, when the national program was restructured and its opposition was removed.

As the League became active in the civil rights struggle of the 1960s, members grew acutely aware of the parallels between the status of women and minorities. Many state and local Leagues pursued women's issues with new vigor, and a strong push for women's issues developed at the national level, culminating in the 1972 Convention's action to support the ERA.

Subsequent Conventions have reaffirmed the League's commitment to the ERA. The 1980 Convention took the League's commitment a step further, voting to use the new supportive ERA position as a basis not only for ratification efforts, but also to work on gender-based discrimination and actively work to bring laws into compliance with the goals of the ERA.

In 1972, lobbying for ratification — and against rescission — on a state-by-state basis became a top League priority at the national and state levels.

In 1979, LWVUS organized the National Business Council (NBC) for ERA, the first formal structure to bring major business leaders into the fight for ratification. In 1981 under an LWVUS/NBC partnership, a volunteer task force of advertising executives developed and produced radio ads designed to "sell" the ERA in seven unratified states. Throughout the media campaign, LWVUS provided extensive technical and financial assistance to state Leagues and ERA coalitions and worked to organize business efforts in the states.

The ratification process was not completed by the June 30, 1982, deadline set by Congress, but the League's support of a constitutional guarantee of equal protection under the law remains strong. The League supported reintroduction of the ERA in Congress in 1982 and helped lead a lobbying effort that culminated in a narrow November 1983 defeat in the House.

In July 1993, the League signed on to an amicus brief in the Supreme Court case, *J.E.B. v. T.B*, which argued that sex discrimination in jury selection is prohibited by the Equal Protection Clause of the 14th Amendment of the US Constitution. League participation was based on support for actions to bring laws into compliance with the ERA. In 1994, the Supreme Court agreed, ruling that state laws allowing jury challenges based solely on sex are unconstitutional.

The League continued to work to achieve the goals of the expanded ERA position while laying the groundwork for passage and ratification of the ERA in the 1980s and 1990s. Issues focused on fighting for pay equity and support for the *Economic Equity Act*, which included provisions to eliminate sex discrimination in pensions and insurance. In 1996, the League endorsed the *Women's Pension Equity Act*, legislation designed to make pension law simpler and more even-handed.

At 2018 Convention, the League again voiced strong support for final ratification of the ERA after the support of the 37th state, Illinois, pushed the amendment toward the finish line. In 2020, Virginia became the 38th state to ratify the ERA, crossing the necessary threshold for the ERA to become a constitutional amendment. LWVUS supported legislation introduced in Congress to remove the ratification deadline and a House resolution expressing that the ERA is valid as the 28th Amendment to the Constitution. LWVUS also worked with the ERA Coalition to urge the Attorney General to direct the US Department of Justice's Office of Legal Counsel to withdraw its 2020 memo that said Congress didn't have the authority to extend the ratification deadline.

At the 2022 Convention, delegates voted to add the ERA to the LWVUS program to reaffirm the League's commitment of resources and focus to accomplish its passage. LWVUS continues to connect Leagues across the country working on this issue to push for state-level measures and identify ways to leverage the League network to support congressional advocacy.

On the international front, the League of Women Voters supports the United Nations Convention for the Elimination of All Forms of Discrimination Against Women (CEDAW) and is on the Steering Committee of the NGO UNICEF Working Group on Girls at the UN, which formed an International Network for Girls, a global advocacy network.

Same Gender Equality

The 1992 Convention added language to the Equality of Opportunity position, stating that it referred to "all persons, regardless of their race, color, gender, religion, national origin, age, sexual orientation, or disability."

In July 1992, LWVUS joined the National Endorsement Campaign in calling for the extension of existing civil rights laws by local, state, and federal legislation to prohibit discrimination against lesbians and gay men in jobs, housing, and public accommodations.

In the 106th Congress (1999 – 2001), LWVUS supported federal legislation targeting hate crimes. In 2004 and 2006, the League opposed the Federal Marriage Amendment, which would permanently write discrimination into the United States Constitution by limiting fundamental protections such as health care benefits for same-sex partners. Convention 2010 added language to the Equality of Opportunity position to equalize the rights of same-gender couples to those of heterosexual couples.

During the 117th Congress (2021 – 2022), LWVUS continued its support of federal hate crimes legislations in sending a letter encouraging the passage of *Khalid Jabara and Heather Heyer National Opposition to Hate, Assault, and Threats to Equality Act (Jabara-Heyer NO HATE Act)*.

Education

Integration

The League is committed to racial integration of schools as a necessary condition for equal access to education.

When busing became one means of achieving school desegregation, Leagues worked to ensure that laws were obeyed peacefully — building coalitions, running rumor-control centers, and sometimes going to court to gain compliance. At the national level, the League worked to oppose anti-busing/anti-desegregation initiatives in Congress.

The League served as an amicus in Supreme Court challenges to the desegregation process. LWVEF maintained a desegregation clearinghouse and assembled League leaders and national policy experts for a workshop on metropolitan school desegregation in 1982 – 84.

Quality Education

The 1974 – 76 LWVUS Program included the phrase "equal access to quality education," reflecting League recognition that "equality" and "quality" are inseparable. However, LWVUS has never undertaken a process for determining a common League definition of quality education that could serve as a basis for action nationwide. Therefore, when the definition of quality is a key factor in a state or local community, a local or state League must conduct its own study rather than relying on the LWVUS position to take action. Many Leagues that have member agreement on quality education in specific terms use their positions to support an array of local and state educational reforms. A number of Leagues have used this position to oppose private school vouchers. LWVUS is a member of the National Coalition for Public Education, which opposes vouchers.

Tuition Tax Credits

The 1978 Convention directed the national board to oppose tax credits for families of children attending private elementary and secondary schools. Convention action was based on League support for equal access to education and support for desegregation as a means of promoting equal access. The League is concerned about the negative impact that tuition tax credits would have on the public schools by encouraging flight, particularly from desegregated schools. The League also supports federal efforts through IRS regulation to deny tax-exempt status to racially discriminatory "segregation academies."

Federal Programs

The League supports many federal education programs, some designed to meet the special educational needs of the poor and minorities and others to give women and minorities equal education opportunities. In 2012, the League conducted a study further defining the role of the federal government in education.

The League worked for passage of Title IX of the Education Amendments of 1972, which prohibits sex discrimination in educational institutions that receive federal aid. Subsequently, the League has focused on thwarting congressional attempts to dilute Title IX, as well as on advancing federal enforcement efforts. At the national level, the League was active in major court challenges to Title IX, defending key provisions and urging a broad interpretation of Title IX's scope. In 1983, the League filed an amicus brief in *Grove City College v. Bell*, a major Supreme Court case that narrowed considerably the prohibitions of Title IX. In 1984, after the Court's decision, the League supported efforts in Congress for new legislation clarifying congressional intent on the scope of coverage of Title IX and similar civil rights statutes.

In 2003, the League responded to a Department of Education effort to scale back Title IX. LWVUS opposed attempts to weaken the law and lobbied in support of congressional resolutions affirming that Title IX had made great progress in establishing equal opportunity for girls and women in education and school athletics. In July 2003, the Department of Education affirmed its support for Title IX without change. In September 2004, LWVUS signed on to an amicus brief in *Jackson v. Birmingham Board of Education*, supporting Title IX's original intent of broad and effective protection against gender discrimination by ensuring that individuals who bring discriminatory practices to light are protected from retaliation and reprisal.

Under an LWVEF project to monitor sex equity in vocational education programs in 1981 – 82, several state Leagues evaluated progress toward meeting federal sex-equity mandates. Vocational education programs have significant impact on employment, particularly for women who have difficulty gaining access to training programs for higher paying jobs. In addition, LWV promoted the enrollment of girls and young women in math and science courses to prepare them for the jobs of the future.

In 2020, the League joined civil rights partners on an amicus brief in the case of *Hecox v. Little*, a lawsuit challenging *Idaho's Fairness in Women's Sports Act*. The Idaho law prohibits transgender students from taking part in female sports, and the harms would be felt by trans students as well as by intersex persons, non-binary persons, and many cisgender women and girls. The district court concluded that the Act constitutes a violation of the equal protection clause and the amicus brief highlights that the Act also violates Title IX's prohibition on sex discrimination.

Education Financing

Many state and local Leagues have identified inequities in education financing during the course of their own program studies and have worked for reforms. Action on school financing equity takes place predominantly at the state level, where school financing laws are made.

Federal Role in Public Education

The League's Position

Statement of Position on Federal Role in Public Education as announced by the national board in March 2012:

The League of Women Voters believes that the federal government shares with other levels of government the responsibility to provide an equitable, quality public education for all children from pre-K through grade 12. A quality public education is essential for a strong, viable, and sustainable democratic society and is a civil right.

The League believes that the role of the federal government should include the following:

- **Provide leadership and vision to promote a quality education for all children.**
- **Provide broad common standards developed by educational experts upon which states and local education agencies can build.**
- **Provide a suggested curricular structure or framework as a guide to state and local education agencies to develop their own curricula.**
- **Provide a national assessment that clearly informs teachers, parents, and students about how well individual students have mastered criteria established at the national level.**
- **Provide a national assessment that informs districts how well their populations compare to other populations similar to theirs.**

- Provide a combination of competitive grants and non-competitive funding to states and local school districts to achieve equity among states and populations.

The League of Women Voters believes that an equitable, quality public education is critical for students. While the League recognizes that there are instances where the federal government's involvement is the only way to achieve universal change (e.g., desegregation, special needs population, gender equity), we also recognize that primary responsibility for public education resides with the states. In accordance with the League of Women Voters' position on Equal Rights, the League continues to support equity in public education for all through:

- Broad guidelines for accountability, leaving implementation to the state and local education agencies.
- Adequate funding for sources that support the broad goals of national standards.
- Mechanisms for local and state funding with adequate federal support for mandates that require less-burdensome, compliance-based reporting and regulations.

The League of Women Voters believes a basic role of the federal government in funding education should be to achieve equity among states and populations on the basis of identified needs. This should be done with full understanding that equity does not mean equal, given that some populations are more expensive to educate than others and some localities have specific needs.

The League believes that the federal government should be primarily responsible for funding any programs mandated by the federal government on local education agencies. Although the League recognizes equity in education depends on meeting basic human needs of children and of their families, the costs associated with providing equitable access to safe neighborhoods and secure housing do not belong in the education budget. Major programs of federal funding for public education (i.e., *Elementary and Secondary Education Act*) should be targeted toward children living in poverty and/or children with special needs.

The federal government has the responsibility to monitor and support access to the following:

- High-quality teaching and learning, supported by quality current learning materials and well-maintained educational facilities.
- Access to health care needs (e.g., hearing, vision, dental, immunization, school-based health clinics at the secondary level) and nutritionally adequate food (i.e., school-based meals under "free and reduced meal programs").

The League of Women Voters believes that the first five years of a child's life are crucial in building the foundation for educational attainment and greatly impact success or failure in later life. Additionally, the League believes quality, developmentally appropriate, voluntary early learning experiences should be available to all children, with federally funded opportunities going first to children of poverty and/or with special needs. The League believes that the federal government should support the following:

- Early childhood education programs that include funding for parent education and involve child development, health, nutrition, and access to other supportive services such as mental health care for all children and their families.
- Research that documents quality early childhood education programs.
- Research that demonstrates the importance of linking state and local community partnerships with effective early childhood education programs and services.

League History

Convention 2010 delegates voted to embark on a two-year study of the Federal Role in Public Education. Local and state Leagues across the country participated in the study and a position was announced in March 2012.

Fiscal Policy

The League's Position

Statement of Position on Fiscal Policy, as adopted by 1984 Convention and as announced by the national board, March 1985, January 1986, and June 1986:

The League of Women Voters of the United States believes that federal fiscal policy should provide for adequate and flexible funding of federal government programs through an equitable tax system that is progressive overall and that relies primarily on a broad-based income tax; responsible deficit policies; and a federal role in providing mandatory, universal, old-age, survivors, disability, and health insurance.

Federal Deficit

The League of Women Voters of the United States believes that the current federal deficit should be reduced. In order to reduce the deficit, the government should rely primarily on reductions in defense spending through selective cuts and on increased revenue through a tax system that is broad-based with progressive rates. The government also should achieve whatever savings possible through improved efficiency and management. The League opposes across-the-board federal spending cuts.

The League recognizes that deficit spending is sometimes appropriate and therefore opposes a constitutionally mandated balanced budget for the federal government. The League could support deficit spending, if necessary, for stimulating the economy during recession and depression, meeting social needs in times of high unemployment, and meeting defense needs in times of national security crises. The League opposes a federal budget line-item veto.

Funding of Entitlements

The League of Women Voters of the United States believes that the federal government has a role in funding and providing for old-age, survivors, disability, and health insurance. For such insurance programs, participation should be mandatory and coverage should be universal. Federal deficit reduction should not be achieved by reducing Social Security benefits.

Tax Policy

LWVUS believes that the federal tax system should: be fair and equitable; provide adequate resources for government programs while allowing flexibility for financing future program changes; be understandable to the taxpayer and encourage compliance; and accomplish its objectives without creating undue administrative problems.

The League of Women Voters of the United States believes that the federal tax system, taken as a whole, should be progressive, not proportional.

The League supports income as the major tax base for federal revenues; believes that the federal income tax should be broad-based with minimal tax preferences and a progressive rate structure; and opposes a value-added tax or a national sales tax in the federal revenue system.

Further Guidelines

Under this position, the League of Women Voters would support tax measures that broaden the base and improve the equity of the income tax while working to incorporate progressivity into the tax system, taken as a whole. In evaluating specific tax preferences, the League will use the following criteria: whether the tax preference promotes equity and progressivity; whether the tax preference effectively furthers League of Women Voters program goals; whether the tax preference is the most efficient means of achieving its purpose; and whether the revenue loss from the tax preference is justifiable.

League History

The 1984 Convention adopted criteria for evaluating federal tax policies as a League position and a two-year study of US fiscal policy. The three-part study focused on tax policy, deficit issues, and entitlement funding. League members completed the tax policy portion of the study in time to position the League as a major force in the tax reform movement of 1985 – 86. As Congress debated major legislation to broaden the income tax base, the League became a recognized leader in pushing for passage of reform legislation. The League achieved a major victory after mobilizing League members and activists to urge members of Congress to pass broad-based, fair, and progressive legislation. As part of its strong legislative campaign, the League opposed a value-added tax as regressive. The League supported taxing capital gains as ordinary income and urged the removal of loopholes in the tax law.

The final two stages of the study, concluded in 1986, gave the League new tools for responding to federal deficit and budget issues. Under the deficit position, the League has supported selective cuts in defense spending that target military investment rather than readiness, in accord with the LWVUS Military Policy and Defense Spending position.

In determining what national security crises might call for deficit spending, the League is guided by its International Relations positions, including US Relations with Developing Countries. The League can also, if necessary, support selective cuts in nondefense discretionary spending. In determining its stance, LWVUS will be guided by its Social Policy, Natural Resources, Representative Government, and International Relations positions and priorities.

As Congress continued in 1986 to grapple with extraordinary federal deficits and budget dilemmas, the League took a comprehensive approach to the budget battle that combined support for increased funding for human needs, selective cuts in defense spending and necessary revenue increases. The deficit position enabled the League to oppose a balanced budget constitutional amendment in March 1986.

The deficit position, like the tax policy position, applies only at the federal level. Thus, LWVUS opposition to the line-item veto and to a constitutionally mandated balanced budget applies only to the federal government. Under the LWVUS deficit position, state Leagues will be expected to oppose state legislative resolutions and other actions calling for a constitutional amendment requiring a balanced budget.

Since the state budgeting process occurs under different constitutional arrangements and laws, the conclusions of the federal deficit study do not overrule any current state League positions on state budgeting processes, nor can they be used at the state level without separate state League study and member agreement on the subjects.

The Funding of Entitlements position enables LWVUS to support efforts to expand participation in the Social Security system (including participation by state and local government employees and other excluded groups). The League is opposed to measures that allow individuals to opt out of the system or measures to substitute private programs. The League opposes reducing Social Security benefits to achieve deficit reduction.

In 1990, LWVUS urged the President and Congress to produce actual deficit reductions rather than masking the problem and prodded them to rely primarily on reductions in defense spending and increased revenues through progressive taxes. In 1992, LWVUS urged the President and Congress to address the recession and promote economic development. The League called for tax and budget reform and for rebuilding the nation's infrastructure.

As the federal deficit grew, the "balanced-budget" amendment to the Constitution was introduced in Congress as a political expedient to control the federal budget. The League successfully fought against passage in the House in 1992 and both houses in 1994. The League argued it would dangerously upset the federal balance of powers and hurt the economy.

In 1995, the federal deficit began to shrink, but the push for a constitutional amendment to require a balanced budget grew. The League lobbied and brought grassroots pressure to oppose this dangerous and misleading proposal, arguing that it would hamstring the government's ability to stimulate the economy in time of recession and respond to natural disasters. Amendment opponents prevailed then and in 1996 – 97. League grassroots pressure was key in defeating balanced budget constitutional amendment efforts.

In December 1998, the League and others signed a letter urging President Clinton to use the budget surplus to invest in programs that benefit the American people, including education, health care, human needs, and the environment.

In 1999, when debate over Social Security's future heated up with various proposals to privatize the Social Security system, LWVUS endorsed the principles of the New Century Alliance for Social Security, emphasizing Social Security's central role in family income protection. The League's stance is based on support for a federal role in providing mandatory, universal, old-age, survivors, disability, and health insurance.

In the 108th Congress (2003 – 2005), the League joined with several hundred other organizations, lobbying against tax cut legislation because it was fundamentally unfair and jeopardized the nation's ability to meet its domestic and foreign responsibilities.

Responding to Congressional efforts to cut funding to the poorest of Americans during the 112th (2011 – 2013) and 113th (2013 – 2015) Congresses, the League lobbied in support of principles and programs that benefit Americans with low incomes, while opposing tax breaks for the wealthiest in the country.

The League again activated its grassroots network and lobbied against the balanced budget amendment in 2018 when both chambers of Congress attempted to move it forward.

Health Care

Statement of Position on Health Care, as announced by the national board, April 1993 supplemented by concurrence to add Behavioral Health, June 2016 and updated by concurrence at Convention 2022.

The League's Position

GOALS: The League of Women Voters of the United States believes that a basic level of quality health care at an affordable cost should be available to all US residents. Other US health care policy goals should include the equitable distribution of services, efficient and economical delivery of care, advancement of medical research and technology, and a reasonable total national expenditure level for health care.

Basic Level of Quality Care

Every US resident should have access to a basic level of care that includes the prevention of disease, health promotion and education, primary care (including prenatal and reproductive health), acute care, long-term care, and mental health care. Every US resident should have access to affordable, quality in- and out-patient behavioral health care, including needed medications and supportive service that is integrated with, and achieves parity with, physical health care. Dental, vision, and hearing care also are important but lower in priority. The League believes that under any system of health care reform, consumers/patients should be permitted to purchase services or insurance coverage beyond the basic level.

The League supports regulatory incentives to encourage the development of cost-effective alternative ways of delivering and paying for health care. Delivery programs may take place in a variety of settings, including the home and online, and must provide quality care, meaning consistent with "standard of care" guidelines, by trained and licensed personnel, staffed adequately to ensure their own and patient safety.

As public health crises increasingly reveal, a health program should protect the health of its most vulnerable populations, urban and rural, in order to protect the health of everyone. In addition, all programs should be evaluated regularly.

Decisions on medical procedures that would prolong life should be made jointly by patient, family, and licensed health care provider. Patient decisions, including those made prior to need, should be respected.

Financing and Administration

The League favors a national health insurance plan financed through general taxes in place of individual insurance premiums. As the United States moves toward a national health insurance plan, an employer-based system of health care reform that provides universal access is acceptable to the League. The League supports administration of the US health care system either by a combination of the private and public sectors or by a combination of federal, state, and/or regional government agencies.

The League supports the single-payer concept as a viable and desirable approach to implementing League positions on equitable access, affordability, and financial feasibility. In any proposed health care financing system, the League favors health insurance access independent of employment status.

Although the League prefers a health care financing system that includes all residents of the United States, in the absence of a federal program that achieves the goals of universal, affordable access to essential health services, the League supports health care programs financed by states which include continuation of federal funding and comply with League principles.

The League is opposed to a strictly private market-based model of financing the health care system. The League is also opposed to the administration of the health care system solely by the private sector or the states.

Taxes

The League supports increased taxes to finance a basic level of health care for all US residents, provided health care reforms contain effective cost-control strategies.

Cost Control

The League believes that efficient and economical delivery of care can be enhanced by cost-control methods. Specific cost-control methods should reflect the most-credible, evidence-based research available on how health care financing policy affects equitable access to health care, overall quality of care for individuals and populations, and total system costs of health care and its administration. Methods used should not exacerbate disparities in health outcomes among marginalized residents.

If they meet the above criteria, cost control methods could include:

- Reduction of administrative costs — both for the insurance program and for providers,
- Negotiated volume discounts for pharmaceuticals and durable medical equipment to bring prices closer to international levels — or importing of same to reduce costs.
- Evidence-based treatment protocols and drug formularies that include cost/benefit assessments of medical value.
- Malpractice reforms designed both to compensate patients for medical errors and to avoid future errors by encouraging robust quality improvement processes (at individual and systemic levels) and open communications with patients.
- Investment in well-care, such as prevention, family planning, patient education, primary care to increase health and reduce preventable adverse health events/expenditures.
- Investment in maternal/infant care, chronic disease management, and behavioral health care.
- Provision for short-term and long-term home-care services to reduce institutionalization.
- Regional planning for the allocation of personnel, facilities, and equipment.
- The establishment of maximum levels of public reimbursement to providers.
- The use of managed care.
- Utilization review of treatment.
- Mandatory second opinions before surgery or extensive treatment.
- Consumer accountability through deductibles and copayments.

Equity Issues

The League believes that health care services could be more equitably distributed by:

- Allocating medical resources to underserved areas.
- Providing for training health care professionals in needed fields of care.

- **Standardizing basic levels of service for publicly funded health care programs.**
- **Requiring insurance plans to use community rating instead of experience rating.**
- **Establishing insurance pools for small businesses and organizations**

Allocation of Resources to Individuals

The League believes that the ability of a patient to pay for services should not be a consideration in the allocation of health care resources. Limited resources should be allocated based on the following criteria considered together: the urgency of the medical condition, the life expectancy of the patient, the expected outcome of the treatment, the cost of the procedure, the duration of care, the quality of life of the patient after treatment, and the wishes of the patient and the family.

Public Participation

The League supports public input as integral to the process for determining health care coverage and funding. To participate in public discussion of health policy and share effectively in making policy decisions, residents must be provided with information on the health care system and the implications of health policy decisions.

Behavioral Health

The League supports:

- **Behavioral health as the nationally accepted term that includes both mental illness and substance use disorder.**
- **Access for all people to affordable, quality in- and out-patient behavioral health care, including needed medications and supportive services.**
- **Behavioral health care that is integrated with, and achieves parity with, physical health care.**
- **Early and affordable behavioral health diagnosis and treatment for children and youth from early childhood through adolescence.**
- **Early and appropriate diagnosis and treatment for children and adolescents that is family-focused and community-based.**
- **Access to safe and stable housing for people with behavioral health challenges, including those who are chronically homeless.**
- **Effective re-entry planning and follow-up for people released from both behavioral health hospitalization and the criminal justice system.**
- **Problem-solving or specialty courts, including mental health and drug courts, in all judicial districts to provide needed treatment and avoid inappropriate entry into the criminal justice system.**
- **Health education — from early childhood throughout life — that integrates all aspects of social, emotional, and physical health and wellness.**
- **Efforts to decrease the stigmatization of, and normalize, behavioral health problems and care.**

League History

Given the growing crisis in health care delivery and financing in the 1990s, the League developed a comprehensive position supporting a health care system that provides access to affordable, quality health care for all Americans and protects patients' rights.

In 1990, LWVUS undertook a two-year study of the funding and delivery of health care in the United States. Phase 1 studied the delivery and policy goals of the US health care system; Phase 2 focused on health care financing and administration. LWVUS announced its initial health care position in April 1992 and the final position in April 1993. The 2016 Convention updated the position by concurrence to include behavioral health.

The health care position outlines the goals LWVUS believes are fundamental for US health care policy. These include policies that promote access to a basic level of quality care at an affordable cost for all US residents and strong cost-control mechanisms to ensure the efficient and economical delivery of care. The Meeting Basic Human Needs position also addresses access to health care.

The health care position enumerates services League members believe are of highest priority for a basic level of quality care: the prevention of disease, health promotion and education, primary care (including prenatal and reproductive health care), acute care, long-term care, and mental health care. Dental, vision, and hearing care are recognized as important services but of lower priority when measured against the added cost involved. Comments from numerous state and local Leagues, however, emphasized that these services are essential for children.

To achieve more-equitable distribution of services, the League endorses increasing the availability of resources in medically underserved areas, training providers in needed fields of care, standardizing the services provided under publicly funded health care programs, and insurance reforms.

The LWVUS health care position includes explicit support for strong mechanisms to contain rising health care costs. Methods to promote the efficient and economical delivery of care in the United States include regional planning for the allocation of resources, reducing administrative costs, reforming the malpractice system, copayments and deductibles, and managed care. In accordance with the position's call for health care at an affordable cost, copayments and deductibles are acceptable cost-containment mechanisms only if they are based on an individual's ability to pay. In addition, cost-containment mechanisms should not interfere with the delivery of quality health care.

The position calls for a national health insurance plan financed through general taxes, commonly known as the "single-payer" approach. The position also supports an employer-based system that provides universal access to health care as an important step toward a national health insurance plan. The League opposes a strictly private market-based model of financing the health care system. Regarding administration of the US health care system, the League supports a combination of private and public sectors or a combination of federal, state, and/or regional agencies. The League supports a general income tax increase to finance national health care reform.

The League strongly believes that, should the allocation of resources become necessary to reform the US health care system, the ability of a patient to pay for services should not be a consideration. In determining how health care resources should be allocated, the League emphasizes the consideration of the following factors, taken together: the urgency of the medical condition, the life expectancy of the patient, the expected outcome of the treatment, the cost of the procedure, the duration of care, the quality of life of the patient after the treatment, and the wishes of the patient and the family.

As LWVUS was completing Phase 2 of the study, the issue of health care reform was rising to the top of the country's legislative agenda. In April 1993, as soon as the study results were announced, LWVUS met with White House health care officials to present the results of the League's position. Since then, the League has actively participated in the health care debate.

LWVUS testified in fall 1993 before the House Ways and Means Subcommittee on Health, the Energy and Commerce Committee, and the Education and Labor Committee, calling for comprehensive health care reform based on the League position. The League joined two coalitions — one comprising consumer, business, labor, provider, and senior groups working for comprehensive health care reform, and the other comprising groups supporting the single-payer approach to health care reform.

Throughout 1994, the League actively lobbied in support of comprehensive reform, including universal coverage, cost containment, single-payer or employer mandate, and a strong benefits package. The League emphasized LWVUS support for the inclusion of reproductive health care, including abortion, in any health benefits package.

LWVEF initiated community education efforts on health care issues with the Understanding Health Care Policy Project in the early 1990s. The project provided training and resources for Leagues to conduct broad-based community outreach and education on health care policy issues with the goal of expanding community participation in the public debate. In spring 1994, LWVEF and the Kaiser Family Foundation (KFF) undertook a major citizen education effort, Citizen's Voice for Citizen's Choice: A Campaign for a Public Voice on Health Care Reform. The project delivered objective information on health care reform to millions of Americans across the country through local and state League-sponsored town meetings in major media markets nationwide, involving members of Congress and other leading policy makers and analysts in health care discussions with citizens. In September 1994, LWVEF and KFF held a National Satellite Town Meeting on Health Care Reform. They also undertook a major television advertising promotion of public participation in the health care debate.

In 1997, LWVUS joined 100 national, state, and local organizations in successfully urging Congress to pass strong bipartisan child health care legislation (CHIP). In 1998, LWVUS began working for a Patients' Bill of Rights, aimed at giving Americans participating in managed care health plans greater access to specialists without going through a gatekeeper, the right to emergency room care using the "reasonably prudent person" standard, and a speedy appeals process when there is a dispute with insurers and other rights.

In 1998, LWVEF again partnered with KFF and state and local Leagues on a citizen education project, this time focused on Medicare reform, patients' bill of rights, and other health care issues. In the first phase, more than 6,500 citizens participated in focus groups, community dialogues, and public meetings. Their views were reflected in How Americans Talk About Medicare Reform: The Public Voice, presented to the National Bipartisan Commission on the Future of Medicare in March 1999. In spring 2000, LWVEF and KFF developed and distributed two guides, Join the Debate: Your Guide to Health Issues in the 2000 Election and A Leader's Handbook for Holding Community Dialogues. The project focused on five issues under debate in the election: the uninsured, managed care and patients' rights, Medicare reform, prescription drug coverage, and long-term care.

In the late '90s, LWVUS lobbied in support of a strong Patients' Bill of Rights. Despite close votes in 2000, Senate opponents continued to block passage. At Convention 2000, League delegates lobbied their members of Congress to pass a strong, comprehensive Patients' Bill of Rights, but it was shelved as the 2000 election drew near.

In the 108th Congress (2003 – 2005), the League lobbied in support of the Health Care Access Resolution. In 2003, the League opposed the Medicare Prescription Drug bill, which the President signed into law, because of provisions that undermined universal coverage in Medicare.

In May 2006, the League urged senators to oppose the *Health Insurance Marketplace Modernization and Affordability Act* (HIMMA), which purported to expand health care coverage, while limiting critical consumer protections provided in many states.

From 2007 through 2009, the League urged reauthorization of the State Children's Health Insurance Program (SCHIP), which in 2007 provided health care coverage to six million low-income children; the efforts were rewarded with reauthorization in early 2009.

In 2010, after two decades of work to ensure access to affordable, quality health care for all Americans and protect patients' rights, the League celebrated success when the *Affordable Care Act* (ACA) was signed into law. The League remains vigilant considering current efforts to repeal or diminish the law in Congress and the courts.

In the 112th Congress (2011 – 2013), the League continued to fight attempts to repeal the ACA and to limit provisions that provide health and reproductive services for women. State Leagues began to work with their legislatures to implement the ACA, and LWVUS signed on to an amicus brief in the challenge to the *Affordable Care Act*, which was upheld by the US Supreme Court.

In 2013, as opposition to the ACA was raised in the legislative, regulatory, and judicial processes, LWVUS submitted comments opposing religious exemptions for contraceptive services. This debate continued in the courts, and the League joined with other concerned organizations opposing broad religious exemptions to the requirement that all insurance plans provide access to contraception as basic care in the 2014 Supreme Court case of *Burwell v. Hobby Lobby Stores*.

Judicial action continued in 2015 as supporters including the League submitted an amicus brief in the case of *Burwell v. King*, which challenged the availability of tax subsidies for people who purchase health insurance on a marketplace administered by the federal government. The ACA gave states a choice not to administer their own marketplaces. The brief outlined how tax subsidies are essential to women's health and critical to the ACA's continued viability.

The League continued to support implementation of the ACA at the state level and expansion of the Medicaid program, as provided by the ACA. The League also continued its strong support for continued funding of CHIP.

The League opposed several attempts by Congress to repeal the *Affordable Care Act* in the 115th Congress (2017 – 2019), including the Graham-Cassidy Plan, the *Better Reconciliation Act*, and the *American Health Care Act*. The League activated grassroots supporters and the LWVUS Lobby Corps on these efforts and was a key member of the coalition that worked to stop passage of a final bill in the US Senate.

The League also opposed attempts in Congress to destabilize the health care market by defunding cost-sharing-reduction payments. And the League worked to spread awareness about the open enrollment period after decision by the executive branch to decrease the outreach budget, limit sign-up during the ACA open enrollment period, and reduce funding for the Navigator program.

Following the 2018 election, the League urged congressional leadership to pursue an agenda that ensures that the best health and health care are equally accessible and affordable to all in the 116th session of Congress (2019 – 2021).

In 2020, as Congress began to address the crisis caused by the COVID pandemic, the League joined other organizations asking the House and Senate to pass legislation that provided state and local aid for essential services. Along with public health advocacy groups expressing grave concerns regarding the US Government's decision to terminate relations with the World Health Organization (WHO)

In early 2021, LWVUS joined an amicus brief in support of plaintiffs in a trio of US Supreme Court cases challenging the imposition of work requirements on Medicaid recipients. We joined LWVTN in contacting the Director of the Centers for Medicare and Medicaid Services (CMS) opposing the approval of a Medicaid block grant in Tennessee that would limit the state's ability to provide access to critical healthcare.

The League lobbied Congress in 2022 to take action to improve health care affordability and address health inequities impacting women and families.

At Convention 2022, delegates concurred with the LWVNY Health Care update, amending the LWVUS Health Position to include updated criteria for evidence-based cost control measures that don't exacerbate DEI disparities, highlight the need for access to healthcare for underserved areas, patients, and populations to improve both equity and public health, and make LWV support for single payer explicit, including allowing states or regions to enact universal health programs that meet certain criteria. The new position also supports separating access to health care from employment, expanding delivery options, ensuring safe staffing, centering the decisions of patients including decisions made prior to need, regular evaluation of health programs, and public participation in determining health care funding and coverage.

Immigration

The League's Position

Statement of Position on Immigration, as announced by the national board, April 2008:

The League of Women Voters believes that immigration policies should promote reunification of immediate families; meet the economic, business, and employment needs of the United States; and be responsive to those facing political persecution or humanitarian crises. Provision should also be made for qualified persons to enter the United States on student visas. All persons should receive fair treatment under the law.

The League supports federal immigration law that provides an efficient, expeditious system (with minimal or no backlogs) for legal entry of immigrants into the United States.

To complement these goals, the League supports federal policies to improve economies, education, job opportunities, and living conditions in nations with large emigrating populations.

In transition to a reformed system, the League supports provisions for individuals already living in the country without legal permission to earn legal status.

The League supports federal payments to impacted communities to address the financial costs borne by states and local governments with large immigrant populations.

Criteria for Legal Admission to the United States

The League supports the following criteria for legal admission of persons into the United States:

- Family reunification of spouses or minor children with authorized immigrants or citizens.
- Flight from persecution or response to humanitarian crises in home countries.
- Economic, business, and employment needs in the Unites States.
- Education and training needs of the United States.
- Educational program opportunities.
- Lack of a history of major and/or violent criminal activity.

Administration and Enforcement

The League supports due process for all persons, including the right to a fair hearing, right to counsel, right of appeal, and right to humane treatment.

The League supports:

- Improved technology to facilitate employer verification of employee status.
- Verification documents, such as status cards and work permits, with secure identifiers.
- Significant fines and penalties for employers who hire unauthorized workers.
- Improved technology for sharing information among federal agencies.
- More-effective tracking of individuals who enter the United States.
- Increased personnel at borders.

The League also supports programs allowing foreign workers to enter and leave the United States to meet seasonal or sporadic labor needs.

US Residents Without Legal Permission to Earn Legal Status

In achieving overall policy goals, the League supports a system for individuals living in the country without legal permission to earn legal status, including citizenship, by paying taxes, studying civics, and meeting other relevant criteria. While policy reforms, including a path to legal status, remain unachieved, the League does not support deporting these immigrants who have no history of major and/or violent criminal activity.

League History

The 2006 Convention voted to undertake a study on immigration. After study and consensus, the new position was finalized in 2008 and sent to members of Congress.

In the 111th Congress (2009 – 2011), the League lobbied in support of the *DREAM Act* (Development, Relief, and Education for Alien Minors) that would provide a path to citizenship for young immigrants who complete a college degree or serve in the military, thereby enabling them to be a fully productive part of American society. The legislation passed the House but lacked enough votes to overcome a filibuster in the Senate.

Because of a request made in 2016, the League clarified part of its position on immigration "to mean that simple illegal re-entry is not considered a 'serious crime' for League advocacy purposes."

In the 115th Congress (2017 – 2019), the League opposed the rescission of the Deferred Action for Childhood Arrivals (DACA) policy by the Trump administration. In response, the League again advocated for passage of a clean *DREAM Act* in Congress. The LWVUS Lobby Corps lobbied both the House and the Senate on this issue.

The League also opposed the *Securing America's Future Act of 2018*, which would have put immigrant youth at risk of deportation while supporting actions at our borders to separate children from their families and funding a wall at our southern border. During the 2018 Convention in Chicago, League members marched in support of immigrants and families while protesting this and other pieces of related legislation.

The League also opposed the Trump administration's Public Charge Rule, which directed immigration officials to limit the entrance of immigrants who they deemed would become more dependent on government funding to meet their basic human needs.

In early 2019, LWV joined a coalition of 44 organizations to file an amicus in *Department of Homeland Security v. Regents of the University of California, et al.*, a trio of cases involving whether the US Department of Homeland Security's decision to end DACA without a pathway for DACA-eligible individuals to remain in the country legally was legal. The US Supreme Court ruled in June 2020 that DHS's decision to end the program did not properly follow the *Administrative Procedure Act* and the majority court held that the agency failed to provide relevant factors associated with ending the program, making the agency's actions arbitrary and capricious. LWV issued a statement commending the court on the ruling and encouraged Congress to pass comprehensive reform legislation on immigration that includes a pathway to citizenship. At the start of the 116th Congress, the League supported passage of the bipartisan *DREAM Act of 2021*. At the same time, the organization supported *The New Deal for New Americans Act*, which would expand access to citizenship, fund workforce development and English-language learning programs, and increase the number of refugees the United States resettles, while rebuilding the capacity and infrastructure of local communities to welcome refugees.

In early 2021, the League joined immigrant rights advocates in successfully urging senators to oppose amendments denying economic impact payments to mixed-immigration-status families. The League also asked the Biden administration to uphold basic due process and human rights for Haitians seeking asylum at the US border. At the same time, the League asked the administration to provide Temporary Protected Status or Deferred Enforced Departure for Cameroonians living in the US. The League urged the administration to designate Mexico for Temporary Protected Status.

Meeting Basic Human Needs

The League's Position

Statement of Position on Meeting Basic Human Needs, as revised by the national board, January 1989, based on positions reached from 1971 through 1988:

The League of Women Voters of the United States believes that one of the goals of social policy in the United States should be to promote self-sufficiency for individuals and families and that the most-effective social programs are those designed to prevent or reduce poverty.

Persons who are unable to work, whose earnings are inadequate, or for whom jobs are not available have the right to an income and/or services sufficient to meet their basic needs for food, shelter, and access to health care.

The federal government should set minimum, uniform standards and guidelines for social welfare programs and should bear primary responsibility for financing programs designed to help meet the basic needs of individuals and families. State and local governments, as well as the private sector, should have a secondary role in financing food, housing, and health care programs. Income assistance programs should be financed primarily by the federal government with state governments assuming secondary responsibility.

Preventing and Reducing Poverty

In order to prevent or reduce poverty, LWVUS supports policies and programs designed to increase job opportunities; increase access to health insurance; provide support services such as child care and transportation; provide opportunities and/or incentives for basic or remedial education and job training; decrease teen pregnancy; and ensure that noncustodial parents contribute to the support of their children.

Access to Health Care

LWVUS believes that access to health care includes the following: preventive care, primary care, maternal and child health care, emergency care, catastrophic care, nursing home care, and mental health care, as well as access to substance abuse programs, health and sex education programs, and nutrition programs.

Access to Transportation

LWVUS believes that energy-efficient and environmentally sound transportation systems should afford better access to housing and jobs and will continue to examine transportation policies in light of these goals.

Further Guidelines and Criteria

Criteria for Income Assistance

- Eligibility of all low-income individuals for assistance should be based on need. Eligibility should be established through simplified procedures such as a declaration of need, spot-checked in a manner similar to that used in checking the validity of income tax returns.
- Benefit levels should be sufficient enough to provide decent, adequate standards for food, clothing, and shelter. Minimum income standards should be adjusted for regional differences in the cost of living and should be revised periodically to take into account changes in the purchasing value of the dollar. Until a federal welfare program achieves an adequate level of benefits, some states will need to supplement federal payments.
- There should be increasing emphasis on cash assistance, but in-kind assistance (e.g., food stamps, housing subsidies, medical aid) should be continued to help assure that these needs are met.
- Under a revised program, participants should not have their benefits reduced.
- Privacy of participants should be protected. All administrative procedures should be conducted with respect for the rights and dignity of the individuals.

- Work should be encouraged: participants' total income should increase as earnings increase. Counseling, realistic training for actual jobs, and financial incentives should be the links between job programs and income assistance.

Criteria for Supportive Services

- Supportive services should be available — but not compulsory — for participants in income assistance programs. Most important among these are child care, counseling, transportation, family planning, health care, and legal services.
- Fees for supportive services should be based on ability to pay and be free where necessary.
- Facilities and services for participants should be the same as for the general public.
- The federal government should exert leadership in setting standards for eligibility, the quality of services, and adequate funding.
- Participants in the programs should be included in program development and implementation, and the administration of social services programs should be responsive to the needs of the people being served.
- Wherever possible, these services should be conveniently located in the neighborhood.
- Transportation systems should afford better access to housing and jobs and should also provide energy-efficient and environmentally sound transportation.
- Government programs that require recipients of assistance to engage in work-related programs would be acceptable only if the following protections are guaranteed to the participants:
  - Job training.
  - Basic education.
  - Exemptions for primary care givers.
  - Supplemental support services such as child care and transportation.
  - Equitable compensation to ensure that program participants earn the same wages and benefits as other employees performing similar work.
  - A disregard of some earned income for purposes of calculating benefit levels.

Criteria for Housing Supply

- The following considerations can be applied to programs and policies to provide a decent home and a suitable living environment for every American family:
- The responsibility for achieving national housing goals rests primarily with the federal government, which should:
  - Assure that our economic system is functioning to produce and maintain sufficient decent housing for citizens at all income levels.
  - Compensate for any failure or inadequacy of the system by building, financing, renting, and selling homes to those citizens whose housing needs are not being met.
  - Give a variety of incentives to local jurisdictions to encourage them to provide within their boundaries an adequate supply of decent housing for low- and moderate-income groups.
  - Withhold federal funds from communities that fail to encourage such housing.
- State and local governments should assist by establishing effective agencies to aid, promote, coordinate, and supplement the housing programs of the federal government and the private sector.
- Government at all levels must make available sufficient funds for housing-assistance programs.
- When families or individuals cannot afford decent housing, government should provide assistance in the form of income and/or subsidized housing.

- Government programs providing subsidies to the building, financing, and insuring industries for housing for lower income families should be evaluated in terms of units produced rather than in terms of benefits accruing to these industries.
- Government at all levels should develop policies that will assure sufficient land at reasonable cost on which to develop housing and that will assure fulfillment of other goals such as access to employment, preservation of open space, environmental cleanliness and beauty, and other aspects of a suitable living environment.
- Regional and metropolitan planning should be promoted to prevent haphazard urban growth, and housing for low and moderate income families should be provided as a part of all planned neighborhoods or communities.
- Lower income families should not be segregated in large developments or neighborhoods. As their economic status improves, lower income families should be enabled to continue to live in the same units as private tenants or as homeowners, if they are so inclined.
- Housing should be designed to meet human needs and should be built with amenities that will encourage economic integration within apartment buildings as well as within neighborhoods.
- Publicly assisted housing should be included in viable, balanced communities, with provision for quality public services and facilities (e.g., schools, transportation, recreation) that will encourage integration and stability.
- Zoning practices and procedures that will counteract racial and economic isolation should be promoted.
- State and local governments should adopt and enforce:
    - Uniform building codes with standards based on performance.
    - Housing codes to protect the health and safety of all citizens.
- State and local tax structures should be examined and revised to:
    - Benefit communities that build housing for lower-income families.
    - Encourage private owners to improve their homes.
    - Reduce speculative land costs.
- Government, industry, and labor should encourage innovative building techniques to reduce the cost of housing production.
- Rights of tenants to negotiate for proper maintenance, management of facilities, and services should be protected.
- Housing programs should be administered by individuals trained for the jobs and sympathetic with the needs of their clientele.
- Citizen groups should participate in the development of publicly assisted housing programs by:
    - Evaluating performance.
    - Activating nonprofit sponsorships.
    - Supporting legislation.
    - Developing public awareness of housing discrimination and need.

League History

After adopting the Meeting Basic Human Needs position in 1988, the League reorganized the Social Policy program in 1990. This reorganization combined several existing positions to address the basic needs of all people for food, shelter, and access to health care and transportation. The Meeting Basic Human Needs position encompasses previous positions on income assistance and transportation. The issue of housing supply was separated from the fair housing position, still under Equality of Opportunity, and put under the Meeting Basic Human Needs position.

In 2015, the LWVUS Board voted to interpret the Meeting Basic Human Needs Position to include support for a living wage. After considerable program debate at the 2014 LWVUS convention, the Advocacy Committee took up the issue and agreed to call attention of Leagues to the Meeting Basic Human Needs position to suggest that the position can be used in communities in "working toward an income that meets basic human needs." Additionally, the Committee agreed that specific issues in relation to a living wage and income levels should be decided by Leagues working in their communities.

Income Assistance

The 1970 Convention adopted a study of alternatives to welfare. As a result of the study, members agreed to support a system of federalized income assistance. The position, adopted in 1971, suggests criteria for such a system and for minimum uniform standards of eligibility for both cash benefits and supportive services (in-kind benefits). The position is closely linked with the Employment position in encouraging work and in emphasizing the responsibility of the federal government to help those who can't find work, those whose earnings are insufficient to meet basic needs, and those who are unable to work.

Adoption of the position coincided with a congressional effort to make major changes in the welfare system in 1971 – 72. The League mounted an all-out lobbying effort, despite recognized shortcomings in the legislation. In the late 1970s, the League attempted unsuccessfully to strengthen a number of federal welfare reform proposals. The League has supported a variety of specific programs for income assistance and in-kind benefits — food stamps, low-income energy assistance, child-care legislation, reform of unemployment compensation and Aid to Families with Dependent Children programs, and housing subsidies. Comprehensive child care remains an elusive but critically needed support service for women seeking employment. In each case, the League has pressed for uniform minimum federal standards of eligibility, uniform standards for benefits based on need, and standards for quality of services.

The League has opposed cutoffs of Medicaid funding for abortion, on the basis of the supportive services provisions of the Income Assistance position and because such actions clearly discriminate against economically disadvantaged women and people who can become pregnant.

In the 1980s, national League action on income assistance focused primarily on opposition to funding cutbacks, dilution of the federal role, and changes in eligibility requirements for income maintenance programs and support services.

In 1986 – 88, the League worked in support of welfare reform legislation in Congress, culminating in passage of the *Family Support Act of 1988*. The League had supported the House version, the *Family Welfare Reform Act*, which included provisions for education, training, and employment of welfare recipients. The final bill followed the Senate version, which the League joined the national Coalition on Human Needs to oppose, citing inadequate funding and mandatory participation quotas. Since passage of the Act, states continue to face implementation decisions.

The League lobbied successfully in support of the *Family and Medical Leave Act* (FMLA), designed to guarantee workers unpaid leave for illness or the birth or adoption of a child. Through the years, the League has supported the Earned Income Tax Credit (EITC) as a necessary form of income assistance.

Other League efforts include lobbying the 102nd Congress (1991 – 1993) to pass the *Mickey Leland Hunger Relief Act* and the *Freedom from Want Act*, both designed to alleviate hunger in the United States. In 1988 – 90, LWVEF coordinated an 18-month Hunger Advocacy Project designed to help state and local Leagues develop and carry out model, targeted activities to document or alleviate hunger. A guide, Fighting Hunger in Your Community, provided information on replicating such activities.

In 1989 – 90, LWVEF promoted discussion of a Ford Foundation report on social welfare, The Common Good. Local Leagues held three regional workshops on issues raised in the report and conducted related community education activities.

The League actively opposed welfare reform legislation proposed in the 104th Congress (1995 – 1997). During summer 1996, the White House and Congress agreed on legislation to essentially hand over welfare to the states. Despite the League's strong lobbying effort with a particular focus on the President, the bill was passed and signed into law in August 1996. State Leagues across the country monitored the implementation and effects of reform efforts at the state level to ensure that the benefits were provided where needed and that recipients' civil rights were protected.

In fall 2005, the League responded to the Hurricane Katrina disaster, urging Congress to protect basic human needs of those affected by securing essentials — jobs, income when work is not available, health care, food, education, child care, and housing — while also protecting and expanding the capacity of the federal government to respond by preserving and increasing funding for vital services and not sapping revenues through misdirected tax cuts.

As the 113th Congress (2013 – 2015) cut funding and changed eligibility formulas for the Supplemental Nutrition Assistance Program (SNAP), (formerly the Food Stamp program), the League joined with other organizations to urge Congress to strengthen the program, not weaken it.

Housing Supply

During the late 1960s and early 1970s, the League worked for a number of federal housing reforms. In 1974, League support was channeled into aspects of the *Housing and Community Development Act*, which consolidated federal assistance under a block grant approach. The League fought against congressional action to weaken the Community Development Block Grant program through drastic cuts in the full range of authorized low- and moderate-income subsidies for both rehabilitation and new housing.

Throughout the 1980s, the League continued to support increased funding to add to and maintain the existing stock of federally assisted housing people with very low incomes. LWVUS efforts included working as a member of the National Low-Income Housing Coalition to urge passage of 1987 legislation authorizing the Department of Housing and Urban Development's low-income housing and community development programs, as well as endorsing the 1989 Housing Now march on Washington.

As a member of the Low-Income Housing Coalition's Women and Housing Task Force, LWVUS endorsed recommendations predicated on the conviction that every person and family should have decent, safe, affordable housing. State and local Leagues have worked to increase the supply of housing for people with low and moderate incomes through efforts to change zoning laws and set up shared housing services.

In 2002, LWVUS formally endorsed legislation to establish the National Housing Trust Fund, using surplus funds from the Federal Housing Administration (FHA) to create new housing for families with low incomes.

Transportation

LWVUS concern about public transportation grew out of efforts on behalf of equal opportunity for employment and housing. The 1971 Air Quality position added another dimension to this concern by urging "measures to reduce vehicular pollution . . . and development of alternate transportation systems." In 1972, the LWVUS Board responded to questions of interpretation by synthesizing the two positions into a unified Transportation position. In 1976, following League concurrence on the Energy Conservation position, the LWVUS Board reaffirmed the national League's Transportation position. In 1979, the Urban Policy position reinforced the theme that federal aid for highway construction should be reduced; the Transportation position language was revised to make that point clear.

The League first put the position to work by backing a national coalition's efforts to amend the *Federal Aid Highway Act of 1972* to permit financing part of the costs of urban mass transit from highway trust funds. The League also supported the *National Mass Transportation Assistance Act of 1974*. Later the focus shifted to prevent stalling or cutting of federal assistance to mass transit systems.

In response to the urgency to improve and promote public transportation systems, the 1980 Convention voted to give greater emphasis to the Transportation position. In 1988, it was incorporated into the Meeting Basic Human Needs position. Leagues continue to use the Transportation position with their own local or Inter-League Organization (ILO) positions to back local and regional moves to improve mass transit and support other alternatives, such as express lanes for buses and carpools.

Child Care

The League's Position

Statement of Position on Child Care, as adopted by the 1988 Convention, based on positions reached from 1969 through 1988:

LWVUS supports programs, services, and policies at all levels of government to expand the supply of affordable, quality child care for all who need it, in order to increase access to employment and to prevent and reduce poverty.

League History

The League has long recognized that child care programs are a key supportive service for families in need.

The 1988 LWVUS Convention adopted child care as a priority and separated the child care position within the Social Policy position. The League supported a compromise child care bill, signed by the President in 1990, which provided financial assistance to low incomes for child care; increased the availability of child care through resource and referral programs and training for child-care workers; and required states to establish health and safety standards for day care. Then Leagues across the country monitored and commented on the regulatory process as the Department of Health and Human Services wrote implementing regulations.

LWVEF activities included a 1990 – 91 School-Age Child Care Project. The goal was to help local Leagues serve as catalysts in targeted communities to increase the availability of affordable, quality school-age child care for low- and moderate-income families. In 1992, LWVEF published a community action guide using the model League projects to help other communities implement similar programs.

In summer 1998, LWVUS and other groups urged congressional action on child care and the passage of a substantial increase in guaranteed funds for the Child Care Development Block Grant.

In early 2002, the League joined other groups in support of legislation to reauthorize the Temporary Assistance to Needy Families (TANF) program and provide for comprehensive reforms to help those on welfare become self-sufficient. It was not adopted.

Early Intervention for Children at Risk

The League's Position

Statement of Position on Early Intervention for Children at Risk, as adopted by the 1994 Convention:

The League of Women Voters of the United States believes that early intervention and prevention measures are effective in helping children reach their full potential. The League supports policies and programs at all levels of the community and government that promote the well-being, encourage the full development, and ensure the safety of all children. These include:

- **Child abuse/neglect prevention.**
- **Teen pregnancy prevention.**
- **Quality health care, including nutrition and prenatal care.**
- **Early childhood education.**
- **Developmental services, emphasizing children ages 0-3.**
- **Family support services.**
- **Violence prevention.**

League History

The position on Early Intervention for Children at Risk was adopted by concurrence at Convention 1994; it was based on state and local League work.

In 1995, LWVEF published a comprehensive kit designed to help Leagues and other groups advocate and work for children in their communities. In June 1996, the League endorsed the Stand for Children, a national day of commitment to improving the lives of children throughout the country.

Violence Prevention

The League's Position

Statement of Position on Violence Prevention, as adopted by the 1994 Convention:

The League of Women Voters of the United States supports violence prevention programs in all communities and action to support:

- **Public and private development and coordination of programs that emphasize the primary prevention of violence.**
- **The active role of government and social institutions in preventing violent behavior.**
- **The allocation of public monies in government programs to prevent violence.**

League History

The 1994 Convention adopted by concurrence a position on Violence Prevention, based on state and local League work. The League subsequently endorsed the *Violence Against Women Act*, which Congress passed and the President signed in 1994 as part of a comprehensive crime bill. In the 2010s, the League supported authorization of the *Violence Against Women Act* through a stand-alone bill and as a part of the appropriations process. After the *Violence Against Women Act* expired in 2019, the League joined coalition partners pushing for reauthorization of the legislation through stand-alone legislation. The League also pushed for reauthorization of the legislation through the appropriations process.

In 2019, the League supported the *International Violence Against Women Act of 2019* (IVAWA), which seeks to take effective action to prevent and respond to violence against women and girls around the world as a matter of basic human rights and to promote gender equality, economic growth, and improved public health around the world.

LWVUS UN Observers also hosted a forum with member of Congress in conjunction with the Interparliamentary Union on the topic of Violence Against Women Politicians. The forum provided insight on how violence against women in politics impacts democracies, discussed preventive action, and shared best practices utilized around the world.

Gun Policy

The League's Position

Statement of Position on Gun Policy, as adopted by 1990 Convention and amended by the 1994 and 1998 Conventions:

The League of Women Voters of the United States believes that the proliferation of semi-automatic/automatic weapons in the United States is a major health and safety threat to its citizens. The League supports strong federal measures to limit the accessibility and regulate the ownership of these weapons by private citizens. The League supports regulating firearms for consumer safety.

The League supports licensing procedures for gun ownership by private citizens to include a waiting period for background checks, personal identity verification, gun safety education, and annual license renewal. The license fee should be adequate to bear the cost of education and verification.

The League supports strong limitations on access to semi-automatic/automatic weapons, enforcement of strict penalties for the improper possession of and crimes committed with handguns and assault weapons, and allocation of resources to better regulate and monitor gun dealers.

League History

The 1990 Convention took the then-rare step of adopting the gun policy position by concurrence. Proponents had sent two informational mailings to all Leagues before Convention. Spirited debate on the Convention floor persuaded the Convention to concur with the statement proposed by the LWV of Illinois.

Following the Convention action, LWVUS wrote to all members of Congress announcing the League's new position on gun control and urging passage of federal legislation to control the proliferation of handguns and semi-automatic assault weapons in the United States. In 1991, the League joined with other organizations to support legislation banning semi-automatic assault weapons. In 1992 and 1993, the League supported congressional passage of the Brady bill, to institute a five-day waiting period and background check for the purchase of handguns. Following enactment of the Brady bill in November 1993, the League stepped up its efforts in a successful 1994 House campaign to force inclusion of the assault weapons ban in the final conference report on omnibus crime legislation.

The 1994 Convention addressed constitutional arguments affecting gun policy by voting to amend the position on gun policy based on federal court decisions limiting the meaning of the Second Amendment's "right to keep and bear arms." This section of the position was nullified by subsequent US Supreme Court decisions in *District of Columbia v. Heller* and *McDonald v. Chicago* and was removed from the position language.

Throughout 1995 – 1996, opponents of the assault weapons ban and Brady bill pushed for repeal, but the League and others convinced Congress otherwise.

The 1998 Convention again amended the position with: "The League supports regulating firearms for consumer safety."

The 106th Congress (1999 – 2001) defeated LWVUS-supported gun policy measures to close major loopholes in the law: mandating background checks for all gun show purchases and child safety locks on guns.

LWVUS endorsed and League members joined the Mother's Day 2000 Million Mom March that demonstrated citizens' call for common-sense gun policy measures.

In 2004, the League voiced strong concern over the *Protection of Lawful Commerce in Arms Act*, which would grant special protection for the gun industry by barring city, county, or individual lawsuits against gun manufacturers and dismiss pending cases.

The League supported legislation to extend the Assault Weapons Ban, which expired in September 2004. LWVUS also supported language to close the gun show loophole to require all dealers to run criminal background checks at gun shows.

In the 2000s, the League opposed congressional attempts to repeal District of Columbia gun safety laws because such action interfered with the right of self-government for DC citizens.

The League again jumped to action in the 2010s in response to a lack of congressional and executive action after a series of mass shootings across the country. The League continues pushing for passage of closing the gun show loophole, universal background checks, limiting magazine size, banning "bump stocks" and assault weapons, increasing penalties for straw purchases of guns, and funding research and reporting on gun violence in America. In the 115th Congress (2017 – 2019), the League opposed the *Concealed Carry Reciprocity Act of 2017*.

In 2018, the League endorsed the March for Our Lives rally in Washington, DC, which was organized by students around the country. The League supported the rally by encouraging our members to attend and sponsor sister marches around the country. LWVUS also used this as an opportunity to encourage our online grassroots advocacy list to contact their members of Congress regarding the need to change gun policy around the country. In the 116th Congress (2019 – 2021) the League supported the *Bipartisan Background Check Act*, and the *Background Check Expansion Act*, to require Brady background checks for all firearm transfers.

Urban Policy

The League's Position

Statement of Position on Urban Policy, as announced by the national board, June 1979 and revised by the national board in 1989:

The League of Women Voters of the United States believes that it is in the national interest to promote the well-being of America's cities.

Sharply targeted federal assistance to distressed cities should be central to this policy. The federal government should give highest priority in urban policy to measures that enhance the economic base of cities. The League also favors supplementary federal aid for cities in distressed fiscal condition and grants for program areas as strategies to counter the problems of hardship cities.

The fiscal health of cities depends on the active cooperation of all levels of government. The federal government should provide incentives to encourage states to take an active role in promoting the fiscal viability of their cities.

The League is committed to an urban environment beneficial to life and to resource management in the public interest.

Further Guidelines

Economic Development Assistance

The cornerstone of a national urban policy is a commitment to helping cities achieve economic strength. Federal programs to encourage private reinvestment in central cities should counter an eroding tax base and provide jobs for the inner-city unemployed. Therefore, the League supports the following federal strategies:

- Target community development programs to cities most in need.
- Encourage businesses to locate or expand in distressed cities through such financial incentives as investment tax credits, loan guarantees, subsidies for hiring the long-term unemployed, and interest subsidies.
- Expand middle-income housing while not diminishing attention to low-income housing needs.
- Target federal purchasing and location of federal facilities in distressed cities.

General Financial Assistance

The League supports a variety of federal strategies, including direct general assistance, targeted to distressed cities. Such a program should include aid to counter recession. In providing federal aid for particular program areas, grants offer city governments the best opportunities to meet local needs.

- In order to increase the availability of funds to city governments for capital expenditures, the federal government should use mechanisms to reduce the cost of borrowing.
- Aid to cities should include technical assistance to improve management capacity.

League History

Recognizing that the League's program already had many urban implications, the 1976 Convention added Cities/Urban Crisis to the national program as a "specific focus for information and action on urban problems." Members examined urban connections among existing League positions in order to open new action opportunities to address the desperate plight of many urban areas.

The 1978 Convention reaffirmed the League's interest in the urban problem by adopting an "evaluation of urban policy options, with emphasis on fiscal policy." Leagues drew on their preliminary explorations of urban problems for a more structured study of the appropriate federal role in the intergovernmental responsibility for cities. In June 1979, the national board announced a new position, enabling the League to take a strong stand on targeting federal assistance to distressed cities, especially through urban economic development assistance programs to encourage private reinvestment in cities. It also supports general and targeted direct financial assistance to cities.

During the consensus process, it was made clear that restoring economic health to the nation's cities requires combined state, local, and federal government efforts. State Leagues have used the position to work for targeted state aid to distressed areas, and local Leagues have pushed for improved city management to make better use of diminishing resources.

The League's first national action campaign under the position involved the 1980 reauthorization of General Revenue Sharing (GRS). Building on the previous monitoring and action to strengthen GRS (see Equal Access position), the Urban Policy position reaffirmed support for strong civil rights, citizen participation requirements, and auditing standards, and for a more equitable distribution of funds. The League worked with a coalition toward these ends and was successful on all but the last issue.

Under the Urban Policy position, the League supported expansion of economic development programs and the reauthorization of Urban Development Action Grants (UDAG). In efforts to bring more jobs to urban areas, the League also has supported the location of federal facilities in distressed cities.

Local and state Leagues implemented the position on the home front, fighting to save downtown businesses from extinction, commenting on local UDAG applications, working for public/private cooperation in the revitalization of city neighborhoods, and undertaking citizen education activities to spur interest in improving the quality of urban life.

In 1979, under a grant from the National Endowment for the Humanities, LWVEF and several local Leagues worked to increase public awareness of urban problems and solutions. Another grant enabled LWVEF to sponsor an exchange between Leagues in the industrial heartland and the Sunbelt.

The 1980 Convention changed Urban Crisis to Urban Policy. A new focus on urban transportation united the League's long-time concerns about access to jobs, air quality, land use, and energy with newer concerns about urban economic development and municipal finances.

Death Penalty

The League's Position

Statement of Position on Abolition of the Death Penalty, as adopted by the 2006 Convention:

The League of Women Voters of the United States supports the abolition of the death penalty.

The League's History

At Convention 2006, delegates voted to adopt a position supporting abolition of the death penalty via concurrence. Since that time, state Leagues have used the position to support initiatives to abolish the death penalty in their states.

Sentencing Policy

The League's Position

Statement of Position on Sentencing Policy, as adopted by the 2012 Convention:

LWVUS believes alternatives to imprisonment should be explored and utilized, taking into consideration the circumstances and nature of the crime. LWVUS opposes mandatory minimum sentences for drug offenses.

The League's History

At convention 2012, delegates voted to adopt a Sentencing Policy position by concurrence. The position is based on the Sentencing Policy of the LWV of the District of Columbia. In late 2013, LWVUS supported the *Smarter Sentencing Act*, a Senate bill that would reduce federal sentences for non-violent drug offenders, but the bill did not come to the Senate floor. In 2017, the League supported the *Sentencing Reform and Corrections Act of 2017*. This legislation aimed to give judges discretion to reduce juvenile life-without-parole sentences after 20 years, allow compassionate release of more people over the age of 60, and essentially ban juvenile solitary confinement in the federal system.

Human Trafficking

The League's Position

Statement of Position on Human Trafficking, as adopted by the LWVUS 2014 National Convention:

The League of Women Voters opposes all forms of domestic and international human trafficking of adults and children, including sex trafficking and labor trafficking. We consider human trafficking to be a form of modern-day slavery and believe that every measure should be taken and every effort should be made through legislation and changes in public policy to prevent human trafficking. Prosecution and penalization of traffickers and abusers should be established, and existing laws should be strictly enforced. Extensive essential services for victims should be applied where needed. Education and awareness programs on human trafficking should be established in our communities and in our schools.

League History

At Convention 2014, a Human Trafficking position was adopted by delegates via concurrence. The League has continued to weave advocacy on this issue through our work at the United Nations.

Made in the USA
Monee, IL
25 June 2023